CLARITY, CUT, AND CULTURE

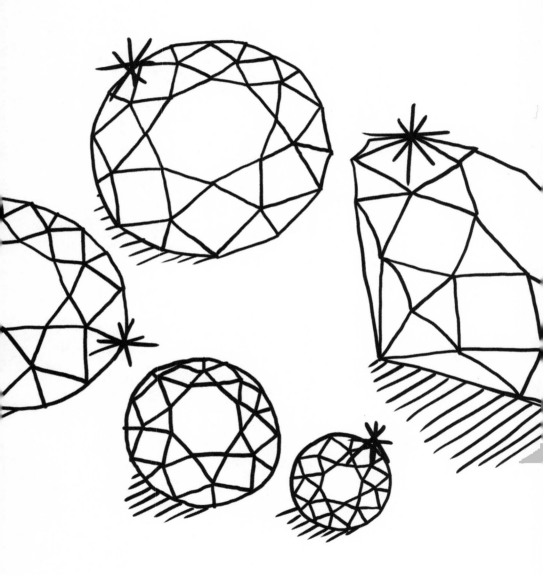

CLARITY, CUT, AND CULTURE

THE MANY MEANINGS OF DIAMONDS

SUSAN FALLS

NEW YORK UNIVERSITY PRESS

New York and London

NEW YORK UNIVERSITY PRESS
New York and London
www.nyupress.org

References to Internet websites (URLs) were accurate at the time of writing.
Neither the author nor New York University Press is responsible for URLs that
may have expired or changed since the manuscript was prepared.

LIBRARY OF CONGRESS CATALOGING-IN-PUBLICATION DATA

Falls, Susan.
Clarity, cut, and culture : the many meanings of diamonds / Susan Falls.
pages cm
Includes bibliographical references and index.
ISBN 978-1-4798-1066-6 (hardback) — ISBN 978-1-4798-7990-8 (paper)
1. Diamonds—Social aspects. 2. Symbolosm. 3. Identity (Psychology) I. Title.
GT2254.F35 2014
155.2—dc23
2014000833

New York University Press books are printed on acid-free paper,
and their binding materials are chosen for strength and durability.
We strive to use environmentally responsible suppliers and materials
to the greatest extent possible in publishing our books.

Manufactured in the United States of America
10 9 8 7 6 5 4 3 2 1

Also available as an ebook

FOR DARE, ZIM, AND TYROO

CONTENTS

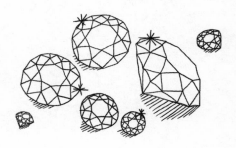

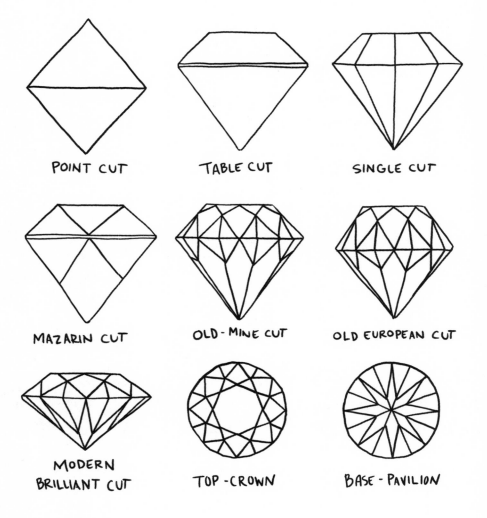

POINT CUT   TABLE CUT   SINGLE CUT

MAZARIN CUT   OLD-MINE CUT   OLD EUROPEAN CUT

MODERN BRILLIANT CUT   TOP-CROWN   BASE-PAVILION

FIGURES

I have chosen to use hand-rendered images in this book for several reasons. First, I have found acquiring permissions for corporate imagery
associated with diamonds to be nearly impossible. Second, hand-rendered images, singular as they are, echo the uniqueness of consumers'
perspectives. I also find them visually appealing. And, the photograph
is often thought to be seared with reality in a way that renders it highly
ideological while the drawing is more clearly a reflection of the artists'
understanding.

PREFACE: THE EMPTINESS OF DIAMONDS

My grandmother, whom we called "Nonni," used to wear a ring adorned with a big, winking diamond. I liked to touch that gemstone, given to her by my granddad after they were married in the 1920s; I remember being fascinated by its rainbow lights. She always called it a "friendship ring," to distinguish it from her engagement ring, which she later gave to my brother in hopes that he would eventually use it in a marriage proposal. (He did!) Nonni wore the friendship diamond until she passed it on to me. I hesitated to accept it then—I didn't want to be rude and refuse the gift—but it was a part of her, and I dreaded the implications of her giving things away. She insisted that it was better for me to have the ring "while there was still time for us to enjoy it," for us to see it on my hand instead of hers, instead of "waiting until it was too late." I was uneasy with the coded reference to her death, but honored by the gift.

Older now, and well aware of how marketing affixes glamour, wealth, matrimony, and status to diamonds, I understand them differently than I used to. And so, while my grandmother's diamond was transformed into an heirloom by her giving it to me, it remains an object whose significance is nested simultaneously within my own biography and a larger cultural milieu. This diamond ties me to her, to the grandfather I never knew, to my greater extended family, and to memories of the past and ideas about the future shared by my grandmother and me. It radiates, unites, and calls forth all of the stories we have made together over the years, creating in me a powerful sentimental attachment to this ring. I wear it only on important occasions, when I want to feel special or just close to her, and especially when we are together.

Around the time that I started wearing my grandmother's diamond, I attended a class on Tibetan Buddhism at an elementary school near my apartment in Manhattan. During his lecture on "The Wheel of Life," Geshe Roach held up a pen and asked, "What is this?" People shifted around in their seats, wondering how to answer this weird question that seemed to have an obvious answer, too obvious to be the right one. Finally someone volunteered, "It's a pen." "Yeah," Geshe Roach affirmed in his customary colloquial way, "that's right, you know this is a pen. It writes and it's got ink in it and I can squiggle lines and that's what it is, it's a pen." He let that sink in, and continued, "But, I mean, so what if you were a dog? If you were a dog what would this be?" He held it high for all to see and then . . . silence. "OK, If you were a dog," he argued, "you come up to it and you look at it, and to you this is not a pen, this is a chewing stick, you see, you can chew on it and it feels good and you probably don't even know what a pen is anyway and so this thing is a stick. This thing is not anything from its side, it is only from your side that it becomes a pen or a chewing stick or whatever."

Geshe Roach's explanation drew attention both to the nonessential nature of things and to the power of perspective in determining meaning. Nonessentialism is, of course, not unique to Buddhism, but the way Geshe Roach illustrated how we give meaning to the things we encounter was elegant and powerful. These ideas resonated as I thought about my ring, in part because I had been reading about interpretation in the work of philosophers Charles Saunders Peirce (see Hartshorne and Weiss 1931–1935) and Hans Gadamer (1975). In their works, both Peirce and Gadamer explore how experience, context, and prior understanding structure, or shape, interpretation. I was impressed by Geshe Roach's use of a simple and concrete example to demonstrate how one's perspective, operating within various constraints, determines meaning.

This attention to subjective perspective is not the same as the cultural relativism outlined and propounded by the great anthropologist Franz Boas, who argued that meaning is pegged to cultural definitions and values. Geshe Roach's lesson highlights instead a distinction between meaning making as a process of imputation—where we "put" the meaning on something—versus one of discovery—where we come to know a predetermined meaning, a meaning that already exists.

The difference between imputation and discovery here is not unlike Roland Barthes' (1974) delineation between "writerly" and "readerly" texts. Writerly texts require an active, creative reader—one who imputes meaning onto the text—while in a readerly text, the reader is restricted to just reading, decoding, or discovering what is already there. The critical distinction between these terms lies in the way they describe the relationship of people to an object, or what we might call a "sign," defined by Peirce in a deceptively simple formulation as something that means something to someone.

How do objects come to have a meaning to someone? Where does meaning come from? Is our relationship to signs like diamonds or other kinds of commodities one of discovery or one of imputation? In the case of Nonni's diamond, for example: do I simply decode ready-made meanings, or do I create and impute other meanings onto it?

Where meaning making is a process, or act, of discovery, it exists externally and prior to us. Here, we come to learn what something means—both the word and the thing itself—by participating in society. We absorb cultural meaning through the process of enculturation. For example, we learn that apple pie means American nationalism. Meaning can also be a process of imputation, where we "put" or assign meaning onto things instead of learning a preexisting code. Attending to imputation allows for greater focus on the ways in which individual experience, history, local context, and contingency all impact the way each of us understands and acts in the world. Studying imputation shows us how meaning is fluid and indeterminate—that apple pie, for example, could be associated with a particular event or person rather than the generic idea of nationalism.

In the case of diamonds, people use both discovery and imputation to do cultural work. Understanding how this happens is important because it illustrates how we negotiate the tension between individual experiences and wider cultural practices, and demonstrates how interpretive idiosyncrasy is a way for people to perform identity, demonstrate disagreement, and generate new ways of relating to others. Making meaning is, in short, a site of agency.

So what do diamonds mean? Diamonds like mine are similar to Geshe Roach's pen in that they are simultaneously historically and culturally situated objects, but with significance that is also deeply subjective and contextual. In Buddhism, the diamond is a metaphor for "emptiness," a special term used to highlight the shifting nature of all things.[1] This Buddhist concept of the diamond is very different from the way I think about my own diamond, which is different, again, from the way diamonds are rendered by the "A Diamond Is Forever" advertising campaign.

In listening to my grandmother talk about her experiences with my grandfather—memorialized by this stone—I realized that the diamond had been changed into a particular kind of object through her interpretive work. It had been transformed from a metaphor—the generic "diamond is forever"—to a specific, unique, "this diamond" when it became integrated into her life, her story, and her way of being in the world. I wondered about the roles taken on by other diamonds in other lives. I had presumed that diamonds, perhaps like all commodities, were "empty"—we add meaning to them with unique combinations of shared, public knowledge and personal life events—but, I wondered, what might we learn from delving into the dichotomy between public and private?

To understand how people go about making meaning in specific instances (this particular diamond) of generically known things (the idea of a diamond in general), I gathered stories about diamonds, and examined them within the context of diamonds' production and use. There is, of course, a massive marketing operation for diamonds, but I wanted to track its reach. How much does diamonds' marketing—movies, fashion ads, wedding industry brochures, and so forth—determine their meaning? How is it that diamonds came to be embedded in American life at the end of a sprawling global production chain? Moving beyond "A Diamond Is Forever," I wondered how these rocks came into our lives as super-valuable gems in the first place. Because we are simultaneously entrenched in large-scale sociohistorical dynamics, microlocal circumstances, and everything in between, we cannot help but draw upon shared cultural ideologies. And yet, at times, people can see the world in ways that are incongruent with shared patterns. Tracing this tension allowed me to discover what Webb Keane (2003, 419) calls the "semiotic ideology" of diamonds—that is to say, what kinds of signs we take diamonds to be—and, more importantly, to illustrate the creative aspect of our interaction with material culture.

In contemporary American society, material culture consists mostly of commodities, things that we buy. We live around them, with them, and through them. These things mean something to us; they anchor us in the world. And while the question of why things have meaning at all is a metaphysical question, one not easily answered using anthropological methods, we can use ethnography to investigate how things work as cultural objects. In unpacking the way meaning is made within the representational economy, which Keane (2003, 410) describes as "the dynamic interconnections among different modes of signification at play within a particular historical and social formation," we gain an appreciation for how agency, imagination, humor, and poesy enhance everyday experience.

Knowing how meaning operates with regard to material culture— and in the case of an advanced capitalist society, this generally means highly advertised commodities—helps illuminate the way we engage the stream of mundane moments that constitute experience. And while the methods (ethnographic study, archive and historical analysis, and examination of markets and marketing) employed in this study could be used to examine virtually any kind of object, they are especially well suited to deal with commodities subject to intense symbolic elaboration through advertising, or those used as identity markers in denoting and communicating gender, race, sexuality, ethnicity, and class. Because we both express ourselves and learn about others through the medium of material culture, semiotic analysis can help tell us who we are and how we got to be this way.

Enchanted one day, mystified the next, I experienced a spectrum of attitudes toward diamonds as I worked through this research. But looking at my grandmother's ring, flashing on my finger as I write, I realize how much I have come to appreciate its lovely rockness as a result of this project. It is my hope that other kinds of objects will also be made more full, as we better understand the cultural work we accomplish through them.

ACKNOWLEDGMENTS

This has been a long project in the making and would never have been completed without a great deal of generosity, guidance, and help from many people. First of all, I would like to thank those who shared with me their diamond stories, both during the period of intensive fieldwork and ever since.

Financial support was provided by the City University of New York Graduate Center. I thank CUNY for being so openhanded: the Writing Across the Curriculum (WAC) fellowship and the Instructional Technology (IT) Fellowship yielded so much more than economic assistance. Archive work at Duke University Special Collections library was funded by the J. W. Thompson Archive Research Fellowship, which I deeply appreciate. The wonderful staff at the Duke library helped to ensure that this phase of my work was fruitful.

I am extremely grateful to everyone who read and commented on various versions of this manuscript (and there were many). I would like to especially acknowledge Michael Blim, Vincent Crapanzano, Shirley Lindenbaum, Jane Schneider, Setha Low, Jeff Mascovsky, Webb Keane, Paul Stoller, and Robert Eisinger. I also owe an enormous debt of gratitude to my amazing colleagues at the CUNY Graduate Center: Larisa Honey, Julian Brash, Suzana Maia, Jean Murley, Roberto Abadie, Melis Ece, Nathan Woods, Aysecan Terzioglu, Klāvs Sedlenieks, Jimmy Weir, Khaled Furani, David Vine, Chris Lawrence, Peter Hoffman, Roger Rawlings, and Pelligrino Luciano gave me inspiration, laughter, and honest feedback. Erin Martineau has remained an especially constant and brilliant critic of my work. I owe a special debt to the late Dr. Richard Smythe, who at UNC–Chapel Hill introduced me to the works of Charles Saunders Peirce. And to Dr. Walter Scott, who made sure that I was able to develop initial drafts with all of my pieces intact.

I am so thankful to Geshe Michael Roach, Venerable Ani Pelma, Khongla Rato Rinpoche, Guy Donahue, K. Patabi Jois, Greg Tebb, and Venerable Nicholas Vreeland, who encouraged me to think in new ways. Dr. Duba at the Museum of Natural History also provided invaluable assistance, as did my instructors at the Gemological Institute of America.

Jennifer Hammer and her colleagues at New York University Press made the entire publishing experience a pleasure and helped in countless ways to improve and to prepare this book. I would also like to thank the anonymous reviewers for their many insights and excellent suggestions.

Some of the ideas presented in this book have appeared in published articles: an article on type/token distinction entitled "Diamond Signs: Generic Stones and Particular Gems" appeared in *Social Semiotics,* and an article on conflict stones (a topic I do not cover in this book) entitled "Picturing Blood Diamonds" appeared in *Critical Arts: South-North Cultural and Media Studies.* Aspects of this material have also been presented as paper presentations in various panels at American Anthropological Association and Society for Anthropology of North America conferences. I appreciate those who attended and responded with care—I learned so much from your questions and comments.

There is no way to express the value of ongoing encouragement from Missy Stancil, Elizabeth Leech, Mclean Brice, Shannon Burke, Lisa Young, Capri Rosenberg, Jessica Smith, David Stivers and Kate Newell, Liz Sargent, Mary Doll, John Valentine, Desire Houngues, Mary Lou Davis, Julie and Joel Varland, Tim Jackson, Christoph Kluetsch, and Paul Abbruzo. Stefan Kochs deserves a very special shout out because he provided moral, financial, and spiritual support throughout the drafting and redrafting of this manuscript.

And finally, I would like to thank my parents and grandparents (especially Anna Lee Elmore Falls) and Darrell and Angie Dukes, as well as Lee Falls, Katherine and the Mengedoht Gang, Zimri and Tallulah, Roy and Jupe. But without Dare's love, patience, encouragement, and sense of humor, this book would never have been even remotely possible.

INTRODUCTION: LITTLE ROCKS

A rock!!! It's just a rock, OK? So, I mean, what's it
all about anyway?
—Tom, diamond consumer

In one sense, diamonds are just little rocks. But they are extraordinary rocks, jam-packed with value and significance. This book explores what diamonds mean, how those meanings come about, and what our interactions with these stones can tell us about ourselves and our relationships with material culture, especially mass-marketed, mass-produced, and mass-consumed commodities. Examining the way people relate to diamonds, we gain insight into the way we make sense of all kinds of commodified goods, the kinds of feelings and even self-understandings they evoke, and the way cultural contexts—like advertising strategies and historical narratives—influence our engagement with ordinary objects.

Like many other commodities, diamonds are instantly recognizable to most Americans, especially the round "brilliant" cut.[1] Even the smallest stones can be cut with fifty-eight facets, causing light to bounce around inside the stone, which is itself clear, but not transparent. It attracts the eye, but does not allow the gaze to penetrate. In many ways, the qualities of a cut stone mirror the diamond as a cultural artifact. The industry is infamously opaque, while its goods are carefully manicured and marketed. And like a brilliant cut with its many facets, diamonds are

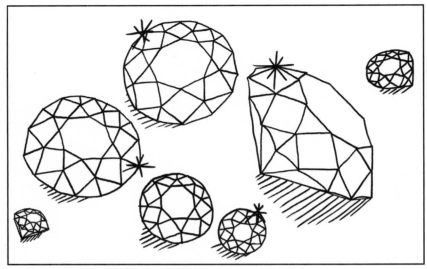

Figure I.1. Cut diamonds. (Illustration by Kay Wolfersperger, used by permission.)

polyvalent, which means that they carry many meanings: gemological, monetary, sentimental, and geological, just to name a few.

Their polyvalence makes diamonds objects of fascination. But what are they, anyway? Just bits of compressed carbon? On the one hand, the industry promotes evaluating diamonds based on the "4 Cs"—clarity, cut, color, and caratage (weight)—which help determine a diamond's grade, and ultimately its price. Marketing campaigns attach notions of love, status, and romance to them. And diamonds really are exceptional minerals, holding special interest for students of geology. They are hard to find and difficult to mine. But rare as they are thought to be, diamonds are everywhere (Zapata 1998). And everyone who has a diamond has a story to tell about it. These stories reveal what we do with these stones, but, more importantly, they suggest how we create value, meaning, and identity through our interactions with what we might call "stuff" (see Miller 2009a; see also Miller 2005).

Consider an excerpt from Carla's story (told in more detail in chapter 6). When she first married Gene, she refused to wear a diamond. Then her Aunt Margaret gave her a small but well-shaped stone. Because it was a gift from a family member, Carla felt obliged to wear it, explaining that it alerts other men that she is married and stops them from hitting on her ("usually") but that at first she was not at all interested in even having a diamond, much less one that she did not find visually appealing. She held the stone up for inspection, moving her hand slightly from side to side in a gesture meant to playfully mock television ads featuring engagement rings. We both laughed, then continued the interview.

Diamond stories, invoking kinship, gender, aesthetics, and desire, as in this excerpt, develop within a complex cultural landscape. Idiosyncrasy, agency, and creativity shape these narratives, which in turn explain, interpret, and ultimately make social worlds happen. Our interactions with things, such as commodities, simultaneously reflect and reshape our experience. This "social work" of diamonds constitutes a pragmatic dimension of consumption (see Dant 1999).

We live with and through things that become meaningful because of our interactions with them, but how do people go about making meaning? In what ways are diamonds good examples of material culture in general? How do people who are positioned within a globalized political economy and a compelling universe of advertising interact locally with these polished rocks? How are those rocks transformed into something unique? What can we learn from an analysis of consumers' stories about the production of identity, creation of kinship, and challenges to the status quo? How does material culture help actualize selves and social relationships?

To answer these questions, this books draws on the work of the American philosopher Charles S. Peirce (1839–1914). While the full Peircian semiotic project is extremely complex in both its content and mission, I hope to demonstrate how one apparatus of the Peircian theoretical toolbox, what is known as the Second Trichotomy (icon-index-symbol), can be fruitfully employed in the study of material culture in general, and applied in the case of diamond consumption in particular. Peirce noted that the Second Trichotomy was the one he used most frequently, and declared that it had the greatest impact on social analysis (Parmentier 2009, 143). In this study, using data collected during fieldwork with industry insiders and consumers in New York City, I explicate how the Second Trichotomy can be mobilized to illuminate how people create meaning. To contextualize these narratives within the history of diamond production, I provide a description of contemporary industry dynamics, an ethnographic report on a grading school, and an exploration of diamond marketing archives. This larger context surrounds us, influencing the semiotic ideologies we use, that is to say, what kinds of signs we take things to be.

My intention is not to provide a definitive analysis of the diamond as a cultural artifact, nor to illuminate a typology of signs, but rather to reflect upon and critique the way the consumer is constructed in social theory. This approach starts with an assumption that similar cultural signs, such as diamonds, from disparate times and places—and even those from the same place, or held by the one individual at different times—may not have consistent cultural meanings (see Parmentier 2009, 153). I take the individual as the locus of investigation rather than starting with the group, which illuminates how agency, often in the form of creativity or resistance, resides in ordinary acts of consumption. Many anthropological studies of consumption assume that consumers' ideas about commodities are in some way reducible to the aims of advertisers or to the ideologies on which advertisers draw. By beginning with consumers' agentive acts and then critically examining the semiotic mechanics behind individual variation, my approach traces and situates the unpredictable process of identity formation within a powerful matrix of historical and cultural discourse.

Identifying different modes of semiosis (meaning making) observed in diamond stories allows me to carve out a space for idiosyncratic meaning making and to argue that consumers use diamonds as a cultural resource to "do" things, by developing their own interpretations as an exertion of agency in an ad-burdened universe—rather than simply imbibing corporate ideologies. We are thus invited to revisit the way we identify, think about, and treat difference, agency, and the politics of consuming material goods. This book is, therefore, in dialogue with (a) semiotic anthropology, particularly those studies that use Peircian sign theory for ethnographic research, attend to individual differences (best exemplified by Johnstone [2000]), or interrogate meaning-making practices (such as work by Vincent Crapanzano [2001] and Webb Keane [2003]); (b) consumption theory, especially with regard to the use of Saussurean theories of meaning that have guided the study of commodities; and (c) research on material culture concerning production, sensuality, and use.

Semiotic Anthropology: Making Sense of Signs

In her review of semiotic anthropology, Elizabeth Mertz (2007) takes up the shifts and themes characterizing the field since the publication of *Man's Glassy Essence* (1984), in which Milton Singer calls upon scholars to use a Peircian lens to integrate social context into the anthropological analysis of meaning. Mertz's review is illuminating in its coverage of the benefits of this strategy, but there is no section devoted to reviewing the study of material culture, and of the more than one hundred references, there are only a handful showing how one might use Peircian theory to look at meaningful *things*. Interestingly, not one deals with consumer semiosis.

Most of the material front and center in semiotic anthropology is theoretical, and often presented in ways that are frustratingly hard to penetrate. When it is ethnographic, it usually focuses on linguistic encounters or language itself (or both). Much of this work builds upon linguistic anthropologist Michael Silverstein's (1979, 1995) analyses that account for pragmatic and indexical aspects of both language and culture. His theoretical work has served as a foundation for much fine-grained ethnographic research on language acquisition, socialization, and identity production.

As Mertz (2007) points out, emerging concerns with power, history, practice, and agency in anthropological theory have also shown up in semiotic paradigms that question the limits of creativity within linguistic structures and the exertion of agency within cultural contexts. What

Silverstein calls the meta-pragmatic structure of language—that is, the description of what language does, or is believed to do, not just as speech but also as action—is just one of the latest advances in the area of semiotic linguistics.

But semiotic lenses contain powerful tools that can brought to bear in anthropological studies of all kinds of material culture (Kockelman 2006), from Walbiri graphics (Munn 1962) to real estate signs (Gottdeiner 1995) to olive oil (Meneley 2008) to the practice of archaeology itself (Preucel 2010). For example, Carol Hendrickson's *Weaving Identities: Construction of Dress and Self in a Highland Guatemala Town* (1995) draws on a Peircian typology of the icon to analyze images of Guatemalan weavers, exploring the space between the image and its purported object of representation in her critique of capitalist interests. A little further afield, Paja Faudree (2012) argues that approaching language-music "semiotically will promote . . . holism in anthropological practice if coupled to the joint effort of attending to textuality while decentering its primacy" (519). And Galina Lindquist (2001) uses a Peircian semiotic to show that New Age Russian healing is a matter of harnessing the iconic and indexical features of diagnosis. But with regard to objects, one can look beyond *sign types* (index, icon, etc.) to *semiotic ideologies*. In the case of diamonds, we will be looking at both sign types and people's expectations for how diamonds can or should work as vehicles of meaning—their semiotic ideologies, or meta-pragmatic structures, if you will.

There are many kinds of signs: conventional, indexical, imagistic, symptomatic, diagrammatic, metaphoric, poetic, onomatopoeic, and so forth. Each works according to its own logic, and exploring the range of sign types in ethnographic (Daniel 1984, 1996; Riggins 1994; Rumsey 1990) or even literary material (Fischer and Nänny 2001) reveals different aspects of semiosis. People make, respond to, and understand their surroundings through signs like words, visual representations, and objects. Logos are signs. Photos are signs. Cars are signs. And diamonds are signs too. Examining diamonds as signs through personal stories illuminates the complexities of sign play, showing the extent to which basic semiotic activities can be highly creative.

In celebrating the creative aspect of human language, Chomsky noted that the majority of lengthy utterances are original and unique. This is partly because people play with the rules and not just the pieces, to draw on the Saussurean metaphor of language as a game of chess. Linguistic theories based on the work of Saussure focus on the symbolic elements of language, but cannot easily account for communication that bends the rules, subverting or exceeding standard codes of meaning. And, as Paul Kockelman (2006) points out, "while most Saussurean categories can be understood in terms of Peirce's categories ([semiology] may be framed in terms of semiotics), the converse is not true. . . . Saussure's theory has fewer dimensions than the processes it seeks to theorize" (83–84). Identifying these other processes helps us to understand creativity in the face of an encompassing social milieu that is powered by the requirements of advanced capitalism, including some rather convoluted consumption practices.

Consumption

There has been a tremendous amount of work done on contemporary consumption by scholars across many disciplines. Of especial utility to consumer studies has been work connecting goods to identity, global exchange and circulation, inequality, value, agency, capitalism, branding. Much of this work advances Bourdieu's *Outline of a Theory of Practice* (1984) to detail how we not only produce but are in a sense *produced by* the commodities with which we interact.

To interrogate the conditions of consumption, this study is launched from lines of inquiry that focus on production (Baudrillard 1975; Gereffi and Korzeniewicz 1994), marketing (Applbaum 1998; Chaudhuri 2001; Davila 2001; Nixon 2003; Williams 1980; Williamson 1978), identity (Friedman 1994; Lunt and Livingstone 1992; Qureshi and Moore 1999), and even shopping (Fiske 1994; Lehtonen 1999; Miller 1998, 2001).

Heavily indebted to the "culture as text" analogy articulated by Clifford Geertz (1977), most of this literature (wittingly or unwittingly) treats commodities as language-like units that refer to codified meanings, as Saussure suggested. People certainly do interpret diamonds in this way (where diamonds mean romance or glamour), but this is only part of the story. But because people use material culture in ways that exceed Saussurean semiology, I decided to work with the broader Peircian theoretical project as a starting point. What I most appreciate about using this approach is that it opens up more space for taking seriously individual responses to history and discourse from which broader insights about creative agency might be gleaned.

Making Sense of Material Culture

The field of material culture studies is a highly interdisciplinary endeavor that addresses empirical and theoretical questions related to the roles that things play within social organization and in subjective experience. Material culture represents an extremely important but oddly under-examined area of study, perhaps because, as many have pointed out, the ubiquity of material culture makes it easy to overlook. Since most commodities are also at least partly material, the field of material culture studies intersects in significant ways with research on consumption. This book is in dialogue with scholars of material culture whose work is constantly reconfiguring our understandings of subject/object relations, practices of acquisition and divestment, and processes of interpretation, resistance, and alienation with regard to the commodity worlds we inhabit.

The history of material culture scholarship is grounded in nineteenth-century museum work, archaeology, exhibition practices, colonialism, and consumerism (Buchli 2002). Methods of anthropological research have been revised since then, the notion of "culture" has undergone almost fatal critique, and the use of structuralist, and even poststructuralist, theory to explicate nonlinguistic "texts" has become strained. Now, the "material turn" has generated new questions about the nature, function, and study of materiality (Hicks and Baudry 2010; Ingold 2012). I have been inspired by work along these lines that explores materiality through the close study of particular objects, revealing how people live with material culture in surprising ways (Chin 2001; Myers 2002; Scheld 2003).

One research strategy for people-object relations is to start with broadcasted images and sociological identity categories, rather than individual voices; people do sometimes read material culture in ways predicated on standard assumptions about categories of difference, especially class and gender. But, even the term "material culture" itself suggests a paradox, simultaneously pointing to physicality, which can be observed and understood through use of the hard sciences along with historical, political, and economic analyses; and meaning, which can be studied through anthropological, sociological, psychological, philosophical, and even literary lenses. In this vein, studies of material culture can be classed as "hard" or "soft" (Prown 1996; see also Hoskins 1998). "Hard" studies, such as Robert Hazen's (1999) history of synthetic diamonds, focus on an object's material configuration, from observable qualities, such as color and texture, down to molecular arrangements. "Soft" approaches begin with an investigation of implicit and explicit cultural meanings reported from a subjective position, like Mukulika Banerjee and Daniel Miller's (2008) analysis of the relationship between women and their saris.

Combining a "hard" with a "soft" approach to diamonds, as Andrew Walsh (2004) has done in his work with Malagasy sapphire producers, or as Brian Brazeal (2012) accomplished in his visual ethnography of the Indian emerald trade, this book focuses on the subjective consumption end of the commodity chain. Consumers' stories refract—sometimes only tacitly, sometimes with full-fledged critiques—fascinating histories (Arkansas Diamond Company 1908; Birch and Norhthrop 1899; Carstens

2001; Joris 1986; Kanfer 1993; Lenzen 1970; Oppenheimer 2002; Worger 1987); cultural significances highly mediated by advertising (Epstein 1982a, 1982b; Hay 2004; Westwood 2002); and material presented in a blizzard of marketing and pop culture books and movies (Fleming 1956, 1957; Zoellner 2006; Zwick 2006).

A discursive universe, including advertising, has established a narrative that ties diamonds to romance and glamour, but when I began conducting interviews, I was surprised by the high degree of thematic and structural variation within consumers' stories. My semiotic analysis, accomplished by coding each vignette, showed that these stones are routinely interpreted over and above, alongside, or sometimes against the normative themes that are promoted in ads and historical accounts; that diamonds are used in the service of many kinds of personal and even political projects related to identity production, poesy, and the management of social others; and that people's expectations for how diamonds should work for others as vehicles of meaning varies widely.

So ads have not been entirely successful on a meta-pragmatic level: marketing has not been able to establish a privileged semiotic ideology by which consumers always interpret diamonds as symbols referring to the values that marketers promote. It does, however, provide consumers with a framework for thinking about how other people, especially strangers, are using these things as symbols. This projection of meaning is further explained by the contrast between the way we understand a particular object (our own diamond) and the way we understand a more generic one; in a phenomenon known as a "token-type distinction," we sometimes value tokens (a specific diamond) differently from the ways in which we think about a type (diamonds in general). The way an object is ushered into token-hood from type-hood has to do with experience, use, memory, and belief about a particular object, for example, its scarcity (Falls 2008).

While diamonds are often described as scarce, the contemporary global diamond industry extracts over 120,000,000 carats of rough diamonds annually, although at least 70 percent is "bort," poor-quality stones used for industrial purposes. Still, sale of the remaining gem-quality goods exceeds $72 billion every year. From the 1880s through the 1990s, most "rough"—unpolished diamonds—moved through a pipeline controlled by De Beers Consolidated Mines. De Beers's first-quarter production of 2012 was reported to be over six million carats, with rough sales in the first half of the year estimated at an astonishing $2.83 billion (Krawitz 2012).

While independent rough dealers began mounting real challenges to De Beers's long-held monopoly in the 1990s, the company remains the most important industry player. De Beers is especially active as a leader in sales vocabulary, in marketing strategies—such as the "right-hand ring" campaign—and in designing the Kimberley Process (KP), an international certification system that has helped to reduce the number of "blood diamonds" (diamonds being traded outside of the licit pipeline for weapons used in civil conflict), which have historically made up somewhere between 3 and 20 percent of the trade (see Falls 2011).

Because diamond has a high per-carat value and is easily smuggled, a lively black market has thrived since even before the formation of the modern industry, which is marked by the 1867 discovery of diamonds in South Africa. Early on, these African gems were absorbed by European elites, but the Great Depression left global sales in a slump. Demand was rejuvenated in 1947 when De Beers hired the advertising giant N. W. Ayer to develop an American middle-class market for diamonds, and copywriter Frances Gerety coined the "A Diamond Is Forever" tagline. The plan worked: about 90 percent of American women own at least one diamond, and most own multiple diamonds; the American market absorbs most of the polished goods sold every year on the global market—its $27 billion revenue is twice that of the number two market (China) and three times that of the third largest (India) (Bain 2012b).[2] The heart of the U.S. market is New York City's "Diamond Row," located on Forty-seventh Street between Fifth and Sixth avenues, just a few blocks south of Rockefeller Center and close to the high-end stores of Fifty-seventh Street and Fifth Avenue. This spot is where my research began.

Figure I.2. Diamond lamps on Forty-seventh Street in New York City. (Photo by Chrystian Rodriguez, used by permission.)

Diamond Row

Most diamonds sold in the United States come through the New York market—also called the "bourse," or "exchange"—inside the Diamond Dealers Club (DDC). In 2004, I visited with a DDC officer who gave me a tour of the trading floor, where packets of polished stones are bought and sold. "You're not taping this, are ya?" he asked me, in a room of the utterly nondescript, high-security building, underscoring the covert nature of diamond trading. Not only is Diamond Row home to the DDC, but the entire block—all the storefronts and all the office space above them—is occupied by some type of diamond operation. Walking there, you will see hundreds of stores selling loose stones and jewelry at all price levels. Right around the corner, luxury retailers like Harry Winston, Tiffany and Co., and Movado sell their signature wares.

The Gemological Institute of America (GIA) is also located on Diamond Row. A final authority on polished grading and identification, GIA maintains the 4 Cs and is an essential partner in the production of value. Grading diamonds based on the 4 Cs is an elaborate affair, which requires years of training and experience to do well. The 4 Cs are sometimes accompanied by a fifth C—a certificate, or map, issued by the Gemological Institute of America detailing every relevant characteristic of an individual stone, and conferring additional value. This is why jewelry is sometimes advertised as "GIA Certified!" But certification is not just a marketing ploy. Although GIA does not set prices, the characteristics graders identify on these certificates help determine final costs. And minute discrepancies can be expressed in significant monetary differences. Price tags up and down Forty-seventh Street, and all over the world for that matter, are legislated and legitimized by this system.

GIA also trains students. When I enrolled in their Diamond Grading Course as part of my fieldwork, I met retailers and other industry employees, learned how polished diamonds are produced, and was of course taught the fundamentals of grading. I learned business jargon and how to recognize "features" and "inclusions," like black spots, cracks, or chips. Instructors showed me how to use a loupe (a small magnifying glass), a pointer, a gem microscope, master stones, and special lights to plot characteristics on maps. I was introduced to grading "fancy" cuts (nonround shapes such as marquise, oval, or pear), colored stones (diamonds come in virtually every color of the rainbow), and techniques for identifying diamond simulants such as cubic zirconia and Moissanite.[3] And while there is a subjective aspect to grading, after practicing on hundreds of examples, I was able to create basic maps of simple stones comparable to those produced by specialists. Having the ability to discuss the particulars of grading was extremely useful in my work with both retailers and consumers.

As an institution dedicated to supporting industry interests, GIA also offers instruction in marketing and sales. My teachers frequently outlined the language retailers should use. For example, one instructor told us as he held up a tiny gem, "This one is junk, but to the customer, you know, 'Every diamond is beautiful!'" I guess everyone thought this was pretty funny because it was followed by a hearty round of laughter, but the humor hints at the fragility of a deeply constructed system.

Browsing along Forty-seventh Street, in the old diamond district at Bowery and Canal streets, and in high-end stores like Harry Winston, estate merchants such as ABC, or discount stores like Zales, I routinely heard salespeople echoing ideas advanced at GIA, coaching customers in how to look at these objects—although, as one downtown retailer named Mandy told me, nowadays people come in knowing more about what they want: "Women are smarter about these things now. It used to be that nobody knew that much. Just yesterday a guy came in here with his girlfriend and she had done all the research, I mean you can get this information online now, and she knew exactly what cut and size and so forth." When people arrive having already accepted the grading system, Mandy and other retailers are relieved of doing the "education" that legitimizes different prices charged for goods that look identical to the untrained eye.

Consumer education at the counter is buttressed by extensive ad campaigns. One archive in the Special Collections Library at Duke University is dedicated to De Beers's marketing history, and contains an extensive record that plainly tracks the "A Diamond Is Forever" campaign with its sustained repetition of themes related to scarcity, glamour, and romance. Even though the people I talked with joked constantly about taglines like "diamonds are a girl's best friend," they were not constrained by grading or marketing discourse when it came to telling their own diamond stories. Understanding these stories requires celebrating the uniqueness of each person while taking cultural tropes seriously. Doing so exposes how we use these tiny rocks—just like we use other kinds of commodities—to do the important work of being in the world. It is through our interactions with material culture, such as diamonds, that we forge and texturize our everyday experience.

While scholarship on both material culture and the experience of the everyday is becoming more prevalent in the social sciences, this book offers a somewhat unusual ethnography because while the people I worked with are linked by their interaction with a single kind of good, they do not make up a community per se. I did not decipher what, if any, characteristics were present among all the people I interviewed, most of whom do not know one another. Instead, I examined the mechanics of interpretation through an analysis of more than forty interviews with people I found using "snowball sampling," asking friends and acquaintances to put me in contact with others in their social network and in turn asking them to introduce me to others. Some people I already knew, and others I met in casual settings, at parties or other social gatherings, who after hearing about my research said, "I'd love to be interviewed" or "Oh, I have story for you—" and launched into a detailed anecdote, or told me, "You should really talk to . . . " (offering to introduce me). I worked with both women and men, mostly white women, between the ages of twenty-five and forty, who fell into the gross category of the educated middle-class (as do I). This is demographic data I surmised, both visually and on the basis of what people said, directly and indirectly, about themselves. The group represents the target market for advertising; my findings about the ways their meaning making diverges from cultural discourse are therefore all the more suggestive.

The vast majority of my interviews were unstructured and open ended. I nudged people to address certain issues, but allowed them considerable freedom in taking a direction and using a vocabulary all their own. I did not systematically request information about salary, class, age, religion, sexual orientation, marital status, or cost of diamonds, though sometimes these things came up. Instead of pursuing detailed life histories, I asked for narratives that included circumstances of acquisition, possession, loss, recovery, and plans for future divestment for their diamonds. We talked about how their diamonds are cared for, when they are worn or displayed, how they compare to other things, how those who wear diamonds believe other people read them, and how their stones gathered or lost significance. I sometimes pressed people to pursue trains of thought only parenthetically introduced (and, of course, these parenthetical remarks sometimes turned out to be the most fascinating).

Coding, a method well suited to studies of subjectivity, allowed me to manage the data. Patterns of variables emerged as interviews were coded and then recoded. Complicating the coding process was the fact that interviews are odd social interactions: people are simultaneously indexing who they are and who they think I am; performing identities threaded with ideas about aesthetics, gender, class, and ethnicity; and either creating or disarticulating a power-rife relationship with me (see Crapanzano 1985). I coded data with a sensitivity to meta-level properties (for example, an interviewee who is "telling" me that she feels herself to be cosmopolitan through dismissive statements about suburbanism, while not using any of those particular words), but only insofar as it applied to the way people were placing themselves in the world through their interpretive work. Shelves of scholarly and popular literature covering social, political, and economic facets of the industry (Bergenstock and Maskulka 2001; Du Plessis 1960; Carstens 2001; De Boeck 1998; Dickinson 1965; Harlow et al. 1998; Kanfer 1993; Worger 1987) provided additional variables.

My data was gathered not as an experimental sample to enumerate frequencies but as a pool of narratives analyzed to yield conclusions about the semiosis of material culture. I immediately recognized a bent toward idiosyncrasy, performance, and creativity, and worked to determine how these elements might be explained by means of existing paradigms. It was not an easy fit. A straight political-economy approach misses the imaginative layer of consumption. A celebration of consumer agency misses the way the issues of race, class, and gender inequality that are obviously part of the context can shape people's interpretive practices. And many consumption theories are predicated upon a "culture-as-language" analogy wherein language is conceptualized as "referential." Here, linguistic communication is conceived of as an activity that simply denotes and describes the world as it already is. Language is understood as a tool of propositionality, rather than as pragmatic or rhetorical. The variation in meaning making evident within diamond narratives suggests that consuming material culture is better understood as a practice operating beyond the referential model; it is also pragmatic and rhetorical.

The method I lay out to analyze diamond consumption can be used, with some modification, for virtually any commodity, in the service of different theoretical concerns, or to further investigate the claims I will be making here. Ultimately I argue for an approach that begins with understanding commodities as historically and discursively situated but that recognizes creative agency in the cultural work of the everyday. Identifying the tactics people use allows us to rethink assumptions usually taken as starting points in the study of consumerism, and supports renewed attention to the role of creativity in making experience intelligible.

This case study is meant to show how an understanding of culture can be gleaned by examining the sometimes incongruent relationship between shared cultural registers and the beliefs, practices, and values of individuals within it. These incongruencies can be accounted for by emphasizing what Dell Hymes called the "foundational status" of individuals and individual differences from which culture is ultimately abstracted (Hymes 1979), while still considering the contextualizing, and sometimes defining, social worlds in which we operate. In a more speculative vein, I suspect this line of inquiry will eventually provide support for the idea that objects are best conceived as events rather than as persistent things, and that cultural norms—in a manner not unlike the ways in which common sense turns out to be not very common— are weaker than we might have imagined, abstracted as they are from different streams of experience by subjects who deploy a range of semiotic strategies.

What Do Diamonds Mean?

Diamonds, carbon molecules compressed into regular octahedrons, precede human existence by millions of years, perhaps even hitching a ride to earth on meteorites. Little is known about their first uses, but they are described as early as 300 BCE in written accounts like the *Arthasastra*, an Indian manual for administration and taxation (Harlow 1998). The English word "diamond" first appeared in print around 1310 in Thomas Wright's "Specimens of Lyric Poetry": "Ichot a burde in a hour ase beryl so bryht . . . Ase diamaunde the dere in day when he is dyht" (Simpson and Weiner 1989). The association between stars, dew, or frost and diamonds is now well known, as in Jane Taylor's early-nineteenth-century classic, "Twinkle, Twinkle, Little Star." And they routinely appear as metaphors related to hardness, refractivity, or preciousness:

> What precious drops are those
> Which silently each other's track pursue,
> Bright as young diamonds in their infant dew?
> —John Dryden, *The Conquest of Granada*, part 2, act 3,
> scene 1 (1672)

> As the diamond is the crystalline
> Revelator of the achromatic white light of Heaven,
> So is a perfect poem the crystalline revelation of the
> Divine Idea.
> — Thomas H. Chivers, Preface to *Eonchs of Ruby* (1851)

> Every tooth in a man's head is more valuable than a diamond.
> — Miguel De Cervantes, *Don Quixote* (1605)

"Diamond" is also a shape, a baseball field, a card suit, and a textile stitch. In each case, a resemblance between what is being described, for example, the shape of the baseball field defined by the relationship between the bases, is thought to resemble a diamond crystal. The personal name "Diamond," means "precious" or "valuable," and reflects how symbolic meanings advanced in marketing campaigns can be transferred through naming onto a person, in a kind of sympathetic magic.

So the term "diamond" suggests glamour, sex, romance, and wealth to one person; greed, conventionality, suburbanism, and pretention to another. How are these various ideas generated and maintained? How can disparate sources of meaning—history, memory, poetry, metaphor, formal (even geological) characteristics, and production chains, in addition to marketing discourse—be contained under a single rubric? How do these stones act as prisms through which we see ourselves?

Since consumption is an important cultural activity, understanding how experience is mediated by mass-produced, mass-marketed, and mass-consumed material culture in the context of advanced capitalism has become a priority in social theory (see Appadurai 1986; Journal of Material Culture 1996; Miller 1995; Paterson 2005; Schor and Holt 2000; Howes 1996; McCracken 1990; Ritzer 1996), one approach is to think about diamonds alongside similar kinds of goods (though even as commodities, they do have some very special qualities). But there is surprisingly little research focused on revealing practical relationships between consumers and commodities as such relationships are articulated by consumers themselves (see exceptions in Miller 2009a and Chin 2001). As Tim Dant (1996, 2000) has pointed out, this is particularly the case once things have been integrated into everyday lives, which is striking since this is where the meanings of commodities become particularly salient. So, in putting diamonds in the context of consumer capitalism but focusing on subjectivity, this book is a response to Dant's call to study commodities in their "postacquisition" phase.

Because of their visibility in contemporary society, there are several theories of the commodity, each with its own aims and suppositions, strengths and contributions. In analyzing the diamond trade—embedded in a tangled web of capitalism and implicated in the reproduction of unequal global and domestic relationships—the most useful theories are those that understand consumption as exemplary of advanced capitalism; that explode categories such as "gift," "luxury," and "consumer sovereignty"; and that recognize how indeterminately we absorb messages promoted through marketing. Frankfurt School scholars like Theodor Adorno and Max Horkheimer (1944) and Walter Benjamin (1969), the Cultural Studies approach led by Stuart Hall and Tony Jefferson (1975), and Terence Hopkins and Immanuel Wallerstein's (see Gereffi and Korzeniewicz 1994) commodity chain model all highlight the dynamics of capitalism by linking commodity meanings to exploitative class relations. These scholars show how commodity circuits are related to asymmetrical relationships among the actors within them—including consumer and producer—which is an important first step in establishing how gems accrue value. To explore this context, chapter 1 details the sprawling transnational commodity chain that helps transform lowly rocks into valuable gems.

It takes many years to become a skilled grader, but doing so is fundamental to making gems. Chapter 2 examines how the act of grading choreographs each gem into uniqueness, and thus enhances its market value. Workers doing various jobs in the production process, be they miners, cutters, or retailers, pay particular attention to grading and pricing, but most consumers have a poor grasp of both. The average person cannot distinguish high- versus low-grade, natural versus simulated, fine versus poor, or pricey versus inexpensive diamonds, even with close inspection.

Understanding the history and architecture of production is crucial to appreciating how gems are integrated into larger systems, such as labor networks and political relationships, and how they came to have such a visible presence in the United States. But since the meanings people associate with diamonds may or may not be related to their knowledge of production processes, and because consumers sometimes introduce ideas that have nothing to do with political economy, an approach that demystifies the commodity by laying bare the realities of production only partially explains what diamonds mean to people "on the ground." One must also consider how they are acquired and how they are used.

That there are mutually exclusive differences between the gift and the commodity can be traced to Marcel Mauss's *The Gift* (1922), which explains the social construction of objects, including what they mean, by virtue of their exchange as gift or commodity.[4] This is a false distinction when taken as a binary opposition. Diamonds are special in that they are often received as gifts—but the mere fact that something is acquired as a gift does not necessarily mean that it does not maintain features of a commodity with regard to its history, meaning, social role, and cost. Furthermore, as Dant argues, acquisition by gift or by purchase does not necessarily predict, confer, or constrain meaning, although clearly it can impact interpretation. Looking at exchange and the value of gifted objects as embedded in social relationships, as David Graeber (1996) has done with beads, helps us focus on diamonds in terms of their local trajectories, while remaining open to the possibility of a gift/commodity distinction, a factor that may or may not be relevant to consumers.

Rather than take "gift" versus "commodity" as mutually exclusive categories that determine the role of goods in social relationships, diamonds can be defined by virtue of manufacture and marketability within capitalist production where consumer interpretation is the terminal stage. And although people might see these gems as moving in and out of "commodity-hood"—in and out of a state for which there is a fair cash equivalent—they are clearly produced and consumed within a society in which luxury is valorized (see Kopytoff 1986).

Because diamonds are routinely linked with luxury, and thus with a related binary distinction between want and need, some people told me that diamonds are frivolous expenses that fail to meet any "legitimate" requirement.[5] Echoing these consumer ideologies, discussions about frivolity are found throughout the sometimes morally charged sociological literature about what counts as "need" as opposed to "want." But even if we accept an analytic distinction between need and want, and the related association of luxury with desire, are diamonds really luxury goods? They are sold at every price point, from Harry Winston to Walmart. The industry has tried to persuade us that diamonds are essential in the engagement ritual (and the engagement ring market does drive the market), while simultaneously fostering the idea that they are lavish (and thus only for the wealthy). This strategy has been fairly successful, since many view diamonds, paradoxically, as both necessary and luxurious (un-necessary). The delineation of need versus want by consumers, on the other hand, can structure the way people judge one another in terms of conformity or aspiration, especially in relation to class, because they may assume that others have internalized not just the meanings but also the semiotic ideology advanced by marketing.

Clearly drawing on the content of advertising campaigns, many people told me things like "diamonds are for rich people," and "nothing says money like a diamond." This is not surprising; we do absorb marketing language and can be mesmerized by what Raymond Williams (1980) called the "magical quality of advertising."[6] And the De Beers campaign has been extraordinarily magical. Most adults I talked with knew the taglines and frequently remarked upon the scarcity and status value of diamonds promoted by ads. But the degree to which consumers are more deeply ensnared is less obvious. Their stories contained overt claims of sovereignty and resistance, and showed people as independent, calculating, self-actualized agents of their own destiny, even though they are, without question, operating within a social universe fraught with marketing, most of which asserts class consciousness as part of a brand identity.

As branding techniques have become more sophisticated, commodities that are similar on the surface, like Pepsi and Coke, compete to gain value through symbolic loads constituted through advertising "sign wars" (Goldman and Papson 1991). Purchasing an object may even become a mere alibi for the acquisition of a brand or logo, like the Nike Swoosh; the sign itself arguably is the primary object of purchase. The Forever Mark—a new brand by De Beers in which gems are etched with a logo and unique number—seeks to become a "lovemark," a brand that "reaches your heart as well as your mind, creating an intimate, emotional connection that you just can't live without. Ever" (Saatchi & Saatchi 2013). Burning icons onto polished gems with a laser confirms diamonds' place among other objects subject to the latest techniques of branding. The use of branded gems for social signaling is, however, complicated by the fact that the logo is literally microscopic.

Brand consumption constructs and communicates identity according to characteristics such as generation, class, gender, sexuality, nationality, ethnicity, or race. Commodities express purported membership in identity categories both to known and to unknown others, but few ethnographic studies focus on the subjective aspect of this experience (see Halle 1996 as an excellent exception). Most work in this vein tracks meaning from the top down. Robert Foster (1999), an anthropologist who explores how marketing draws on nationalism, closely reads Coke, Pepsi, and Shell gasoline ads in Papua, New Guinea, and argues that insofar as consuming these products is an everyday experience, consumption is inserted into a "micropolitics of belonging" (263). Here consumption serves as the basis for an imagined national community, and Foster does an excellent job of exploring the mechanisms of branding. But, however compelling his analysis, it would be made even more so had we heard from Coke drinkers themselves. Marketers clearly try to use nationalism as a selling point, but how do the people living in one of the most culturally and linguistically diverse countries in the world interpret this? How do they understand their consumption of soft drinks or gasoline in relation to the nationalism being promoted?

But First, Some Technical Terms

Taking the question of subjective experience into consideration, chapters 3 through 6 track consumer perspectives. I found that the most effective way to accomplish this is through a pointed, thorough semiotic analysis. This treatment requires using some technical terms that I begin introducing here.

Semiotics, as we have seen, is the study of signs. And, following Peirce, a *sign* is anything that means something to someone. Anything can become a sign. And signs can have multiple meanings. They can be linguistic, gestural, or material. There are various kinds of signs, and each kind functions in its own way. People understand diamonds as at least four kinds of signs: symbolic, motivated, poetic, and performative.[7] Chapters 3 through 6 each focuses upon one of these modes. Following Peirce's Second Trichotomy (icon-index-symbol), a *symbol* is a kind of sign that operates by virtue of convention. That is, we learn to associate a certain meaning with a symbol. We are taught that a red octagon means "Stop!" Or that the word "cat," or "*la gata*," refers to the idea of a furry, whiskered creature that likes to chase mice. With symbols there is no necessary or obvious relationship between the significance (Stop!) and the sign itself (red octagon), so the meaning can be described as unmotivated. Another way to think about this is that the form of the symbol is not intrinsic to, or motivated by, the idea to which it refers. Chapter 3 investigates diamonds as symbols.

For motivated signs—such as icons or indexes—there is a discernible relationship between the form of the sign and what it actually means. *Icons* operate by resemblance: a street map of the city resembles the urban layout in some ways (though not in all ways, for example, because maps are much smaller than the terrain they depict). A portrait works iconically when it looks like its subject in some important way. Onomatopoeia is an iconic linguistic sign; a loud crash of objects against a wall motivates us to describe it as "Bam!" The word resembles what it means. *Indexes*, another class of motivated signs, work through causality. A footprint in the sand means (indexes, or points to the fact) that someone walked here. A weather vane swings north (indexes the fact that the wind is blowing north) because the wind pushed it in that direction. Stories collected in chapter 4 show how diamonds work as icons or indexes.

Linguistic theories based on the work of Ferdinand de Saussure, an important linguist and father of the field he called "semiology," focus on the symbolic elements of language, but cannot easily account for poetic communication that subverts or exceeds standard codes of meaning (see Bally et al. 1986). Special devices such as irony, parody, sarcasm, and *ostranenie* remain mysterious and underexplained. *Ostranenie*, literally "making strange," a term developed by Russian literary theorist Viktor Shklovsky, is a device of defamiliarization, and is yet another lens through which we might understand diamond semiosis (Lemon and Reis 1965). Chapter 5 illustrates how "bling" (big, flashy diamonds in unusual settings that are worn in ways that cut against standards of gender and style promoted in industry ads) works partly as a symbol of glamour or status, but by calling attention to itself and its sign-hood, invites a critical, questioning engagement. Bling is a poetic device that instead of reflecting, or even pretending to reflect, cultural norms has the potential to create new knowledge, ideas, and relationships.

Linguistic studies have continued to augment our understanding of the way culture works even as the study was for a time hobbled by inattention to some of the nonsymbolic aspects of language (such as icons, indexes, and poetics). Linguistic anthropologists such as Webb Keane (2003) have explored how these elements of language might be used to understand cultural dynamics. In a related line of inquiry, J. L. Austin (1962), in his seminal *How to Do Things with Words*, explores the pragmatic dimension of language. Demonstrating how language operates beyond representation, Austin argues that language "does things," such as confer titles, create relationships, and dissolve obligations: language is, in this sense, *performative*. Combining insights garnered from Austin's work with a focus on linguistic idiosyncrasy (which assumes the individual as the locus of meaning production [Johnstone 1996, 2001]), chapter 6 shows how diamonds, like linguistic utterances, are both in and of the world, and as such, are used performatively. In short, diamonds "do things."

"The Fullness of Diamonds," the concluding chapter, revisits questions opened in this introduction, reviews themes suggested by ethnographic materials, and discusses how this framework might be expanded. Reflecting on the main arguments advanced in each chapter, which are organized heuristically in terms of iconicity, indexicality, symbolism, and performance, the conclusion shifts in scale, from a close discussion of diamonds to commodities in general, to explore the larger implications of this case study.

Investigating—instead of assuming—how signs are interpreted provides us with a method for understanding how people navigate the various social worlds in which they inevitably participate. In deciphering the unpredictability present in consumer narratives, and what it might suggest for anthropology as a discipline, I call for a keener interest in idiosyncrasy: far from trivial, and without lauding "individualism" as a political or social position, idiosyncrasy makes living in society not just bearable but also intelligible. Its presence must, therefore, be integrated into cultural theory.

But there is an even more vital political point to be made here. Semiotics is not only about interpretation; material culture is not simply a blank slate for unconstrained meaning making. Material culture also motivates and expresses activity. By casting local variations against larger cultural patterns, by paying attention to the particular within the general, we open a theoretical space for creative agency—for recognizing that alternative ways of being are often hidden in plain sight.

1

FROM ROCK TO GEM

Anthropology and Value

Once they are cut and polished, diamonds are quite valuable—especially considering how small they are. But how do we get from "just a rock" to "such a gem"? Where does a diamond's value come from? How is its value defined, produced, and recognized? What is "value" anyway?

Moving beyond economic models of value that hinge upon exchange, anthropological theories of value consider a broad array of variables such as labor, use, sentimentality, morality, semiotics, and more. The anthropological lens is multivalent, even kaleidoscopic. As Paul Eiss and David Pederson (2008, 283) point out, "from Smith and Ricardo to Marx and Mauss, and by way of Simmel and Saussure, the category has been used in varied ways to illuminate ethical, economic, aesthetic, logical, linguistic, and political dimensions of human life. . . . The value of value may lie in its ability to elucidate and move across boundaries of many kinds." Value is, thus, a foundational category, and deserving of exploration across all domains of activity and experience.

Many anthropological theories start with Marx and develop "value" in ways that attend to some aspect of labor, use, or exchange with regard to contemporary capitalism. David Graeber, in *Toward an Anthropological Theory of Value: The False Coin of Our Own Dreams* (2001), for example, combines theoretical innovations by Marcel

Mauss and Roy Bhaskar to argue for value as a form of creative action. Contributors to Fred Meyers's (2002) edited volume, *Empire of Things: Regimes of Value and Material Culture*, challenge the implications of Annette Weiner's (1992) theory of inalienability within a capitalist context, utilizing Arjun Appadurai's demonstration that objects take on different meanings as they move through different cultural contexts (Appadurai 1986). These texts show us that value can be used as a theoretical lens to transcend the restrictions of binary categories (like production vs. consumption, or gift vs. commodity), and that value can provide an analytic device to address how groups of people might be linked by their interaction with a set of goods even when separated by time or space. Using value in this way usually requires, however, a sustained consideration of historical context.

And just as different notions of value appear in theory, there are many iterations of "value" in the vernacular of the everyday. It is a term whose meaning at once expands and dissolves upon closer inspection; even as a concept, value is never inert. Its force is felt across every domain of social life—from the political and economic to the aesthetic, the religious, the scientific, the semantic, the moral, and the personal. Insofar as subjective value, or meaning, takes place in a cultural context in which many forms of value and valuation are operative, any study of value must consider a range of questions concerning the forms, sociality, and production of value. What are the relationships among various forms of value, and how might one form of value be translated into the terms of another? How does the notion of intrinsic value operate? Are there forms of value that are epiphenomenal to others—and if so, what is the nature of these secondary forms? How might value serve as a source of social action? Are there hegemonic forms of value in different social activities, and how are they produced and maintained? If there are gatekeepers of value, who are they and how are they established? How might cultural agents seek to shape or wield the standards of value to their own purposes? How do historical and discursive constructs restrict or enable alternative semioses? And finally, how do conceptions of value within anthropology itself reflect larger disciplinary issues, as well as direct research? I will return to these questions at the conclusion of our adventure into the value of diamonds, a journey that begins now with the story of how these rocks became gems. This is a good place to start because besides being impressively serendipitous, it helps explain how the industry choreographs diamonds' value and provides a backdrop against which consumption takes place.

Romance, Status, and Glamour

The association of diamonds with romance, status and glamour is, actually, relatively recent. And you might be surprised to learn that diamonds were not always for women. It was only in mid-fifteenth-century France that King Charles VII, defying sumptuary laws prohibiting women from wearing them, gave a diamond pendant to his mistress, Agnes Sorel. As soon as she started wearing it, she was emulated by her peers, starting a new trend in the court.

If we go further back, the particulars of diamond wear become somewhat murky. Indian Dravidians knew of diamonds by the seventh or eighth century BCE, but even as late as 4 BCE, Buddhist texts referring to diamond as a precious stone contained few clues about where it was found, how it was used, or what it meant. The Bible also seems to reference diamond, though it is possible that authors were referring to magnetite, corundum, or rock crystal quartz, using terms that were subsequently mistranslated as "diamond." Pliny's *Natural History* (77 CE) is one of the earliest texts that appears to portray diamonds as a cultural artifact, but the text has also been subject to questions regarding translation issues.

Greek, Indian, and Chinese legends all allude to diamonds' magical qualities, describing their use as poisoning or healing agents, or as cutting and bead-drilling tools. Through a kind of contagious magic, diamonds were thought to bring virility to men on the battlefield and in the bedroom. The fantastical story of Alexander the Great rescuing a stockpile of diamonds from a snake-guarded pit, and a similar tale celebrating Sinbad the Sailor's escape from Diamond Valley, are universally related in books on diamond lore. Other legends, like the naming of the Koh-i-Noor ("Mountain of Light"), a huge 108.93-carat Indian diamond, or the discovery of diamonds in South Africa by Erasmus Jacobs, contribute to a history generally construed as a sequence of wondrous incidents.

Our ongoing fascination with carbon gravel is demonstrated by the success of trade publications that court the industry at large, lionize individual diamondeers (often hagiographically),[1] and even spotlight single stones. Early on, merchants and visitors to Brazil and South Africa wrote stories of arduous travel to rowdy fields that abounded with scoundrels and scandals, authoring books with exciting titles such as *History of the War in South Africa, Containing a Thrilling Account of the Great Struggle between the British and the Boers; Including the Causes of the Conflict; Vivid Descriptions of the Fierce Battles; Superb Heroism and Daring Deeds; Narratives of Personal Adventures; Life in Camp, Field and Hospital, Etc., Etc.; Together with the Wonderful Story of the Transvaal, the Orange Free State; Natal and Cape Colony; the Kaffirs and Zulus; Richest Gold and Diamond Mines in the World, Etc., Etc.* (Birch and Northrop 1899).[2]

Half a century later, readers continued to be captivated by diamond stories, as ex–security agents penned accounts of guarding booty; *Diamonds Are Forever* (1956) and *The Diamond Smugglers* (1957) were best-selling, nonfictional accounts of the De Beers Security Service, written by former security agent Ian Fleming—most famous for creating the character of James Bond. And British MI5 agent Sir Percy Sillitoe, star of Fleming's *Smugglers*, wrote *Cloak without Dagger* (1955) describing his experience masterminding the De Beers International Diamond Security Organization, which was tasked with halting African illicit diamond buying (IDB).[3] Industry insiders now write about their struggles to control new Canadian fields,[4] while journalists and scholars track diamonds from outsider perspectives.[5] These texts are fascinating in and of themselves, and, taken as a collection, help to explain the larger contemporary industry. Insular, sprawling, and powerful, the diamond business generates huge profits for individuals, corporations, and states across the world, and the gems are implicated in identity formation, social organization, and political violence in diamond-rich areas.

William Crane's (1965) work on Congolese *évolués*, or "evolved ones," locates the emergence of a class that imitated European lifestyles within the context of burgeoning luxury industries such as the Kasai diamond fields. Filip De Boeck's (1998) more recent work connects diamond traffic to commodities, money, and identity in southwestern Congo-Zaire. Also focusing on the emergence of new social groups, De Boeck described the widespread phenomenon of the *bana Lunda'* (the children of Lunda'), the young Congolese urbanites traveling through civil war from southwestern Zaire to the Angolan province of Lunda, in order to dig or dive for diamonds in UNITA-controlled territory. These articles, spanning thirty-five years, demonstrate how Western demand has continued to influence local activities, social formations, and economies in areas where diamonds are mined. To extend consideration of these transnational relationships, I focus on tensions between production and the subjective realm of demand. So how are these gems produced?

The Rise of Diamonds

Diamond mining takes place in a technologically dynamic landscape. Today, most gem-quality diamonds are extracted from highly mechanized mines in Africa, Russia, Australia, and Canada. Some of these mines are new, operational only since 2000. Hundreds of years ago, diamonds were found only occasionally in Borneo, before they were discovered in Goa, India, around the seventh or eighth century BCE (Spencer et al. 1998). These were alluvial diamonds spread around a large area by the forces of erosion; their poor quality and dispersion meant that mining in India never became a high priority. Even during peak production in the late 1600s, India only produced between fifty and one hundred thousand carats per year, only a small percentage of which were gem quality. The rest were used as abrasives in bead drills or just discarded. Indian diamond collecting was eclipsed when diamonds were discovered in Brazil.

Around 1730, just as Indian production was petering out, gold *garimpieros* (miners) in Minas Gerais (southeast Brazil) recognized that the small, greasy-looking stones discarded by panners were not worthless bits of quartz, but diamonds. Brazil was then under Portuguese control, and the Crown tried to manage the diamond-rich riverbeds by taxing miners and their slaves, creating a system in which only a few designated companies could operate. A decade later, Portugal canceled these contracts and got into production itself, tasking royal cashiers with the counting and grading of diamonds shipped to Lisbon to be sorted for distribution (Bernstein 1986). Far more calculating than Indian policy, Portuguese management focused on both production and distribution in order to maximize the prices they could charge their English, French, and Dutch buyers.

As production became more efficient, other Brazilian sites were discovered, but more diamonds invited more pilfering. The small size, liquidity, and high value of diamonds meant that they were easily stolen and smuggled. In much the same manner as occurs today, "leaks" in the legal supply system led to a vigorous contraband market operating outside of the Portuguese trade. There is no way to know how many diamonds moved through black-market channels, but the official market was so lucrative and the effort required to stop the black market was so great that the hemorrhage was more or less tolerated. This same cost-benefit arithmetic was applied in modern times to mines in places like Sierra Leone, until a PR nightmare—generated by the NGO-led "Blood Diamonds" campaign—pushed the industry to take serious steps to halt the black-market exchange of diamonds for weapons. (The industry's efforts have been at least partly successful.)

Portugal's attempt to control mining, distribution, polishing, and sales was eventually replicated by other entrepreneurs. It is interesting to compare how the Portuguese strategy—slowly integrating the product chain first backwards and then forwards—was later mimicked, and extended, by De Beers. The current De Beers branding strategy and Flagship Stores move toward even greater integrated management of production, distribution, and sales.[6]

The flow of Brazilian diamonds into Europe had two important consequences. Indian diamonds, few and highly prized, had been treasures for the elite. Now, not only were they more available because of increased supply, but they were less expensive, to boot. As a result, they were swept into commodity capitalism and, as European royalty became increasingly unable or unwilling to absorb them, the emerging industrial bourgeoisie started to buy diamonds as status goods. Meanwhile, Brazil attained independence and fostered increased production by easing regulations. By 1850, new laws encouraging free enterprise had caused the untaxed contraband trade to ebb, but, at the same time, Brazil's ability to fix prices, set leases, and regulate site fees were weakened. So, even as bourgeois demand continued to rise, looser laws combined with increasing scarcity meant dramatically less production (Bernstein 1986). The diamonds were running out!

As production slowed, supply to Europe and the United States was severely curtailed. Major cutting and polishing outfits in Antwerp, Amsterdam, and France experienced worrisome shortages. How would the cutters survive? Where would retailers find stock? Miraculously— just as the Brazilian supply emerged to replace the dying industry in India—diamonds were discovered in South Africa, just as Brazilian production petered out. According to legend, a game hunter was handed a large, conspicuously glittery stone by the Boer farmer Schalk van Niekerk in 1867. The stone had been found among the pebbles in the Orange River, near the settlement of Hopetown, by his young neighbor, Erasmus Jacobs. Variations of this tale appear in dozens of publications, but what seems certain is that the 21.25-carat diamond, now known as the "Eureka," was displayed at the Paris World Exposition that year.

One might have expected a massive diamond rush to ensue. But rumors that the stone had been planted—a fraud technique known as "salting" that makes barren land seem diamondiferous—kept people in doubt and away. When another diamond was identified nearby, it too was virtually ignored. As it turns out, these were both alluvial finds. No one knew then that water had eroded primary deposits, ferrying the stones far away from their ground source.[7]

As soon as the first primary deposit, known as a kimberlite pipe (after its ore and shape), was discovered between the Vaal and Modder Rivers in 1870, the rush was on! This area became the famous Kimberley Mine. Another pipe, found on the estate of brothers D. A. and J. N. De Beer, became the De Beers Mine. The discovery of more pipes soon followed, and thousands of men from Great Britain and elsewhere came, hoping to strike it rich. Digger committees created rules they hoped would prevent centralized control, while local governments tried to develop and enforce their own laws. In 1871, the British declared Griqualand West a colony of the British Crown, but instead of following in the footsteps of the Portuguese, they legitimized digger committees and their rules for limiting claim size and prohibiting corporate alliances. These rules worked fairly well for alluvial collecting, on the surface and over a large area. But once it became clear that diamonds were not just on the surface but also underground, the men had to work much harder to manage their claims, and limitations on size and collaboration fell into disuse.

The huge Kimberley Mine became increasingly unmanageable as workers excavated at uneven rates. The thin dirt walls separating the claims collapsed, and debris from one level fell or were pushed into the next. Rain and ground water had to be removed. A network of ropes was installed to haul buckets of earth and water in and out. As the entire area became crisscrossed with tangled webs of rigging and heavy machinery, it became more difficult to move men, tools, and water safely and efficiently. By the 1880s, finding a solution to the water problem represented a lucrative business opportunity (see Epstein 1982b, Lenzen 1970). The era of De Beers was about to begin.

"My dear, De Beers IS the diamond industry."

John Cecil Rhodes, a British national there to make his fortune, tackled the water problem by investing in and renting out steam pumps. Combining the profits he made excavating the De Beers Mine with those from his pumping business, he was able to purchase even more claims. He then began building the company that would later become De Beers Consolidated Mines, Ltd. His competitors, meanwhile, were also consolidating claims at other sites. Eventually there were only two major shareholding corporations at the nearby Kimberley Mine: the Kimberley Central, which was a miners' conglomerate, and the Compagnie Française des Mines de Diamante du Cap, known as "The French Company," which controlled the larger portion of the mine.

By 1888, Rhodes had gained control of the De Beers Mine, aiming to adapt the supply of rough diamonds to the market-dependent world demand by centralizing the control of production. Simply put, supply would be adjusted as demand fluctuated. Through price fixing at a level maximally above production costs, effected through collective monopolization, Rhodes also created a stabilizing fund that would cover costs in the event of economic recession and any resultant drop in demand (Bernstein 1986). This strategy has defined the De Beers model to this day.

But his aims extended well beyond mere profit seeking; Rhodes hoped to use revenue to recolonize Africa—and beyond—for Great Britain. In support of these goals, the South African Colonial Office granted him a special charter empowering him not only to build mines but to develop railroads, lay telegraph wires, annex territories, raise armies, and even install governments. And while Rhodes the historic figure is often lauded as a hard-working, nationalistic visionary, Rhodes the man was frequently denigrated as misogynistic, stiff, and calculating. Depictions deriding his behavior and high, squeaky voice stand in stark contrast to those of his rival, Barney Barnato. Practically every account of Barnato, born Barnett Isaacs to a London rabbi, paints the image of a charmed, likeable "bad boy" whose charismatic personality simultaneously elicited suspicion and friendship.

Having followed his brother Harry to South Africa to make his fortune in 1873, Barnato's first swindle involved peddling defective cigars. Ever the entrepreneur, he arranged (and fought in) boxing matches, performed in a cabaret, sold liquor, and invested in imaginative schemes. Like almost everyone else living around the South African fields, Barnato eventually learned to deal diamonds, buying a claim in the Kimberley pit, which almost immediately began to produce. He invested in more claims, taking chances on places that others had abandoned. His strategy paid off: he and his brother soon amassed enough capital to take over the miners' conglomerate, Kimberley Central Company.

There was no love lost between Rhodes and Barnato. Rhodes seems too have regarded Barnato as a talented hoodlum. Barnato thought Rhodes a snobbish prig. In 1888, this antagonism came to a head. Rhodes, with monopoly in mind, cast his eye upon control over the Kimberley Mine. Well connected in the British banking world, he secured enough backing to bring about a takeover of The French Company. Barnato mounted a counteroffer. In ensuing negotiations, Rhodes convinced Barnato that competitive bidding would only benefit The French Company, and he persuaded Barnato to agree to a deal that would allow Rhodes to buy out The French Company's section of Kimberley for the lower bid of £1.4 million, which he would then sell to Barnato in exchange for £300,000 plus 20 percent of the Barnato Brothers' Kimberley holdings. Barnato believed himself the victor. But Rhodes, with the help of financiers in London and a plan to dump diamonds from the De Beers field onto the market to lower prices, started buying up shares of Barnato's company, eventually positioning himself to take over the entire Kimberley Mine. When Barnato realized he had been bested, a consolation deal gave him a lifetime appointment in the newly formed De Beers Consolidated Mines; his tenure ended after less than ten years when he either fell or jumped off a ship headed for home in 1897.

Rhodes easily acquired the rest of the mine. By 1889, De Beers controlled at least 90 percent of world output, but Rhodes took the lessons of history a step further. Although production had been managed successfully through centralized authority in both India and Brazil, Rhodes pushed for central control not just of production but also of marketing and sales. This he would accomplish in several steps, the first of which was to establish the Diamond Pool Committee consisting of about ten firms of dealers in London, three of which were major shareholders in De Beers Consolidated Mining. The group put together packaged boxes of assorted-quality unpolished goods ("rough") to be sold at fixed prices. There are remarkable similarities between the operations of the Diamond Pool Committee and those of the contemporary Diamond Trading Company; the latter now holds London "sights" where about 60 percent of the available global rough is packaged and then distributed to a special group of invited clients, called "sightholders," who process the rough at set prices.

De Beers survived Rhodes's death in 1920. Through a series of property acquisitions and cross-holding arrangements, a major interest was acquired by Sir Ernest Oppenheimer's Anglo-American Corporation. By 1929, Oppenheimer was made chairman of De Beers. The next year, in extending Rhodes's strategy of forward integration, Oppenheimer hired the N. W. Ayer Company to develop a marketing campaign in the United States.

Sir Ernest, who died in 1957, was succeeded by his son, Harry Oppenheimer. Harry served as chairman of Anglo-American Corporation and of De Beers Consolidated Mines until he retired from those positions in 1982 and 1984, respectively. Harry's son, Nicky Oppenheimer, became deputy chairman of Anglo-American in 1983 and chairman of De Beers in 1998. And Harry's grandson Jonathan held various other executive positions until the family sold its stake in De Beers in 2011 (Antwerp Facets Online 2011).[8] Such family dynasties are not unusual in the diamond industry. The nepotism seen within the Oppenheimer family in the management of De Beers is reiterated at every level of the industry, around the globe. As a form of "kinship capitalism," families and close friends employ one another in this business because trust is an absolute necessity (Shield 2002).

Loyalties and common goals have kept the network, sometimes referred to pejoratively as a "syndicate," together for over a century, though changes in production, the global economy, and the efforts of a few individuals outside of De Beers are testing the resilience of the long-standing industry architecture. The growth of a significant polishing industry in India, the discovery of diamonds in Australia and Canada, loss of control over Russian goods, threat of damage to demand by public relations campaigns against blood diamonds, in addition to minor threats to the industry levied by the Clean Diamonds Act and even the PATRIOT Act, have together pushed De Beers to develop strategies such as privatization, "supplier of choice" sight protocols, brand-name marketing, and a partnership with LVMH (an investment group founded as a result of the 1987 merger of Louis Vuitton and Moët Hennessy, which seeks world leadership in branded luxury goods). Still, when I asked a Forty-seventh Street retailer to describe the relationship of De Beers to the overall industry in light of these changes, he just laughed: "My dear, De Beers IS the diamond industry."

Pure Carbon

Diamonds are some kind of crystallized mineral, something
that is black. Which is weird, because they are clear!
—Dana, diamond consumer

People sometimes incorporate what they know about production into their attitudes about commodities. But what are the basic steps in diamond production? Where do they come from? What are they, even? Comprised of pure carbon, diamond's chemical formula is simply "C." But graphite, also pure carbon, is the stuff of soft, gray pencil lead. Graphite atoms share only one valence electron (rather than four); they share that one valence electron with only three of their closest neighbors (rather than four), and in sheets (rather than in all directions). The single electron skips from one neighbor to the next to the next in cycles, in essence time sharing with each of its neighbors. Though each sheet is very strong, there are no strong attachments between sheets. When one is writing with a pencil, the sheets slide off one by one as pressure is applied. Since extreme heat and pressure can change electron bonds, graphite can be transformed into diamond (and vice versa).

A third version of pure carbon, lonsdaleite, is a rare configuration associated with meteor impacts. What makes diamond unlike its pure-carbon cognates in both appearance and behavior is its molecular configuration.

The atomic number for carbon in the periodic table is 6, meaning that each atom has six protons and six electrons. Protons in the nucleus have a charge that keeps electrons in orbit and allows them to interact with other atoms. Four of carbon's six electrons follow an orbit in which they are chemically interactive ("valence electrons"), while the remaining two are inactive; there is "space" for an additional four electrons from neighboring atoms in the orbit. So, carbon has four "valence electrons" (electrons in a position to interact with other atoms). The shell of the carbon atom's orbit is ideally balanced with ten electrons, so each atom has "space" for four additional electrons in addition to the six already there. In diamond, the nucleus is surrounded by a full complement of ten electrons: two inactive and eight valence electrons (four of its own, plus four shared from neighboring atoms). Diamond is exceptionally durable because of its "covalent bond" or "shared-electron" bond, meaning that electrons are shared between adjacent atoms—the strongest possible form of attachment.

A few people I interviewed were not only familiar with diamond's atomic structure but used this knowledge to interpret them. Ian, a well-educated writer in his thirties, did this when he explained his policy on engagement rings. The problem, he said, is that individualized creativity and spontaneity are essential ingredients in personal expressions of emotion, such as love or caring, which is inconsistent with the unbending regularity of carbon atoms. Ian said,

> Diamonds are impersonal. They are about as impersonal as you can get! I mean you go and give some Hasidic Jew guy up on Forty-seventh Street like thousands of dollars to justify an idea of emotional permanence. But seriously, what can be more impersonal than carbon atoms lined up just exactly so and totally standardized like stiff little soldiers? And it's all so cold and rational. I value poems and personal creativity much more. Like having people over to play music or sing or just entertaining yourself based on your own merit and imagination. This is more personal. That's what I mean by personal I guess, and I think it's a lot more gratifying.

It is not only diamond's atomic arrangement that is striking. Carbon is a fundamental building block of life, and its role in making and sustaining life can mirror kinship when diamonds are handed down through generations. Margalit, a married woman in her thirties who wears a family diamond, explained,

> Diamonds are made from carbon, I know that, and carbon is everywhere, so the carbon is recycled . . . just like life is recycled, and so it's like when my husband gave me his grandmother's ring . . . we had it reset, but still it's like a continuation in the family. I mean I am not really that into diamonds, but I am into my husband and I love being a part of his family so this is like making a chain. You know, it's all ashes to ashes.

This "ashes to ashes" concept is salient to a broad audience; Life Gem, a company that manufactures diamonds out of carbon-rich cremation remains (pets and people), has been in business for over a decade.

While taking atomic chemistry into consideration is somewhat unusual, interpretation based on diamonds' more apparent features is not. Everyone knows they are hard and transparent, but sometimes other qualities—durability, color, refraction, luminescence, and conductivity—figure into creative readings. Durability might, for example, be read as "stability."

Extraordinary Features

Diamond mineral has some extraordinary features. It is extremely hard, measuring a ten—the highest—on the Mohs Scale of Hardness, a scientific scale of mineral hardness. A good gemstone is hard for practical reasons. Hardness makes it durable, resisting chipping under knocks and pressures, but one thing to keep in mind is that hardness is not necessarily a good indication of durability because minerals can fracture along cleavage planes. Diamonds are cleavable in four directions, and while cutters preparing gemstones can take advantage of these planes, this quality also makes them brittle.

Some minerals, like opal, are durable but not very hard; using opal for dinner jewelry, where it is less likely to get rough use, is consistent with its vulnerable status. The covalently bonded diamond, however, is perfect for everyday wear, as are other hard and durable minerals like ruby, sapphire, and emerald.

Stephanie, a 37-year-old massage therapist and Iyengar yoga teacher, interprets diamonds' pure carbon and hardness as representing simplicity and marital stability:

> A diamond is like the essence of something and this essence is reflected in the context. . . . Simplicity is part of the whole transaction of meaning because a diamond is pithy essence; it is beautiful and long lasting. It endures anything. Like marriage is supposed to. Of course I know that diamonds can become chipped or crack, but they are so hard, and they basically endure. They can scratch glass, and this hardness is communicated in the stone and it means essence. It means endurance.

And this meaning of "endurance" is key to representing a relationship with her husband, Charles.

Diamonds reflect light, "twinkling" and "shimmering"—what scientists call "refraction." The "refractive index" measures the extent to which light is slowed and bent when it enters and passes through something. Transparent, dense structures, like diamond, have high refractive indices. Cut diamonds twinkle and shimmer because light bounces around inside the stone before flickering out the top. As with its purity, high durability, and density, the refractive index of diamond is exceptional. The degree of refraction, which is correlated to the wavelength of light used to measure it, is different at the extreme poles of the visible light spectrum (red and violet). When well-cut diamonds are placed under a halogen light, as in most jewelry stores, light is highly refracted, separating into a prism. That wavelength of light creates a high "coefficient of dispersion," causing the diamond not only to sparkle but to emit tiny colorful rainbows, an effect known as "fire."

While I did not hear consumers using scientific jargon, they routinely referred to "sparkle" and "fire." Renee, a 34-year-old former stockbroker turned housewife, argued that "diamonds are the best out of all the gems, of all the precious stones, because they are the most sparkly. None of the other gems catch the light the way that diamonds do. I think that I like the pizzazz, the 'Hey, look at me!' factor, because they really draw the eye. Diamonds cry out!"

Imitation or "simulated" diamonds made out of glass, Moissanite, and cubic zirconia can have even higher coefficients of dispersion than diamond, making them look fake; the fire in simulated diamonds crackles neon, with lime greens, lavenders, and pinks rather than shamrock greens, violets, and reds.[9] Synthetic lab-made diamond, although it tends to have coloring and atomic regularity not present in a random sampling of natural stone, is chemical diamond and will behave just like the natural version (and the use of synthetics for industrial purposes reflects this).

Even though Renee and others find diamonds beautiful, and judge beauty by the degree of sparkle and glitter, their aesthetic appeal is far from universal. Glitter can be seen positively, as "festive," "flirty," "attractive," "pretty," and "exciting," or negatively, as "calling too much attention to itself," "teasing," or being "too showy."

Daphne, a visiting nurse in her late forties, detests "sparkling," as she explained in her story about a large, fiery stone she inherited from her mother:

> Diamonds tease—they twinkle at you, they call you, they seduce you, but then there is nothing there. To me that is one of the fascinating things about diamonds. You know, my mother gave me this stone—it's almost three carats—I don't know what the quality is or anything but I would never wear something like this. It's gaudy . . . and diamonds are just not me. I don't like the way that they wink and twink and call you, and then they are empty. I mean you look in there and it's like a well that could suck you in, and you would never come back. . . . That teasing seductive quality is what comes to my mind. I ask people about them sometimes—you know I am a nurse and so I handle people's hands and stuff. Man, they never take them off! And so it's a way to relax them and pass the time. I'll say, "Oh that's a real pretty ring" or "That's a real nice necklace," and they usually talk about who gave it to them or when they got it or something. Some people get more technical I guess, but the main thing I notice is that people are really into these things. . . . Not me, though, like I said, they remind me of a black hole. Diamonds are all talk.

Daphne's views are balanced by Laura's: "Diamonds are just so beautiful, with their clean lines. So bright. So glittery. I just look at them, and I am like, 'Wow! I want that!'" And the clear ones sparkle best, but they are the exception. Although most commercial stones look clear, they come in every hue—most natural stones are somewhere between yellow and brown, but they can be red, orange, pink, green, blue, yellow, gray, and even black or white. Covalences are imperfect, and "purity" is statistical—coloration is caused by impurities or structural irregularity. Impurities are elements captured within the crystal as it forms, most commonly nitrogen, although other substances such as boron are occasionally present. Impurities absorb certain wavelengths of light, giving the stone a shade. Nitrogen, for example, provokes the absorption of violet, blue, and green wavelengths, causing a diamond to look yellow. Boron results in green, yellow, orange, and red absorption, producing a blue tint. The mechanics of diamond coloration for white, red, pink, orange, and some shades of green remain poorly understood.

But impurity or irregularity can have other effects as well. Once in a while, you might see diamonds flashing across the room in a nightclub lit with black lights; this is no optical illusion. They "luminesce," emitting light in response to energetic excitation. Objects that stop emitting light once the light source is removed are called "fluorescent." About a third of diamonds fluoresce under ultraviolet light, flickering across the room, but some "phosphoresce," continuing to glow even after the light source is removed, like "glow-in-the-dark" stars. Luminescence does not change basic color, but it can affect appearance by brightening a yellowish gem or causing a clear stone to look greasy.

Glowing or not, diamonds are excellent thermal conductors and poor electrical conductors, making them good candidates for high-tech computer and spacecraft applications. Diamond's conductivity, in addition to its durability and hardness, make it an industrial tool unequaled by any other. Conductivity causes diamond to feel cold when touched to the lips. Could this sensation, in addition to its resemblance to a tiny chunk of frozen water, explain why it is known as "ice"?

Squished Dinosaurs

The term "diamond" has its roots in the Greek word "*adamas*," meaning "invincible" or "unbreakable," which might explain how it came to be used as a warrior's talisman. But, like love, diamond can chip, break, or crack into thousands of tiny splinters. It can also burn, and at 4,289 degrees Celsius, it evaporates, leaving nothing behind but a puff of gas. Deep underground and during their treacherous voyage to the surface, diamonds can be damaged, melted, or transformed into graphite by volcanic processes. Seen in this light, the miracle of any single stone making it to the surface is an event worth celebrating.

The general knowledge that carbon, heat, and pressure are involved in diamond formation is reflected in statements such as, "Diamonds are made from carbon that has been subjected to extreme heat under great pressure over long periods of time"; some people believe them to be "thousands" or "millions" of years old. Brooke, a real estate broker, explained, "Well, I know that diamonds are formed in faults and it's some kind of process having to do with layers of the earth in South America. I know that there are not many diamonds here, but my perception is that they come from South America in vitamin-rich soil." Rosetta told me, "Well, this is probably wrong, but I think it is compressed carbon that has been under weight for a long time. I don't know if it needs heat or not but I know it's way down there, and I, well, I think somehow it gets really hot or something. Um, something about crystals? I have no idea!"

Apart from having just a little familiarity with the way they are formed, mined, or produced, most people feel little need to learn more. In my research, when people were knowledgeable about diamonds, they at times considered that information. Stephanie discussed diamond formation in a way that shows that her knowledge of the physical process enhances the significance of her diamond for her:

> The intense forces that formed it—all that heat and pressure and energy and the live things of the earth like the trees are compressed by nature miles and miles under the ground—into this one beautiful sparkling diamond. So I mean it's all about me and Charles being a part of the whole natural process, part of the whole intense, amazing, cosmic cycle of existence.

When I asked Renee what she knew about diamond formation she just laughed, "Well, I know that they are made of squished dinosaurs. . . ." And while science puts most diamond at about three billion years old, much older than even the oldest of dinosaurs, they are indeed made of the same omnipresent material that constitutes life: carbon.

The eruptions that brought diamonds to the surface took place millions of years ago, but when the kimberlitic lava cooled, it formed bluish, carrot-shaped rock deposits that sometimes contain diamonds. These pipes are deep, but narrow. The surface area of the Orapa pipe in South Africa, one of the largest in the world, covers only 262 acres.

Kimberlite deposits are rare, and few are diamondiferous. Kimberlitic eruptions occur only on very old, deep continental plates called "archons."[10] Sometimes the lava brings diamonds to the surface, along with other rocks and minerals. Magma conditions underneath archons contribute to diamond formation, so prospecting begins by locating diamond-friendly archonic or protonic plates in areas such as southern Africa, Russia, and Canada. Protons, dated at 1.6–2.5 billion years, are unlikely to contain kimberlite pipes, but may have diamondiferous lamproite pipes, as in the Australian Argyle pipe. Tectons, dated at eight hundred million to 1.6 billion years, are unlikely to contain kimberlite or lamproite pipes.

Diamond formation requires very specific mantle temperature and pressure. The range of temperature and pressure within which diamond is formed and sustained is known as the "diamond stability field." Below a certain threshold, carbon forms graphite; above it, diamonds melt. Ideal conditions are a depth of two hundred kilometers and one thousand degrees Celsius, with a pressure of fifty kilobars. There are various types of mantle rock, and some, such as harzburgite and ecologite, are potentially diamond forming. Finding "indicator minerals" such as chromium-rich garnets, associated with those types of mantle rock, is one way to locate pipes.[11] When a pipe reaches the surface, the material explodes outward. Erosion pushes materials back towards the top of the pipe, or away from it, spreading them over a very large area. Erosion can even carry the diamonds out to sea, creating high-quality offshore marine deposits.

While diamonds are produced in about twenty countries, people have varying degrees of knowledge about where they come from. Rosetta, an educated thirty-something, guessed, "Diamonds are from Africa, but I don't know which countries, maybe like Congo or South Africa, or maybe just in South Africa where the market is, and maybe some other places, but I have no idea." Sandy, although extremely well informed about polished gems, knew little about the origins of rough: "Diamonds come from the earth, I mean they are rocks, right? I think they come from Africa and India, but mainly Africa and California."

Marketing that promotes an ideology of scarcity has been successful. People routinely insist that diamonds are "very rare," sometimes to justify price, but how scarce are they? Acquiring accurate statistics on production is difficult due to a combination of industry secrecy, inconsistent reporting techniques, and underreporting of black-market trade. Some underreporting results from a desire to avoid taxation, while overly optimistic numbers encourage investment by creating an impression of mine viability. Nevertheless, the idea that diamonds are scarce is troubled by the fact that global production from antiquity through 2005 is estimated at 4.5 billion carats, valued in the neighborhood of $300 billion, with an average per-carat value of just $67 (Hart 2001). In 2011, miners produced more than 120 million carats of rough diamonds, valued at $15 billion; once out of the ground, the rough moved through the pipeline with a resulting retail value of $71 billion (Bain & Co. 2012a).

On the other hand, it is tricky and expensive to mine and process diamonds. The diamond-to-overburden ("overburden" refers to all the ground-extracted stone) ratio in profitable mines is less than six carats of rough per ton (Janse 2007). Mine viability is contingent upon quality: a site producing few but good-quality diamonds may be more viable than one regularly producing lots of tiny, poor-quality stones. Most rough, upwards of about 80 percent, is "bort," which sells for as little as a few dollars per carat. The monetary worth of diamonds from jewelry and investment-grade stones far exceeds that of bort, which makes mining diamonds economically feasible.

Top diamond-producing countries include Botswana, Russia, Canada, South Africa, Angola, Namibia, Congo, Australia, Lesotho, China, Guinea, and Sierra Leone, with Botswana being the world's largest producer by far. There is no commercial diamond mine in the United States, although the Crater of Diamonds State Park in Arkansas might produce a few hundred carats in a good a year, which means that almost all of the diamond consumed in the United States is imported. Botswana, through Debswana, a joint venture with De Beers, is an exceptionally important producer, contributing around a fifth of total global production.[12] According to estimates, Botswana produces around twenty million carats per year; diamond has fueled Botswana's economic expansion and currently accounts for about 70 percent of export earnings.

Diamonds are Botswana's greatest mineral asset and represent its biggest revenue stream, so market fluctuations can be threatening.

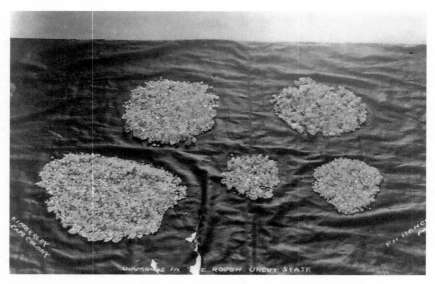

Figure 1.1. Uncut diamonds gathered by five different mines in two days, Kimberley, South Africa. (Photo by F. H. Hancox between ca. 1900 and 1923. Public Domain image Courtesy of the Library of Congress.)

The next two highest-producing states, Russia and Canada, are less dependent than Botswana on diamonds for crucial revenue, and rely less on De Beers for knowledge and market access. Their governments are less imbricated in the De Beers empire and consequently can leverage products outside of the De Beers pipeline. And other viable outside markets are emerging: Robert Wake-Walker, a former employee willing to speak out publicly against De Beers, started his own company, WWW International Diamond Consultants, which trades Russian and Canadian rough (Hart 2002). Another figure in sales outside of De Beers is former De Beers sightholder Lev Leviev, whose strong political connections and business partnerships in Russia, the Middle East, and Africa allow him to trade successfully. Leviev, like other moguls, is rich, connected, and depicted in mainstream press as unusual, charismatic, and mysterious.

Low-quality/high-quantity quantities of rough ("packages") can move without help from De Beers. For example, although occasionally producing valuable pink gems, Rio Tinto's Argyle mine in Australia sells many small brownish stones directly to polishers and dealers in India and Antwerp. Argyle can be profitable partly because of the growth of the Indian cutting industry, in which low-paid workers, who are sometimes very young with good eyes, take small, near-gem rough that would once be considered industrial grade and transform it into gemstone.

Extraction

I asked Henry, a film critic in his early forties, if he knew how diamonds are mined. He replied (in terms befitting a film buff),

> Diamond is a lot like other rocks, granite or cobalt or even chalk and limestone, so you mine it. I can picture it, like gold or coal miners, like those photographs of Sebastião Salgado—he has these photographs of miners in Africa or wherever, and it's heavy chiaroscuro, all black and

white, massive pits filled with workers, so many workers that it is like
an abstract painting, very odd . . . and they take place in various African
nations. Diamond mining, it's like that.

Others also described coal-mining-type scenarios, but there are actually
several types of diamond mining: open-pit and block mining, alluvial
and river digging, and marine extraction (both from the sea floor as well
as from on-shore terraces or beachfront). Although the early South African rush was characterized by thousands of workers hauling diamond,
ground, water, and each other out of the pits, miners in today's heavily
automated mines almost never come into direct contact with ore. And,
besides, miners are now mostly wage laborers, rarely stakeholders in the
claim.

Open-pit mines are on the surface where the kimberlite ore is
dynamited into chunks, then chewed by machinery into smaller, more
manageable pieces from which diamonds are extracted. Jwaneng, in
Botswana, is the world's most valuable open-pit mine, with a recovery
ratio of 1.25 carats per ton of ore. Block mining, similar to coal mining
in that it is underground, is used when open-pit mines become too
deep or unwieldy. But unlike coal veins, diamonds are scattered
throughout the ore, and the "tunnels" are huge theaters where trucks
remove overburden by the ton. When open pits become too deep to
profitably manage, some companies resort to block cutting, where long
shafts are sunk parallel to the mine and then horizontal shafts dug
under the exposed pipe. Workers dynamite the roof and let the debris
fall, collecting it and ferrying it to the surface for crushing. Enormous
amounts of ground, or "overburden," need to be processed just to
recover a few grams of diamond.

The same exploitative working conditions that plague coal industries,
however, characterize many, but not all, diamond mines.[13] In marine
mining, giant tankers literally suck and sift diamond-studded sands
from the ocean floor. Since sea diamonds have passed the tests of
erosion, they tend to be of very high quality. Here, as with other types of

corporate mining, workers almost never come into direct contact with diamondiferous materials.

Ideas about the working conditions of diamond production shape people's opinions of the industry and the politics of consumption. Tom, in his early thirties, works in publishing. When discussing whether men should wear diamonds, he went so far as to suggest, somewhat provocatively, "Well, the only men, or people, that should wear diamonds are black South Africans. They work to get them out of the ground, so they deserve to wear them. I mean they might get one for their birthday or maybe never. I don't know if they ever keep a few or not—but they should." Luke, a computer technician, also worries about working conditions in his critique of rappers wearing "ice." Political messages in rap are, he said,

> very inconsistent, in terms of race, in terms of violence, in terms of the objectification of women and things like that, they are all over the place, and, I mean, how can you talk about progressive politics and then wear those obscene diamonds and still have the gall to be confronted with the realities of the South African diamond trade? It just doesn't make any sense.

Luke and Tom, who spoke explicitly in favor of purchasing diamonds for women, say that we all have a responsibility to be aware of the realities of production. However, in keeping with the basic inconsistency of human behavior in relation to stated norms, knowledge, and values, an awareness of poor working conditions in diamond mines does not necessarily translate into a change in desire. This same dynamic has been demonstrated for many goods.

Sights

After rough is extracted, acid-cleaned, and sorted into categories based on color, size, quality, and cutability, De Beers sells them in Diamond

Trading Company (DTC) "sights." Prior to each event, "sightholders" advise the DTC, through their brokers, about what kinds of goods they want. DTC then prepares and prices client boxes. When clients arrive, they, along with their broker, are escorted into a room to examine the contents. This is an all-or-nothing affair: boxes can be accepted or rejected, but if rejected, the client risks losing his future sight invites.

The problem here is that clients want good-quality stones that will not lose volume in the cutting process, but since De Beers must sell off all its rough, not just the desirable pieces, boxes can contain a mix of goods. Edward Epstein (1982b, 1982c) explains how clients have historically been rewarded for good behavior with the inclusion of specials, large diamonds at a discount, while others might receive junk, small, poorer-quality rock that is hard to polish or will lose significant weight in cutting, if they fail to meet De Beers's expectations.

Because the global rough trade is now open to more participants, De Beers has altered the sight system, now called "Supplier of Choice," as part of its broader management strategy. The *Rapaport Report*, which provides information about pricing and industry news, explained that the new Supplier of Choice system has used the tactic of branding to reduce the number of sightholders who must participate in "adding value" (Rapaport 2004). According to De Beers, sights are allotted on the basis of financial standing, market position, distribution abilities, marketing strength, technical and manufacturing ability, and compliance with the DTC's Best Practice Principles (maintaining, through proper disclosure, consumer and trade confidence against the increasing threat of synthetics and treatments). These new protocols have the effect of both increasing the net promotion of diamonds and passing off marketing costs to retailers.

Processing Rough

Diamonds are cut with strong machines. I know they are
really hard so I guess they are cut with steel machines or
something.
—Dana, diamond consumer

The early use of diamond in men's fashion in India and Greece was accompanied by an unexplained taboo against polishing. But when diamonds were introduced to Europe, the taboo fell away and by the fourteenth century, a lively cutting center had been established in Antwerp. Diamonds were scarce then, under sumptuary law, and used only to complement other gems and semiprecious stones. Technology was to change all of this. Cutters found that shearing off a facet, using a technique called "cleaving," opened the diamond to light. Cleavers rubbed one stone against another to make a narrow channel called a "kerf." To cleave the stone, a flat-edged knife was inserted into the kerf, then

Figure 1.2. Diamond cutting on lathes in Jewish factories in Palestine on Plain of Sharon and along the coast to Haifa. (Tel Aviv. Diamond works, March 1939. Public Domain image Courtesy of the Library of Congress.)

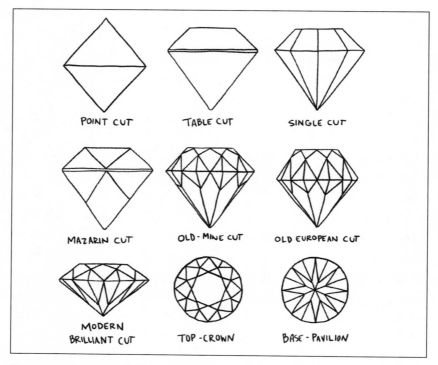

Figure 1.3. Early cuts. Early forms of diamond cutting started with the point, which emulates the point of a natural octahedron, and then developed through the table, rose, and early brilliant cuts. The light reflected by a cut diamond depends upon the number, angle, and placement of facets. (Illustration by Kay Wolfersperger, used by permission.)

carefully tapped. If all went well, the diamond split cleanly. Because they can easily shatter, cleaving diamonds that contain a "gletz" (or fracture), "knot" (a small diamond within a diamond), or "cloud" (area with tiny bubble-like inclusions) is also risky. Cleaving requires tremendous skill and patience, and it remains an expedient way to open up a diamond. As an art, though, the practice of cleaving was threatened by the invention of the saw.

Lodewyk van Berken invented the faceting "scaif" in the late fifteenth century. The scaif, a predecessor to the saw, is a polishing wheel impregnated with a mixture of oil and diamond dust. Stones, cemented in a little cup-like dop, are held against a spinning wheel until the desired area is ground away. The result was that facets reflected light in new ways, and cutters competed to learn scaifing, enhancing Antwerp's status as the preeminent cutting center. And diamonds began to appear more frequently in European regalia during this era; Charles the Bold, Duke of Normandy, became the patron of Van Berken and commissioned him to cut a 137-carat diamond, which became known as the Florentine (Epstein 1982c:102).

It was not until the twentieth century, however, that the saw, a circular blade coated with diamond dust and oil, freed cutters from having to shape along naturally occurring cleavage lines. Sawing is more expensive than cleaving (about one-tenth of a carat of dust is required to saw through a carat of diamond) and more time consuming (it can take days to saw through a moderately sized stone) but is easier to master and allows cutters to lop off bulges or salvage misshapen or twisted stones that cannot be cleaved, or perhaps only cleaved with great talent. In the early 1960s, a De Beers subsidiary introduced the Pieromatic diamond-cutting machine in Antwerp, and, although it still required trained workers, the Pieromatic greatly reduced the need for master craftsmen or even long apprenticeships since, according to the literature accompanying the Pieromatic machine, men could be trained to operate it in a matter of months (Epstein 1982c:104).

As with the decline of skilled artisanship in other fields (Sennet 2008), the small cutting trade in New York is getting even smaller. Jake, a skilled old-school cutter, lamented that "cutting is a dying art in New York. It takes years and years of apprenticing and these kids today don't want to do that, so I don't know what's gonna happen. You can get a setting that looks OK but the real craftsmanship is dying out. We're a dying breed!" By contrast, the mechanized Indian industry, employing hundreds of thousands of people, specializes in producing small, cheap goods. These usually brownish, tiny stones can at times only carry a few facets, although amazingly, through the use of new technology, even the "larger" Indian goods of one point are polished with the full fifty-eight facets. As the Indian industry gains momentum, factories vie for rough. The expansion of small-goods production means that mines producing low-quality rough can now be run economically. Though the cuts are inferior and the stones are junky, making millions of these every year generates enormous profits, and the Indian diamond business is booming.

New mining and cutting technologies, changing geographies of labor, modern taxation schedules, war, the end of apartheid, entrepreneurship by outsiders like Leviev, and the discovery of diamonds in Australia, Russia, and Canada have all impacted the transformation of rock into gem, otherwise understood as the production of value. With these seismic changes taking place, producers must redouble efforts to secure demand by managing the cultural construction of the diamond. This is achieved by deploying a grading system and powerful marketing narratives, both explored in the following chapters.

2

VALUING DIAMONDS

How are differences in price orchestrated and maintained when, to look at them, most diamonds look virtually identical? What's the difference between an investment-grade stone and "junk"? The Gemological Institute of America (GIA) creates meaningful discriminations through a highly contrived grading system that is then mapped onto a grading sheet called a "certificate." Control over grading is assured by the use of specialized jargon, tools, and knowledge, all carefully leaked to the public in an effort to guide perceptions. What grading does, then, is maneuver the seemingly similar into a hierarchy of value.

One place we are taught to pay attention to microscopic differences is at the point of sale. These differences, commonly called "The 4 Cs," are carat, color, clarity, and cut, for which GIA developed stringent specifications in the 1950s. As part of my research, I attended GIA's Diamond Grading course, where I learned about the intricacies of grading and the extent to which valuation remains hidden behind a veil of "expert" knowledge. And while the average consumer cannot discern grade differences, the bulk of diamonds that pass through the retail market are subjected to these standards.

Gemological Institute of America

The Gemological Institute of America is located at the corner of Fifth Avenue and Forty-seventh Street in Manhattan. The building also houses the Diamond Dealers Club (DDC), is full of merchants and others involved in the trade, and is under high surveillance at all times. At the front desk, guards scrutinize visitors, who must produce identification for Xeroxing before passing through metal detectors and listing what floors they intend to visit. Guards closely monitor visitors' movements; the first day I visited the building, when I accidentally got off the elevator on the wrong floor, a sentry was instantly at my side asking, "Hey, what are you doing on this floor?" The DDC, like many diamond businesses, uses two secured doors for additional protection: you are buzzed through one door into a tiny cubicle with a security camera, and only buzzed through the second door after the first one locks shut.

My group met in the lab classroom, which is equipped with microscopes, special fluorescent lights, master stones, and diamond grading tools. The carpet is bright blue: if a student drops and loses a diamond, he must pay for it (luckily the blue rug makes finding the stones—which too easily pop out of tweezers and go flying— much easier). There were approximately fifteen other students there, all of whom were involved in the trade as shop owners, retail clerks, designers, etc.

When I explained my presence as part of a research project, my classmates at first merely tolerated me, but over time they began to talk with me about their experiences. The class was led by two instructors, Avi and Rebecca. "Every diamond is beautiful," Avi said when he introduced the course, "but some diamonds are more beautiful than others!" This won some chuckles, but reminded me that we were here to learn the tactics used to legitimize value. "Of course, you never tell a customer that!" Avi continued, explaining, "In this course you will learn to grade polished stones. We don't price diamonds here, but the grade helps determine price, according to market fluctuations. And the grading is what the certificate reflects."

Geography

Diamond grading is modeled on the "brilliant," a 57-faceted round cut. We began our lesson by learning the geography of the polished diamond. Avi handed a diamond to each of us in exchange for our ID or credit card(!) and showed us how to pick the stone up at the girdle (its widest point) with tweezers. This is not as easy as it sounds. Diamonds are tiny and the girdle is thin: hold it too loose and it drops; hold it too tight and the stone shoots out, hopefully not too far away. We put the stones under a microscope with a bright light. Like anything examined under a zoom lens, a magnified diamond appears as a whole world in and of itself. I was amazed by how complex the facets now appeared, and by the many nicks and chips I could suddenly plainly see. Avi asked us to concentrate on systematically locating all of the internal and surface imperfections and facet irregularities. Later we turned the diamond sideways to scrutinize the girdle. Prior

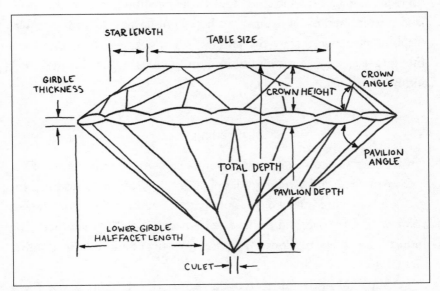

Figure 2.1. The geography of a diamond. (Illustration by Kay Wolfersperger, used by permission.)

to this, I had no idea there were so many details to appreciate, and during the next weeks I was drawn into a bright arena of specialized knowledge.

Diamonds with a GIA certificate are often believed to have special authenticity and prestige (and instructors suggested that certification is fast becoming the fifth "C"). I was later told by more than one by proud consumer that "my diamonds is certified," even though they were unable to interpret the maps. Certificates do, however, contain a great deal of information if you know what the abbreviations stand for, what the target numbers are, and how diamond pricing works.

Two stones may look alike at a glance, but to the grader—with his or her loupe and probe and tweezers and tiny ruler and crown-angle measurer and color stones and fluorescence chart and calculator and diamond thermal tester—no two are identical. Table size, crown angle and depth, girdle thickness, pavilion angle and depth, culet size, facet symmetry, the centeredness of table and culet, as well as the polish itself all influence value. But these characteristics are not just arbitrary; they do really impact how the stone looks. The pavilion angle, for example, is important because it determines how light flashes out of the crown; it should be between forty-two and forty-four degrees. Deviations from this target can cause a stone to look dull, lowering its "beauty" and, ultimately, its price.

Grading

On GIA certificates, stones are systematically mapped in terms of the 4 Cs. Any diamond can be graded, but grading is usually reserved for diamonds that are valued over $1,000, are greater than one carat, have a color of "I" or above, and/or have a clarity grade higher than "SI2." The industry has spent millions marketing not only goods, but the grading system itself.

Perhaps the most objective characteristic—meaning, the most consistently observable by different graders—of the 4 Cs is carat. The word "carat" is derived from the Greek for the pods of the carob (or

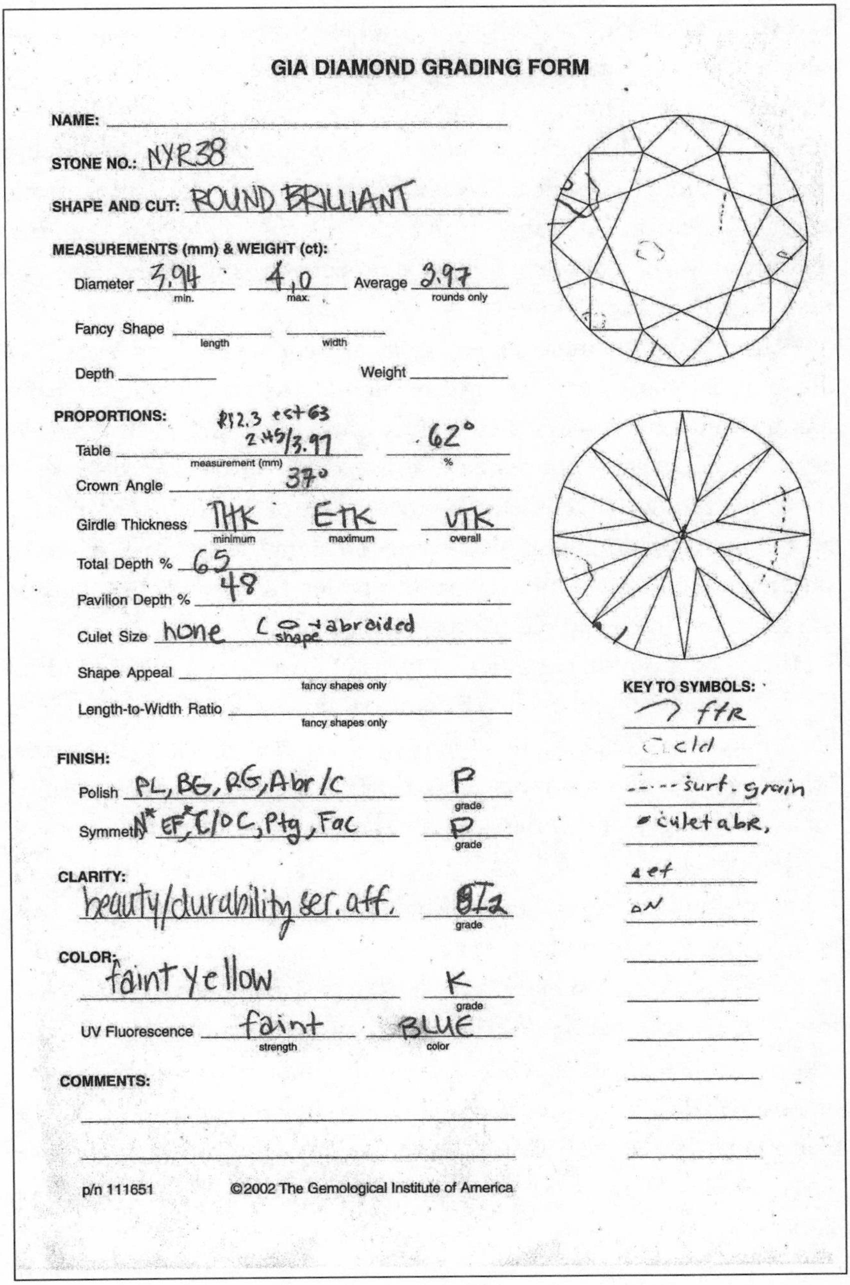

GIA DIAMOND GRADING FORM

NAME:

STONE NO.: NYR38

SHAPE AND CUT: ROUND BRILLIANT

MEASUREMENTS (mm) & WEIGHT (ct):

Diameter 3.94 (min.) 4.0 (max.) Average 3.97 (rounds only)

Fancy Shape (length) (width)

Depth Weight

PROPORTIONS:

Table R12.3 est 63 2.45/3.97 (measurement (mm)) .62° (%)

Crown Angle 37°

Girdle Thickness THK (minimum) ETK (maximum) VTK (overall)

Total Depth % 65

Pavilion Depth % 48

Culet Size none (shape + abraided

Shape Appeal (fancy shapes only)

Length-to-Width Ratio (fancy shapes only)

FINISH:

Polish PL, BG, RG, Abr/C P (grade)

Symmetry N* EF* C/OC, Ptg, Fac P (grade)

CLARITY:

beauty/durability ser. aff. SI2 (grade)

COLOR:

faint yellow K (grade)

UV Fluorescence faint (strength) BLUE (color)

COMMENTS:

p/n 111651 ©2002 The Gemological Institute of America

KEY TO SYMBOLS:

ftr

cld

surf. grain

culet abr.

ef

oN

Figure 2.2. My GIA practice page.

locust) tree, which contain tiny, remarkably consistent seeds that are excellent units of measure; these seeds were used by early traders to weigh diamonds. One carat (abbreviated as "ct.") equals 0.200 grams, or 200 milligrams. Diamonds are now measured to the nearest hundredth of a carat, though American law allows for rounding up at .05 so that a .95-ct. stone can be listed at 1 ct., whereas GIA standards permit rounding up only at .09 ct. All other things being equal, the more caratage, the more expensive the diamond.

Clarity, a slightly more subjective measure, refers to how "clean" the diamond is, that is, how free it is of "flaws." The clarity grade impacts market value when flaws, either "inclusions" (characteristics that are either inside the stone or extend inwards from the surface) or "blemishes" (nonpenetrating characteristics on the surface of the stone) hamper the play of light. Diamonds are first examined from the top, then from the side, and then through the crown and pavilion facets, and any inclusion or blemish is noted and plotted on a map.

There are about fifteen different types of inclusions and ten kinds of blemishes, some more serious than others. For example, an inclusion of black mineral crystal is more deleterious to the play of light than internal "graining," which is an indication of crystal growth. Internal graining looks like a piece of colorless cellophane floating underwater, but you can barely see it, even with a microscope. Other characteristics include feathering on the girdle ("bearding"); nicks and chips of all shapes, sizes, and depths; hazy or milky areas made up of clusters of tiny inclusions ("clouds") or twinning planes ("twinning wisps"); internal breaks and fractures ("feathers," one of the most common problems); included crystals made of diamond ("knots") or other substances (such as garnet or peridot); dots inside the diamond ("grain centers" or "pinpoints"); or places where the stone is unpolished or where a laser has burned a hole.

Depending on the placement, size, color, and the overall effect of flaws, clarity grades fall somewhere between "flawless" (F) and "severely flawed" (SI). Surface blemishes rarely affect the basic clarity grade because these things—tiny abraded areas where the facets meet, small extra facets or unpolished areas, nicks near the girdle, minuscule surface pits, polish lines caused by the scaife, unevenness or surface clouding, scratches or surface graining—can usually be polished out by a skilled cutter. The "best" location (having the least impact on light and transparency) for any inclusion is usually somewhere near the girdle. The worst position tends to be near the culet, where reflection can make a single inclusion look like three or more.

Each feature has an abbreviation, color code, and symbol. Blemishes are drawn in green, inclusions in red, and black is used to delineate extra facets. Surface crumble, for instance, is usually accompanied by tiny feathers on a facet junction, what is known as a "bruise," and is represented by a red "x" on the map and listed as "br" (see GIA certificate in figure 2.2). Looking at the crown ("the crown view"), a grader will map all characteristics found on the crown surface or the girdle onto the crown diagram; those seen only by looking through the pavilion, or inclusions that break the surface of the pavilion, are plotted separately on the pavilion map. A grader will typically start with the largest or most obvious characteristics from the crown view and then systematically work through other features, plotting them relative to the position of the main inclusion, which will set the upper limit of the grade. Graders may spend hours identifying and mapping the flaws of a single diamond.

"Flawless" (F) gems show no blemishes or inclusions when viewed under a 10X loupe and are extremely rare. Flawless gems may, however, have "naturals" (unpolished spots) or laser inscriptions on the girdle, internal graining that does not affect transparency, or an extra pavilion facet not visible from the crown. All things being equal, "flawless" diamonds are the most expensive, and are sometimes used for investment, but are seldom set in jewelry since the slightest blemish can cause a significant price drop. "Internally Flawless" (IF) samples have no inclusions and only minor surface blemishes that can be removed by a good polisher.

Compared to F or IF stones, "Very Very Slightly Included" (VVS1 or VVSI2) stones can cost substantially less. They contain minute inclusions, hard for even a skilled grader to locate under magnification, and are only visible from the pavilion or are extremely shallow. Stones with pinpoints or minute girdle chips may qualify as VVS1. The truly subjective nature of diamond grading is apparent with the VVSI grade: in reflecting the subjective, fuzzy nature of grading, the language describing the difference between VVS1 and VVS2 suggests that it is "more difficult" to remove the flaw with polishing.

"Very Slightly Included" (VS1 and VS2) stones contain minor inclusions "difficult-to-somewhat easy" to see with a loupe, along with pinpoints, feathers hidden near the girdle, small crystals, or clouds. "Slightly Included" (SI1 and SI2) specimens are obviously flawed under magnification, and their flaws might even be seen with the naked eye. "Included" (I1, I2, I3) diamonds are seriously flawed, and have problems easily seen with the unaided eye. "I"-class inclusions, like a large feather—actually a crack, because cracks can look like feathers inside the diamond—can affect the durability of the stone, making it a poor candidate for jewelry because it would be susceptible to breaking. Anything graded less than SI3 (Slightly Included, class 3) is industrial grade ("bort"), about 75 percent of all diamond. Of the remaining 25 percent, only about 5 percent is graded SI or higher. Significantly, differences between SI and the higher grades are not generally visible at a glance, which is how most diamonds are encountered.

Diamonds sold in stores and depicted in ads are almost always clear, and are characterized by science as pure carbon, but rarely, if ever, is this the case. Molecular impurities dispersed throughout the atomic structure, at a ratio as low as 1:10,000 atoms, produce color, as do structural defects within the carbon bonds. As we know, structural irregularities absorb different frequencies of light, causing the stone to appear tinted. So about 90 percent of "clear" diamonds are tinted yellow, brown, and gray, but this is unnoticeable in a good setting. For every one hundred thousand carats of cut diamond, only ten thousand are colorless, and only one thousand have intense, "fancy" color (Harris 1994).

Unusual coloration, like dark red, tends to be very expensive. A fancy purplish-red diamond weighing 2.26 carats (set on a ring) was recently sold at a Christie's auction for $2.7 million; that's $1,180,340 per carat, the highest ever for a red diamond at an auction (Doherty 2007). The Graff Pink, a 24.78-ct. "potentially flawless" pink diamond, was sold by Sotheby's for £28.8 million in 2010 (Evans 2010). Purple, red, and orange diamonds are also pricey, greens and blues less so, and then, least of all, yellows and browns. The grading scale for colored gems, different from that of white diamonds, is based on "hue" (color), "saturation" (intensity), and "tone" (scale from dark to light), but it was not until the 1980s that colored diamonds even appeared in public media. More recently, advertising geared to capture a greater market share by creating "new" products has begun promoting colored diamonds. Yellows and browns that once might have been ground into bort have been reframed as "fancy," with evocative names that lend status, like "cognac" and "champagne."

The white diamonds (which are actually clear) purchased by most consumers are assigned a color grade between D (totally colorless) and N. Grades D, E, and F are basically colorless. Grades of G–J, less expensive than those graded D–F, are the near-colorless stones that make up the majority of the mainstream trade. When facing upwards, these stones appear color free, but a slight yellowing appears when the table is turned upside down. Grades K–M are increasingly yellow. A diamond graded N is obviously yellowish, brownish, or grayish. To determine the color, specimens are compared against a set of small, brilliant-cut, GIA "master stones."

Since fluorescence can affect appearance, after the basic color is determined, the stone is placed under special light and assigned a fluorescence grade of None, Faint, Medium, Strong, or Very Strong. Colorless stones can lose up to 15 to 20 percent of their value as a result of their level of fluorescence. Fluorescence can create a milky or oily appearance, but the appearance of a faintly yellow gem can be improved by a bit of fluorescence.

Finish and proportions determine the fourth "C": the "cut," or "make." Grading considerations for the cut include the polish quality and the details of facet placement. Graders examine size and angle relationships between the facets and other parts of the stone, like the girdle and table. Cutters attempt to conserve "caratage" while maximizing optics and integrity. For example, a cut featuring a razor-thin girdle or no culet may save a few points, but the downside is that it becomes more vulnerable to chipping. Then again, especially when it is not faceted, a thick girdle may become scraped, or "bearded" (which is when it becomes feathered, taking on a roughened appearance); this may make the stone look clunky. A very thick girdle may be harder to set. Plus, a thick girdle easily shows dirt and grease, which reflect back into the stone.

The Tolkowsky cut is the standard by which round gems are graded. This cut is highly specific. It has thirty-three facets on the crown, or the upper part of the diamond; has a table, the large middle facet; and is surrounded by triangular "star" facets, upper-girdle facets, and diamond-shaped "bezel" facets. There are twenty-five facets on the pavilion; twenty-four alternating lower-girdle and main-pavilion facets, plus a tiny flat culet polished horizontally onto the bottom. All of these angles are specified, including the relative proportion of the table size to the stone's maximum diameter, the pavilion depth, the crown height, the width of the girdle, the angle at which the crown and pavilion are cut, the size of the culet, and the shape of each facet. Here, the girdle can be left unpolished, but the ideal cut has a "small"- to "medium"-sized girdle.

When a diamond is cut correctly, light refracts inside the stone several times before dispersing out the top. If the gem is too deep—meaning the angles of the crown or pavilion to the horizontal girdle are too steep—the diamond will look dark, or "sleepy," but if it's too shallow light will leak out the bottom. In both cases the gem will lack fire and brilliance, so tolerance for deviance from the ideal specifications is very limited.

GIA instructors explained that the art of cutting lies in the ability of an artisan to "imagine himself as light inside of a diamond, bouncing from plane to plane, and then shimmering through the top." Depending on the

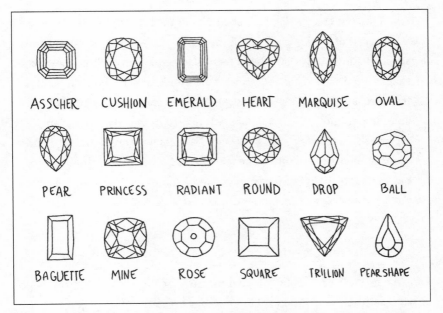

ASSCHER	CUSHION	EMERALD	HEART	MARQUISE	OVAL
PEAR	PRINCESS	RADIANT	ROUND	DROP	BALL
BAGUETTE	MINE	ROSE	SQUARE	TRILLION	PEAR SHAPE

Figure 2.3. Various diamond shapes, many of which are adaptations from the Tolkowsky design. (Illustration by Kay Wolfersperger, used by permission.)

shape and condition of the rough, a cutter may use an alternative shape such as the octagonal "emerald," the pointed oval "marquise," the triangular "trillion" or the squarish "princess" to maximize fire. Round diamonds are almost always the most expensive per carat because the consumer is paying for the gem plus the 40 to 60 percent that has been ground away.

Most retail diamonds are round, but that cut is not always the favorite. The shapes themselves, the most visible of the 4 Cs, can be interpreted rather idiosyncratically. As we sat at my kitchen table talking, Renee, who knew a lot about diamonds (for example, names of the various facets, such as culet or table, and how cut affects appearance), told me that she likes to study the setting and shape of other people's jewelry, which she judges aesthetically and uses to understand their class or style:

There are shapes that I truly cannot stand, like the marquise . . . ugh, it's soooo ugly and redneck looking, and I just think it looks really cheap.

And I am not crazy about baguettes a lot of the time, though I will wear that [cut]. But I really don't go for the elongated stones. I like round and square. I don't know what it is but there is something gross about the other shapes. I prefer brilliant and princess cuts, and I am also not crazy about triangles, but they can be interesting I think. I look and see how it is set and I might think, "Oh, that looks sort of nice," and I have seen triangles set in really interesting ways, but I would still not want one for myself. And I look at the size sometimes, and sometimes I try to study it [to see] how big it is, but it's hard to tell sometimes and I know you can have a big table but a shallow cut and then it just looks bigger than it really is.

New Developments: Lasers, Specialty Cuts, and Branding

Verena, a retired travel agent, had recently become engaged to George, a successful cabinet maker. He gave her a diamond engagement ring, which she, as is the custom, showed me when we met. As I inspected the ring, we talked about its beauty and about the setting, and so forth. She explained to me that it is a Lucida cut from Tiffany's, so she can go to get the ring cleaned whenever she likes, and that it "is laser inscripted. You can only see the inscription with a microscope but there is a message there—I don't know exactly what it says, but I know that it's there. And it means that this diamond is unique." Laser inscription, a practice that burns logos, corporate names, serial numbers, or personal statements on the girdle, has developed in concert with aggressive marketing and new designs. New cuts, branding, and sales are enhanced by specialized technology like laser saws, particularly in the areas of bruting and faceting.

Laser saws can create unusual shapes or cuts that would be impossible to produce with conventional saws. Lasers blast out impurities, leaving holes to be filled with molten glass. In the 1970s, Lev Leviev began utilizing this technique for his trademarked Yehuda diamonds to improve clarity grades. His computer software, Strela 6, produces three-dimensional images of rough and evaluates potential yield. Leviev developed another program that maps a series of yields, then predicts, on the basis of dynamic pricing and demand statistics, which shape will generate the most profit (Berman and Goldman 2003).

Other machines calibrate facet smoothness, while software like Brilliant 3.1 optimizes cut specifications. The Octopus-system, an automatic polisher, works out round and fancy shapes up to a finished weight of five carats. The uniting of these new production techniques with marketing helps support perceptions of a value hierarchy.

The Lucida, for example, is Tiffany's fifty-faceted, cut-cornered, square diamond in a special setting. It was launched in 1999 amid much fanfare (Tiffany and Co. n.d.). With the Lucida being marketed as a "modern classic," shoppers are given the hard sell on their Fifth Avenue diamond floor. Other retailers like Zale's and Hearts on Fire have their own signature cuts. Zale's, marketing to less affluent consumers, patented the democratically named, and much less expensive, 128-facet "People's Diamond" (Beres 2002). The Hearts on Fire cut, or "make," supposedly glimmers and sparkles with heart-shaped flecks of light (Hearts on Fire n.d.). In all cases, consumer buy-in is absolutely crucial to the construction of value.

Besides round, oval, marquise, and pear, the last twenty years have seen a slew of new shapes that have been branded and patented with fantastical names such as the "Baguillion," a brilliant cut baguette. Whimsical shapes, like the "Buddha" and the doughnut-shaped "Torus," or gems with a profusion of facets, like the 221-faceted "Brilliant Lady," reflect pressures on retailers to be different. In 2003 alone, at least eight designs were awarded U.S. patents, including the "Asprey," designed by Gabi Tolkowsky, great-nephew of Marcel Tolkowsky (Rapaport 1998). Branded cuts can even include text: the "Ten Commandments" cut, sold by the Trillion Diamond Company, is shaped like the two tablets of the Ten Commandments, and has the text of the commandments laser-inscribed on the table facet of the stone (the text is available in different versions for different religions) (Diamond Source n.d.).[1]

The recent explosion in branded cuts can be explained by the need for companies to make themselves appear unique or to "add value," as mandated by the De Beers's Supplier of Choice (SoC) program. Consumers are willing to pay premium prices for branded cuts if they can be persuaded that doing so makes an otherwise nonunique purchase more precious, a practice for which American consumers are well trained, be it for diamonds, blue jeans, or TV sets.

Not everyone is pleased with these developments. I met Carmen at a film screening, and after I told her about my project, she started explaining that she had been in the Foreign Service in Israel, where she had learned "all about the industry." She and her mother had recently been on Forty-seventh Street, and her mother stepped on something hard wrapped in a white paper sheath. The "something hard" turned out to be a diamond! They had the stone appraised, "and it's over 1 carat, but it's an old cut, I forget the name. . . ." Carmen went on to say that "some of these new cuts, well, they have too many facets," they are "too sparkly," while the one they found is "plain." She prefers "to be able to look down into the stone, without all of those facets."

Retailer cuts are often heavily branded and marketed, in keeping with other commodities under advanced capitalism (Klein 2000; Foster 2007). But lasered logos can't be seen by the naked eye, unlike the Nike Swoop or the La Coste alligator, which serve to differentiate one object from apparently virtually equivalent others. Cuts are similarly "invisible" in that most people are unable to recognize a standard brilliant cut versus a more complex round cut. Branding and specialty cuts orchestrate the perception of difference between things that are outwardly identical, impacting price, even though the public sign value of these qualities is severely constrained by visibility.

"Nature's Signature"

Sitting with Tom at a coffee shop, I asked him what he thought diamonds say to other people. He replied,

> Diamonds say, "I have arrived, I am rich, I am valuable," but the thing is that diamonds are meant to be worn on the outside, you don't keep them

in a drawer and invite someone over to look in your drawers. I mean you might say come look in my drawers and that would be a different show, but diamonds are to be worn on the outside for the public. And who knows the difference?

I prompted him to continue, saying, "So, what is the difference?"

I mean if they are real or fake. Crappy, or worth like $12,000. Only a jeweler can tell the difference. I see stuff on Home Shopping Channel or at Macy's or whatever, and is it diamond, zirconia, or whatever? I can't tell the difference. So a lot of this has to do with a person's belief in whether it's real or not. Like in that story—you know that story "The Necklace" by Maupassant? She couldn't tell. . . . Someone lent her a necklace to wear and she lost it, and then she spent her whole life making enough money to buy another one, and then she was ruined. And then she found out that the necklace wasn't even real. But she thought it was. So maybe the fact that it is easily fake-able plays into the whole thing. I never thought about that, but maybe part of it is about convincing people that it is real. And that depends on who is wearing it.

Tom highlights how discerning a real diamond from an imitation is expert knowledge. The materials that simulate diamonds, including glass, cubic zirconia, and Moissanite, look like diamond to the casual observer, but lack the weight, refractive index, and hardness of actual diamonds. Of course, traders have techniques for spotting an imposter—coloration is a good place to start. Moissanite, for example, turns yellow when the gem is held to a flame. Synthetic gem labs like Gemesis manufacture diamond for industrial and technological purposes, and at least one company, Life Gem, makes diamond out of carbon from cremated pets and even people; until very recently, these tended to be bluish. In reality, though, it can be hard even for experts to identify a fake.

The industry responds to the fake and the simulant market with ads extolling the profound uniqueness of natural diamonds. Internally, the

2004 Antwerp Diamond Conference considered threats to consumer confidence from advances in gem-quality synthetic manufacturing. There the Antwerp Diamond High Council argued that banning the synthetic trade wouldn't work: "The industry must instead educate the public about the uniqueness and wonder of natural diamonds" (Trachtenberg 2004). The threat to the natural diamond industry will ultimately depend upon being able to identify natural stones and convincing the public that natural is indeed superior to simulated or synthetic.

Treated stones that have had inclusions removed by laser and then filled, or that have been radiated, coated, or manipulated for color, also pose problems. Regulations insist upon disclosure, and a talented grader might recognize a treated diamond, but the use of these enhancement technologies challenges the value hierarchy that is based on the distribution of features in natural gems—with clear, flawless gems being rare, prized, and the most expensive. Were a synthetic, simulated, or treated diamond to become as acceptable as a natural stone, the industry could find itself on shaky ground. Retail usually involves a salesperson explaining the 4 Cs, sometimes using full-color brochures to persuade customers. Echoing GIA instruction, they explain that all diamonds are beautiful, unique, and special, but some are more beautiful, unique, and special than others. Salespersons ask for a consumer's budget, then present goods starting at that price or just above, using euphemistic language like "nature's signature" to describe flaws in ways that transform the meaning of an inexpensive, low-quality gem into something more unique and interesting—and valuable.

Though much of De Beers's business is in the rough trade, retail demand pulls that rough through the pipeline. The rough trade is, thus, managed according to demand and the pricing of polished gems—the goal being to maintain and, when possible, increase the price of diamonds at both rough and retail levels so that each step in the commodity chain remains maximally profitable. If not for these tactics, prices would probably be lower and the role of diamonds would be more like that of semiprecious stones.

Market Value

What would happen if diamonds suddenly lost their market value? Both De Beers and business students argue that the monopoly "works out for everyone, including the consumer," who, they argue, wants diamonds as a direct result of their high price (Chang et al. 2000). Further, consumers want the price of diamonds to stay high to stabilize the value of their outlay and maintain the appeal of being able to possess a luxury good.

The strength of this claim is undermined by several points. First, the resale value of diamonds (other than investment-grade stones, which are very rare and not worn as jewelry) is negligible compared to their cost, so the market value of diamonds once purchased is largely imaginary. Second, one can buy inexpensive or fake diamonds and no one other than the buyer is the wiser, complicating the purchase of diamonds meant to be read by others as a luxury good and status symbol. Thus the pleasure derived from spending is not necessarily contingent upon the manipulation of diamond prices. And thirdly, many people buy, are given, inherit, or otherwise acquire diamonds, despite the fact that they cannot afford them. In reality, some consumers resent being made to feel that they should make such an expensive purchase and would rather pay less, which is why discount outfits for diamonds do a brisk business. All three of these factors are related to market pricing, but to argue that the monopoly benefits the consumer obliges qualification.

It is unclear to consumers how diamonds accrue value, though many offer a simple supply and demand calculus, in which scarcity determines cost. People routinely state that diamonds are expensive because they are "very rare." Meanwhile, the DTC sold $5.5 billion worth of rough in 2003, at a retail value of about $60 billion. Most people I talked with have a poor idea of the cost of single diamonds, but generally believe them to be "very expensive." Karina, a well-educated stockbroker's wife, accurately guessed that an extremely fine one-carat diamond would cost about $25,000. Then she went on to say, "but the real question to me is where it gets its value, I mean does it come out of the ground like that?

Or is it just once it gets in the store? I don't know if that $25,000 is the price for the raw one or what."

Value increases exponentially as it moves from extraction to consumption In an example of the price of a 0.5 gemstone moving through the commodity chain, Ariovich shows the value of mining at $62 per carat while retail sales are somewhere between $290 and $550 per carat (Ariovich 1985). Even though the numbers in this example are a little dated, the cutters and retailers I interviewed agreed that mark-up is approximately the same now, though recently the price of rough has increased, cutting into profit margins downstream. Retail is where the largest mark-ups take place, but to make the pipeline viable, people at each node must be rewarded.

As Berman and Goldman (2003) report, a fine ten-carat stone can cost about $15 per carat to extract. A sightholder might then pay for that colorless, flawless stone, at $5,000 per carat, before it is cut (and loses anywhere from 50 to 70 percent of its original caratage). A retailer then pays around $75,000 for the stone, which is now only 3.5 carats. Two years after the stone is taken from the ground, a customer spends $125,000, or more if the stone is colored, bears a specially trademarked cut, or has been brand lasered.

Several factors determine final pricing. Large stones are difficult to price, and profits at each node are proportionally enlarged because of the risks associated with taking large stones from rough to retail, but in general prices increase exponentially with size. Two one-carat stones may cost substantially less together than a single two-carat stone of the same make. "Specials," or larger stones, may be sold outside of sight lots as single stones: bids may be made without any cuts to the stone, but it is hard to predict how a stone will finally polish. It's a gamble because the stone might explode on the cutting wheel, undetected inclusions could become ugly and dangerous, or knots could make cutting overly laborious. There are additional snags when it comes to colored stones. They command a high price, but when they are cut, the value-giving color can leak out, transforming, for example, an expensive rich, dark blue into a cheaper pale shade (or, conversely, the color may improve).

Consumer Education

Retainers, we know, help get consumers on board with grading and pricing by highlighting color, branding, and specialty cuts. Emphasis on grades by retailers has resulted in increased demand for certificates, leading to the emergence of new grading companies and marketing practices. Retailers use scientific-looking technology to convey grade information to shoppers, often in spectacular ways. For example, the "DiaScribe," developed by Sarin Technologies, is a machine with a viewer that allows people to see inscriptions on a monitor without a microscope or loupe, when usually the branding text is inscribed on the girdle, which they may never actually see again. The "Brilliant Eye 'S' Series" enables retailers to show images of a stone in an animated display that quickly creates a colorful diamond report (Murray 2004). There is even software that produces a musical analysis of a stone. Efforts to enhance the buying experience are well received by retailers, all of them competing to move the same product by making consumers go "gaga" over flashing diamonds.

And yet, branding and sales techniques are some of the least crucial areas of change. New production strategies, transformations in the global political and economic landscape, the discovery of new diamondiferous areas, and the desire of entrepreneurs to operate outside of the De Beers syndicate have all altered the trade.

Even the success of De Beers's branding mission has been uneven in terms of name recognition, partly because people's knowledge about De Beers and its association with the industry varies. I asked people what, if anything, they knew about De Beers. "De Beers? What's that?" "De Beers? Oh sure . . . that's the big diamond company!" "De Beers is a big outlet store or chain . . . right?" "It's a big wholesaler." "I don't know . . . well, I know that De Beers is a quality brand." Others, having seen television shows about blood diamonds, complained that "De Beers is evil" or, "There is something very strange about De Beers. . . . I don't know what their motivation is because there are ways to make money without being a monopoly, but I think they are trying to hide something." Jenny, a secretary in a real estate company, told me, "I don't know much about De Beers but I think they are very high-quality diamonds and they have a really good commercial that I like to watch, and so I remember the name." And Renee reported that "De Beers is a company in South Africa, and it's a monopoly, and I think maybe it was publicly traded but now it isn't. I think I learned about it in a movie—yeah, that's right, it was about some gorillas or apes that were guarding the gems of Africa, I don't remember the name of it." As De Beers retail stores gain visibility, the brand will find greater recognition among consumers, particularly in New York. Regardless of what people know about diamond production, grading, specialty cuts, or brands, everyone knows "A Diamond Is Forever." The following chapter explores the mechanics of diamond advertising.

3

A DIAMOND IS FOREVER

As ever more diamonds have been mined over the last seventy-five years, the industry has needed to develop a market willing to absorb new stocks (while making sure that there was little or no resale value). To achieve this, De Beers has spent millions of dollars each year on advertising through its marketing arm, the London-based Diamond Trading Company (DTC), and the Diamond Information Center (DIC).[1] The DTC sets goals that are then executed by an ad agency, partly by using the DIC as a mouthpiece. For example, De Beers's online site (www.ADiamondIsForever.com) keeps site visitors, over two hundred thousand per month, up to date on the latest DTC initiatives, offers a free download of a "bridal app," and endorses itself by citing the "Diamond Information Center." Print, web, and video ads are complemented by contests, billboards, and product placement in high-profile media events like the Academy Awards.

De Beers has consistently manipulated price and demand through strategic production and distribution; alongside such tactics, its marketing efforts have been wildly successful: over 70 percent of all American women own at least one diamond.[2] As displayed in advertisements, diamonds symbolize romance, status, and glamour. Ads also intimate that scarcity, beauty, and naturalness increase diamonds' value. Of course ads encourage us to go purchase diamonds, but how much do they determine what we think about the meaning of these gala minerals? Ad content certainly played a role in many stories I heard, particularly when we talked about other people's diamonds. But other factors also shaped the way consumers talked about their own jewels: how they acquired the diamond, their relationship with the person from whom the diamond was received (in cases of gifting), attitudes about why it was purchased, and the biography of both the wearer and the stone. While most theory usefully observes consumers as members of identity groups (like those based on class or ethnicity) rather than as individuals, this chapter shows that, far from being batches of passive absorbers, consumers creatively interpret discourse in ways that may cut against their membership in identity groups. Combining analytic and ethnographic approaches, consumers can be productively theorized both at the level of individuals and at the level of groups.

Individuals and Groups

Consumption studies have successfully explored the symbolic potential of commodities, especially in terms of (re)producing ideology, in which people use commodities to construct national, racial, or ethnic identities. And a focus on differences among individuals is often called for in some studies, especially when ethnographic materials are present, as in Elizabeth Chin's (2001) work on Barbie dolls and children of color in Connecticut. Meanwhile, persuasive deconstructions of advertisements, like Robert Foster's (1999) work on brands in Papua, New Guinea, clarify how social categories or ideologies are maintained through marketing. In tracing the rise of advertising itself, Raymond Williams (1980) argues that ads, as powerful psychological tools that ensure economic reproduction, are "magical" in that they hide the conditions of production while transforming objects into "mere signs," where to consume is to sign(al) rather than to use (although I would argue that this is a somewhat false opposition, since signaling *is* using). In such works, consumers are molded by forces of discourse arising out of the relations of production.

People, said to be written by ad discourse, lack agency, individuality, and subjectivity, and there is little consideration of how local conditions impact the interpretive encounter between individuals and the commodities that ads tout.

In linking ad language to political economy and the discursive production of subjects, Betty Friedan (1963) was one of the first to explicate a relationship between advertising and identity, arguing that ads have the potential to create and communicate not only status but also (feminine) gender. Friedan reserved special ire for marketing aimed at housewives. Ads (attempt to) make housewives feel indispensable to the running of the house, a job, she asserted, that could be done by any "half-wit" and that requires only a "strong enough back and a small enough brain" to recognize and purchase household products and appliances. But the underlying framework of this argument, that women—or that people—passively soak up ad copy, is an untenable position.

Since Friedan's publication of *The Feminine Mystique* in 1963, the gendering potential of ads has been continuously and vigorously interrogated in academia. Most ads do depict diamonds as strongly gendered. And while many people I talked with agreed that "diamonds are feminine," some argued that this is only the case because almost all jewelry is feminine, and that men should not wear any jewelry other than "traditional ornaments" such as cufflinks, watches, and wedding bands. So, while diamond ads are strongly gendering, even defining of femininity, this needs to be contextualized within overarching attitudes toward jewelry.

Working from another angle, theorists in the 1960s and 1970s examined advertising through the lens of structuralism. Judith Williamson's (1978) work showed how advertising promotes commodity fetishization, where commodities (like shoes or cameras) are social things whose meanings are divorced from their circumstances of production. Marketing can thus be viewed as a value-giving process that transfigures an object into what Karl Marx (1867) called a "social hieroglyph," where the real conditions of its production and value are obscured. A politics of reconnection, in which consumers are educated about the realities of production, can, but does not always, reduce such fetishization.

Awareness about diamond production is uneven, but even the knowledgeable do not necessarily reject diamonds. "I just love diamonds and wearing them makes me feel special and feminine, and, well, like someone cares about me! They are sparkly and wonderful, and they go with everything and you can wear them to turn that plain outfit into something really special," one woman explained, just minutes before summarizing a story she had heard on the radio about "how the meaning of diamonds is manufactured by ads and there is a lot of manipulation involved."

I asked Ray, a fashion photographer in his late thirties, who believes diamonds are "overrated," whether there is a difference between wearing a small diamond and wearing a large one. He replied,

> No, no difference—big, small, it's all the same—people are not educated. Plus it's something—it's like everything actually, it's like politics, the environment—nobody gives a shit, they don't want to know. Even if they did somehow know, people are so cliché in this country they would still want it—they would still want their peanut-size diamond ring. Everyone wants that.

Ray's pessimism is supported by Lisa Bratton's (2001) research on correlations between education and desire. Her study examined whether knowledge about the history of the diamond industry influenced the beliefs, attitudes, purchase intentions, and behaviors of a sample of undergraduates. She found no change in attitudes or behaviors after the subjects learned more about the industry, suggesting a lack of concern for the social ramifications of participating in this commodity chain.

This apparent disconnect is partly explained by the fact that gaining information does not necessarily undermine the metaphors—subtle but powerful linguistic devices—that fetishize products in ads. In the case of diamonds, temporal metaphors rupture the connection between knowledge about diamond production and consumption. Sallie Westwood (2002) shows that the phrase "A Diamond Is Forever" promotes what she calls "diamond time," which is predicated on symbolic associations having to do with romance, status, and heterosexuality. Diamond time simultaneously conceals the labor time of children and factory workers, and the gendering of gem production in India. She argues that the erasure of labor time in ads is essential to the success of other time frames, and thus to continued sales. Consumers, described as "complicit knowing subjects . . . in a fairy tale where we all want to believe that diamonds are forever," use diamonds for signaling to others the messages dictated by the industry and on occasion suggested by celebrity style gurus (Westwood 2002, 36). Looking at how time relates to consumerism through rhetorical deconstruction is an innovative approach, but Westwood's conclusions are not altogether congruent with the way consumers explained their own desires and practices to me, probably because Westwood's claims are based on a theory of meaning that makes it challenging to pick up individual divergences from the rhetorical statements in ads. Ethnography with consumers focused on the postacquisition context is one methodological answer to this problem.

Westwood's work is like that of Jean Baudrillard (1972)—both look at consumption as instrumental to identity formation through signing practices. Said in another way, meaning emerges from the way we use or display commodities, especially branded ones, to construct or perform identity. Within this framework, a commodity's use-value is secondary to its sign-value; it is a sign, intelligible to others (sign-readers), largely identified on the basis of class.

Other work in this vein shares the tendency to obscure individual agency, subjectivity, and history. Arthur Berger (2000), for example, explicitly denies the impact of the particular and the local in arguing that since advertising, on television in particular, broadly shapes people's behavior, its effects must be studied en masse, rather than at the level of the individual. And of course, advertising *is* a significant social force. How could it not be? In the mid-1990s, the number of advertisements

Americans were exposed to on TV, radio, newspapers, and magazines was as high as four hundred per day, and if promotional messages, including logos on products and ads on billboards that we see but may not process, are included, this number could be as high as sixteen hundred. By 1997, this figure had exceeded three thousand ads per day by some estimates (Shenk 1997). Some contemporary estimates exceed even this astronomical figure (Kirn 2007). However, our relationship to marketing is indeterminate: just seeing a message is no guarantee of internalization—that even heavily advertised products fail more often than not is a testament to this point. Consumers may be lured by the symbolic associations ads promote, but they are not rigidly controlled by them. By focusing on the tensions between postpurchase interpretations and ad discourse, we can better understand how commodities work in everyday lives—in ears, on fingers, and around necks.

Consumers use the ideas they glean from ads as one resource among many to make meaning, but are likely to say that other people are less savvy than they are about marketing. For example, Suzanna, a married, twenty-something fundamentalist Christian, parroted a De Beers message when she explained that her engagement ring is "a symbol of our love for one another." But then she continued,

> Some people wear big diamonds, even when they go to the grocery store or to eat at a cheap diner, to show that they have money or whatever, but for me it's not about that. It's about the celebration. I am religious, so, to me, I see God's love for us shining in here. And plus I think I am pretty savvy when it comes to what's on TV, so I am not easily drawn into believing what's in the ads.

There's a logic to the tendency to generalize about generic diamonds while weaving elaborate, situated meanings for specific individual stones. Diamonds *in general* symbolize status and romance, but *this* diamond, the one on Suzanna's finger, in its material particularity, holds ideas, associations, and memories wholly her own. They are situated within her awareness of ads and symbolic meanings, but also reflective of her own life and worldview. So, while the "A Diamond Is Forever" campaign encourages people to purchase and treat diamonds as symbols, people can undermine, ignore, or refuse ad symbolism using other semiotic strategies. Understanding the mechanics of these other strategies requires delving into a bit of technical language, but the payoff is worth it.

Symbolism

Many theorists and cultural critics use the term "symbol" to mean "sign" as it was understood by Ferdinand de Saussure. The Saussurean sign consists of two parts, likened to two sides of a coin that cannot be separated: the *signifier* and the *signified*, the word and the idea.

Saussure theorized the relationship between the signifier and the signified as one of shared convention, but the model poorly captures subjectivity and the singular, often creative and original, meanings of language, gesture, or material objects that make up everyday experience. To understand how commodities operate, then, it is precisely at the level of individuated particularity, contextualized within shared conventions, that focused research is most needed. This requires using a model of the sign that affords space for idiosyncrasy, a feature the Saussurean model lacks.

Luckily, there is an alternative: we can use the sign concept developed by Charles Saunders Peirce (pronounced "purse"). The Peircian model has the advantage of simultaneously explaining shared habits of signification and at the same time, keenly embracing subjectivity.

A Peircian sign has three elements: it stands for something to somebody in some respect or capacity. Unlike Saussure's two-sided sign, the Peircian sign is tripartite, encompassing a *sign-vehicle*, an *object*, and an *interpretant*. The association of the sign-vehicle (or sign) to its object takes place in some given consciousness, in time, and in a particular context. Semiosis is, therefore, a unique event, every time, and, although we draw on experience and our behavior tends to be extremely habitual, we are not merely habit driven—any sign has the potential to give rise to any object for some interpretant.

Signs can thus be analyzed according to the relation of any sign (like Saussure's signifier) to its object (like Saussure's signified). The interpretant, the most powerful and intriguing element of Peirce's account (and which is totally absent from Saussurean theory), is the understanding that we have of the sign-object relation, or the way we translate the sign into object. And what is really special is that these understandings or translations can change considerably according to circumstances. Why? Since meaning comes from the interpretant—emerging from a process of interpretation—it is not a characteristic of the sign-vehicle itself. Here, meaning is more of an event or process than a thing to be apprehended.

Peirce eventually identified over sixty thousand different kinds of signs, but these were largely iterations of three basic types: *symbol*, *icon*, and *index*. Every potential sign has the potential to be treated as a symbol, an icon, or an index, depending on the situation. Similar to the Saussurean sign, a Peircian symbol refers to its object by virtue of a law, habit, or convention. It is an arbitrary association—there is no necessary link between sign and object. For example, a red octagon is a symbol of the imperative "Stop!" To say that a diamond means "love" or "romance" is to treat it symbolically, but this is due to "deeming," one of advertising's primary functions.

Deeming establishes a habitual association of sign to object through repetition and persuasion. Ads attempt to persuade us that some given meaning or association is attached to a product. Diamonds have been deemed a "quintessential symbol of eternal romance," according to one consumer. What happens to these symbolic significations at the individual level, after something is purchased, is not advertisers' particular concern. What does concern them is maintaining the notion of diamonds as a beautiful and necessary component of love, courtship, and status, which is why the industry challenges associations—for example, that diamonds are traded for weapons used in brutal war and then sold to American consumers—that might tarnish their carefully managed symbolic load.[3]

Even when people understand how deeming works, it can remain a powerful force. Allen, a 32-year-old Wall Street broker, explained what he saw as the meaninglessness of diamonds to me:

> [R]omance is not what diamonds are about, or vice versa, even though a lot of people think that, it is just society that believes it. It's like flowers. If you send someone flowers by calling an 800 number and then they are all happy because you did something for them—diamonds are the same. People don't know why they like them, but they are just so darn happy to get one. But actually, it is an object with no meaning. People don't know why they think any of this and so to me it doesn't seem right—it is more or less a ridiculous concept. It is totally random—do you know the movie *Good Will Hunting*? The main star, Matt Damon, is asking this girl out and he is like, "We should go out for some caramels some day," and she says something like, "That's strange," and then he is like, "Well, going out for caramels is just as arbitrary as going out for coffee." Diamonds are just like that. It could have been anything. Why not just write the person you are going to marry a check? Just cut them a big fat check and hand it over?

So, ostensibly believing that diamonds have no intrinsic meaning, Allen rejects their association with romance. Nonetheless, he bought one for his sweetheart, thus fulfilling the aims of marketers that were established when Harry Oppenheimer hired N. W. Ayer to make a concerted push to massage American demand.

Oppenheimer and Ayer: The Rise of Diamond Advertising

In the 1920s, amidst a failing U.S. economy and diminishing demand for luxury items, control over De Beers was usurped by Sir Ernest Oppenheimer, owner of the powerful South African Anglo-American Corporation. In 1938, his son, Harry Oppenheimer, hired Gerald Lauck, president of the New York advertising agency N. W. Ayer & Son, to spearhead a new campaign. At the time, about three-quarters of their stock went to engagement rings in the United States for about $80 apiece, but they were of poorer quality than those sold in Europe, where the market was never, and still is not, particularly robust. Oppenheimer hoped that an ad campaign could persuade middle-class Americans not only that diamonds were integral to courtship but that the purchase of more diamonds at higher prices was a direct expression of love (Epstein 1982a). Ayer took advantage of every kind of medium available to stoke demand.

Ayer's psychologists devised consumer questionnaires for focus groups, while public relations experts hosted special events to promote sales. Account managers even negotiated with film producers to have movie titles reflect well upon the industry—gems were placed in love scenes on the bodies of film stars—and arranged "photo ops" with British royalty. They even commissioned artists like Salvador Dali and Pablo Picasso to develop images for their ads. Using feedback gathered from focus groups, "news" texts containing "historical" information were placed in major media for women to see.

Ayer's "Hollywood Service" provided copy to infotainment media about movie stars' diamonds. These press releases, including portraits of celebrities' ring-wearing hands, stating carat size and cut, were published in newspapers and magazines. Contemporary marketing continues to rely upon these same apparently successful strategies. "News" shows like *Entertainment Tonight* showcase the diamonds celebrities receive or purchase, often stating size and price. Popular magazine articles cover diamond "news," as when rap mogul Sean "P. Diddy" Combs spent almost $1 million on a diamond necklace for pop singer Jennifer Lopez after her break-up with actor Ben Affleck, or when the rings exchanged by actors Brad Pitt and Jennifer Aniston, gold bands studded with multiple stones, were copied by a jewelry distributor, who was then sued by the couple to the tune of $50 million. And the popular website Pinterest contains an entire "pinboard," a section where users can find and add related images, dedicated to "Celebrity diamonds seen at the Oscars, BAFTA's, and Golden Globes," which features photos of stars alongside close-ups of their diamonds.[4]

By 1941, sales had risen by a stunning 55 percent, which Ayer celebrated as the result of a new form of advertising in which no direct sale or brand name is sold, but the idea is impressed upon the public (Epstein 1982a). Continuing through the 1940s, Ayer sent authoritative representatives to high schools to educate young women about the importance of diamond jewelry, and published a portrait series called "Engaged Socialites." Based on a logic of emulation, the portrait series would, as explained in a 1948 agency strategy paper, "spread the word of diamonds worn by stars of screen and stage, by wives and daughters of political leaders, by any woman who can make the grocer's wife and the mechanic's sweetheart say, 'I wish I had what she has'" (Epstein 1982a). And when I visited the Hope Diamond—a blue diamond famous not only for its provenance but also for being cursed (Kurin 2006)—on display at the Smithsonian Museum in Washington, DC, I heard countless women, and even very young girls, using some variation of the phrases contained in that agency paper: "Oh God, I wish I had that," "I would wear that every day," or "I want that soooo bad." Steps away, a red diamond, one of the largest in existence and worth hundreds of thousands of dollars, was virtually ignored while people pushed one another to get closer to the Hope. Countless other stones—not diamonds—of all colors, sizes, and shapes are on display at the museum, but none elicited the excitement and desire expressed about the Hope and the colorless diamond collection featured in ad campaigns, which rely in part on the infamous tagline "A Diamond Is Forever."

Frances Gerety

In 1947, copywriter Frances Gerety came up with the slogan "A Diamond Is Forever." Even though it has been listed by market-watching journalists as the best advertising slogan of the twentieth century, initial response inside the agency was lukewarm. But within three years of the agency using it, an estimated 80 percent of engagements included the exchange of a diamond. Ayer believed the growth of this trend was interrupted only by the desire of women to differentiate themselves from their mothers (a desire discovered through focus group research) and responded with a "Not Your Mother's Ring" campaign. This pattern of marketing to carefully tracked consumer responses continues today in the "Right-Hand Ring" campaign.

Ayer also set up the Diamond Information Center (DIC) as an in-house public relations department and authoritative front from which to release information. Drawing on Thorstein Veblen's (1899) notion of conspicuous consumption, the agency introduced the idea that a woman's ring indexes her partner's success. The persistence of this idea in conjunction with the perception of needing a diamond to legitimize an engagement was reflected in interviews with both men and women. Allison told me that when she became engaged, she informed her fiancé about what she wanted:

> There is no question that I want a diamond. And I told him that I was not going to wear some little chip. So I said straight out, "Don't even bring anything less than a carat around." He didn't want me to wear a small one anyway, as people might think that he was cheap. Of course he didn't want that!

Like Allison, Henry believes that by wearing a big diamond, a woman is "telling the world that 'Hey, I can afford it,' meaning the diamond and lots of other things too," but for him, and other men I interviewed, the connection between diamonds and status is complicated by the fear that too big a diamond is unbelievable or socially unacceptable.

> What I know about De Beers is just the ads I see: A Diamond Is Forever and all that jazz. I see those ads all around town. And I do feel affected by them, but I am a guy, and so what I really want to know is what women think. You know giving someone something like that is a big deal, and you

don't want to screw it up by giving something too small, but something too big can also be wrong. I mean it could be a disaster!

But, I asked, what would he do if he had the money and his girlfriend wanted a big, even huge and expensive one? "Then," he replied, "the sky's the limit!"

There is a sliding range, highly individualized, within which diamonds can or should appropriately reflect status. I saw no consistent factor determining the extent to which people see diamonds as the type of status symbol Veblen imagined, although the idea that size can reflect a man's financial success was very often at play. Allen expressed a belief, shared by others, that evaluating someone's financial success on the basis of jewelry is "wrong because you can never tell if you are dealing with the real thing or a fake" and that "some guys will go into debt to buy something that does not fairly reflect their standing in life. They just want you to think they are up there, but they aren't."

Sally, who comes from a moneyed family and works with inner-city youth, agreed with Allen's basic assessment that reading status is risky, but for a different reason: people's "real" motives are hidden. As she has aged and "started to become aware of class issues," it is increasingly important to her that others not see her as "spoiled, as someone who is pretending not to be spoiled, or even as someone from a privileged class who is pretending to be from a lower class." The diamond earrings she once wore were demoted to permanent residence in a jewelry box in the midst of this "class crisis" because the associations of glamour and rank in the form "of having made it" were not in keeping with the way she wanted to be seen by others.

For Sally, diamonds not only can reflect being spoiled or privileged but also can reveal aspirations toward being middle-class—neither of which she finds desirable:

But you know with diamonds, [class] actually doesn't matter, because people who are really poor and don't have anything will spend their last cent on a diamond, or something that looks like one, so that they will appear as if they have done all the things they are supposed to do and have been rewarded by being securely middle-class. So, as I see it, wearing diamonds is about being middle-class, about wanting to be middle class. And I don't want that.

To Sally, aspiring to look middle-class is "tacky." Wearing a diamond announces "a middle-class mentality" to the world and is for her, therefore, deeply unattractive. These ideas reflect her own class ideologies, social concerns, and experiences, as well as ad content, but are not congruent with the symbolic associations ads advance.

Anxiety about how strangers read gems as an expression of a partner's success was surprising in some cases, but for everyone who worried about such conclusions, another brushed them off since others who "don't know anything" are of no social consequence. This point was reiterated by those whose diamond narratives are known only to themselves, their closest friends, and/or their family. The memories, emotions, hopes, and stories that generate meaning are unknown to social others who misinterpret the stone on the basis of generic symbolic meanings seen in marketing.

During the late 1960s, as production ramped upward and producers looked for market shares outside of the United States, De Beers hired the J. Walter Thompson agency, with its expertise in international marketing, to develop campaigns for markets in Germany, France, Brazil, and Japan. Demand remained weak in Europe and Brazil, but the Japanese operation paid off. Images of Japanese women participating in nontraditional Western activities like biking or mountain climbing while wearing Western clothing and diamonds alongside swanky-looking Japanese men who looked on approvingly fired the imagination of the Japanese public. Within fifteen years, diamond consumerism had increased from less than 5 to over 70 percent, and Japan is now one of the largest diamond markets in the world.

Japanese demand is for small, high-quality stones whose perfection and cleanliness stand as a metaphor for the bride's virginal purity. A mar inside the stone is unacceptable, whereas in the United States, size is sometimes more important than clarity. Evidently, we love big things: a "Bigger Is Better" campaign ran in New York during the market boom of 2004, but the industry has, at other times, promoted small stones. In the 1970s, when their cache of small diamonds grew due to increased Russian production, De Beers launched a campaign that emphasized cut, color, and quality to promote small solitaire diamonds, tennis bracelets, and cluster rings. Consumers were urged to appreciate the sentimental aspect of the gift, rather than the size of the stone. Average carat sizes for purchases plummeted. The campaign was so successful that large stone reserves ballooned. By the late 1970s, campaigns to rebuild desire for larger stones while not erasing small stone demand had to be devised. The solution? Offer multistone jewelry, particularly large solitary stones framed by smaller ones, called "baguettes," a design still popular today.

Marketing has not only worked to encourage desires for differently sized gems but has also attempted to manage demand for color. Diamonds in ads are usually transparent, but because of shading treatments, greater availability of natural and synthetic colored gems, and product placement, colored diamonds—even yellow and brown "cognac" and "champagne" hues—have become fashionable. One night at a barbecue, I met Russell and Paige, a professional couple in their thirties, and told them about my research. While discussing their engagement ring, Russell said he felt sorry they had already purchased a stone when they found out about coloration. He "regretted the purchase of the clear diamond because what we really wanted to get was one of those new colored ones. They are really valuable because they are yellow!" But Paige reassured him, "This one is beautiful, and I wouldn't want anything different." She joked, "It makes me feel so, umm, traditional." Later in private she admitted to me that she really did prefer a yellow one because it "would be something different." Perhaps the coloration ads had successfully provoked a new desire.

Sex Sells

Some people, however, have negative reactions to symbolic deeming and the appearance of diamonds in association with Hollywood stars. Claire, a film editor in her midthirties who describes herself as "not into diamonds," rejects the association of diamonds with celebrity:

> I know that the diamond companies are trying to make you feel like you have to have a diamond to be a legitimate part of society, but anyone can see through that. They are just companies with a really expensive product, and I think the whole Hollywood thing is caught up in it. I have no idea how the whole thing happened, but you see the Oscars or whatever and they are all talking about so-and-so's diamond, and how much it cost, and where it came from, like Harry Winston or whatever, and it's all just really stupid, if you ask me. I mean, who cares?

But although she eschews its symbolic associations with glamour and status, Claire does have a diamond. She says that its meaning is linked to the memory of her partner's grandmother and the close relationship he shared with her, and the hope that her and her partner's relationship will live up to their dreams and expectations (they are "committed, but not married").

Diamond ads, the content of which people are clearly responding to, have risen to the level of a cultural phenomenon, tracked by *Advertising Age* and *Brandweek*, publications that provide an additional layer of visibility to marketing. For example, in November of 2000, *Brandweek* covered the De Beers holiday campaign, reporting that De Beers had spent $15 million in television ads targeted to high-income men between the ages of twenty-five and fifty-four to complement an online contest (Bittar 2000). De Beers had also purchased all 140 available ad spaces in New York's former World Trade Center from which to bombard prospective buyers with "guy-humored" ads containing copy such as "Only her ears need enhancing," followed by, "Of course there's a return on your investment. We just can't print it here."

Many ads insinuate a link between sex and diamonds: The "Ever wonder why so many babies are born in September" ad was posted all over New York City in September 2003. In interviews, people who made an association between diamonds and sexual access usually did so with complicated attitudes. Some women equate receiving a diamond with "being possessed" and understand it as an exchange in which they are making themselves into, or allowing themselves to be treated as, sexual objects. And some men explicitly stated that giving someone a diamond is a way to ensure sexual access: according to Sally, wearing a diamond ring

> is like saying, "I have been bought!" He gave you the ring and now you are his, the whole thing is oriented around him. You are indebted to him and that's it, that's the extent to what you are getting from him, and now you have to spend your whole life paying him back. Gosh, that sounds terrible, but that's what it is all about if you know what I mean. It says, "I am conservative and into home decorating." Emeralds and rubies don't say any such thing. Wearing them, you are more saying, "Here I am, I am exciting and lovely!" I don't think diamonds are very sexy in that sense.

It is interesting to compare Sally's words with what Ian said.

> I was walking past a bus station over on Madison Avenue earlier and I saw an ad for diamonds, and it said something like, "Ever wonder why so many babies are born in September?" and then there is this image of this perfect diamond just reflecting all over with gleaming colors. And I was like, "Wow!"—and it took me a minute—I was truly perplexed, but then I was like, "Oh, OK, so the idea is that you give her the diamonds in December and then she starts fucking you like crazy and the fucking is better and it is so good that you get her pregnant 'cause she is so crazy

to fuck you all the time." But I think that I am like most men, and men want to make women feel good and happy and, you know, turn to you and smile and be glad that they are with you and feel like they are in love with you and enthralled and all that, and the idea of this ad is that you can actually buy that. So in a way you are willing to lay out the dough and that is what people are actually appreciating. It is the sacrifice that turns women on, maybe, which I understand, but then there is the whole symbol thing too.

Ian's understanding of the exchange of diamond for sex is perhaps more generous than that of Tom, who, having seen the same ad, was talking about rap stars and "bling" when the subject of sex came up.

These guys are simple conspicuous consumers. They have the money and they use it to adorn themselves. They don't have money in the bank; they are walking around wearing it. It's not like disposable income like I bought this coffee with. That's all they have. So people can see it and envy them. And women will want to have sex with them. And it's all the same with women, they get diamonds and then they have sex with you for the next thirty years. All women are hos [slang for whores], really— it's like a contract—I will provide for you, entrust you with my money, here's a diamond to prove it, and then you have sex with me. There is an expectation of fidelity, and women wear diamonds to show that they are taken, that they are marked. And there are those ads on TV and billboards all over town. Have you seen that one that says why babies are born? And the whole thing is how you can get someone to have sex with you if you give them a diamond. It's all so visible and out there, now you don't see that for pearls or sapphires, and here it is, a rock. A rock!! It's just a rock, OK? So, I mean, what's it all about anyway?

The way men understand women, sexual relationships, and gifting varies from person to person, but Tom, as it turns out, would give a diamond to a woman, even dipping into his savings to do so, even though he sees the exchange as a kind of sexual purchase. The symbolic marketing of diamonds is ineffective on both Tom and Ian, who both told me that diamonds might be a symbol of love and romance to other people but that they "do not buy into all that" and are "aware of ad techniques."

For each person who finds the ads clever or sweet ("I just love those ads!"), another finds them insulting. Simone described one set of ads, and explained why she found them distasteful:

> [I saw] the ads for diamonds where there is a silhouette of a woman but there is a diamond on it, and the diamond is very present and sparkly but her whole face is erased. To me this is, like, such a major turnoff. I think "suburban" and I hate that. I mean there is supposed to be a person there! But in the ads it's like it's the diamond that matters and the woman is just faceless.

Ads sometimes feature celebrities to generate glamour—which is sometimes about sex but at other times about class or status.[5] In 2003, advertisers organized "tie-in" events—events where certain products are featured—associating diamonds with celebrity, fame, and success. Together with General Motors, De Beers built the "Diamond Cadillac," a car specially retrofitted with professional jewelry cases, studio lighting, and a make-up counter to transport jewels and stars to the Oscar night celebrations. Promoting associations with Hollywood is a mainstay in diamond marketing history: retailers report that designs worn by film, television, and music stars fly off the shelves as soon as celebrity-specific advertisements are broadcast.

Women I spoke with often recited the carat size and color of Oscar nominees' jewelry, or were able to otherwise describe it. A few who were knowledgeable in this way remarked on the "incredible beauty" of the stones. Others were critical: Jessica wondered how "these people get those diamonds, I mean I bet they don't even get to keep them. If they are even real! It's just a publicity stunt. Half the time they don't even look that good." Even though she prefers not to wear diamonds because of the "exploitation of all the people involved," Jessica was quite well versed in who was wearing what. She explained,

> I had a neighbor from Sierra Leone and he only had one arm, and they had this meeting [in her apartment building] where they were talking about what had happened over there. I wouldn't be caught dead wearing a diamond. Especially when it's just that same ring everyone has, with, you know, that same boring setting. But mainly, like Nicole Kidman or whoever, they are just part of the whole machine anyway, so, I mean, who can be surprised that they are wearing diamonds? That doesn't make me want to run out and get one.

Jessica later qualified all of this by stating that when a diamond is handed down or in a very old setting, it is acceptable, even becoming a beautiful and cherished item.

Raise Your Right Hand

Taking another path to stimulate sales, a $6-million advertising campaign, with the tagline "Women of the World, Raise Your Right Hand," posits a feminist sensibility in encouraging women to make purchases in commemoration of career accomplishments. *Billboard Magazine* (Hay 2004) covered the campaign, which became even more visible when it appeared as a story in the *New York Times* (Walker 2004), the *Wall Street Journal* (Yee 2003), and *USA Today* (Carter 2002); celebrity and fashion magazines like *People* and *VIBE* then started covering the purchase of right-hand rings by public figures. The campaign—correlated with increased sales directly to women—received the "They Get It" award from Advertising Women of New York (AWNY), a watchdog group that tracks the construction of gender in ads. These right-hand ring ads feature svelte models wearing diamonds on their right-hand "bling-finger," accompanied by copy such as, "Your left hand says 'We'; Your right hand says, 'Me.'" Others in the series read, "Your Left Hand Rocks the Cradle. Your Right Hand Rules the World" and "Your Left Hand Feeds the Family. Your Right Hand Takes the Cake." Since this campaign is responding directly to the construction of women in most diamond ads, it makes the tacit ideologies in those ads more explicit (where women are family oriented, passive, soft, and subordinate to their male partners).

But it is not just rhetoric that marks this campaign as special. At the level of material culture, the settings differ from solitaire or other engagement-looking jewelry, tending toward vertical, more playful motifs. In addition to the ad blitz, the DIC product-placed these rings on the hands of celebrities like Faith Hill, Julia Roberts, and Sarah Jessica Parker. A right-hand ring ad featuring Halle Berry as Catwoman was even tied into the opening of *Catwoman* in July 2004. Daria, a physicist in her early fifties, wears a right-hand diamond ring. She explained that "nobody was going to buy it for me, certainly not my husband who already gave me one diamond, so I had to buy it myself." Her big-by-any-standard stone is a "yellow diamond, but looks like a topaz, and it is something I did for myself, something different and just a little reward that I felt I deserved." Her explanation closely mirrors the commemoration of accomplishments, the sense of self-esteem, and the rewards for financial success that are suggested in ads.

The idea behind the right-hand ring campaign was to create a new occasion for diamond use by establishing diamonds as a potent expression of a woman's individuality and style in addition to diamonds' better-known symbolic associations with love and romance. Here, advertisers exploit the slippage that exists in symbols between the signifier and the signified to increase the array of diamonds' meanings. But DIC's strategies do not always work. Against the success of the right-hand ring, there have been spectacular campaign flops, such as the attempt to create a market for elegant men's wear.

Gender and Ethnicity

The failure of the men's campaign may be linked to the advertising industry's previous work to gender diamonds as female. Consumers feel that diamonds are for women, that they are "feminine," "sexy," "fun and charming," and "flirty." Giving diamonds an important role in her fashion sensibility, Ruth said, "They are so feminine and delicate, and if you wear anything else it *has* to match this concept of feminine and delicate, so you have to create the whole wardrobe around it. Men should not wear diamonds unless it is done ironically, in a rock and roll spirit." Many white, middle-class women I talked with agreed.

"Listen," Sally said, "any diamond jewelry on men is too much. Ostentatious. Actually, any jewelry on men is too much. Men should only wear, like, brushed steel at the most. Any gem at all looks gaudy and showy and therefore cheap. And it devalues the person." Renee also volunteered views on gender and diamonds. The gendering, and possibly ethnicizing, potential of men wearing diamonds is reflected in her answer to my question about whether men can wear diamonds. She replied passionately,

> No! Now that's what I call ugly and vulgar, but, then again, I don't think women should wear mustaches. Because that's not ladylike and, you know, I think it's OK for men to stick with a watch and a wedding band. That's it. I'm not a big fan of diamonds and onyx pinky rings. If I see that that tells me, "Hey, howya' doin', Vinnie Baggadonuts." Like a Mafia guy from Jersey or something. It tells me: slime factor. And then I start wondering if he has on a strapper t-shirt under there somewhere. You know, a "wife-beater," one of those white, ribbed Fruit-of-the-Loom things. So, no, I don't like that. Diamonds are not for men.

Renee's friend Allison echoed her assessment when asked what she thought about men wearing diamonds:

Uggghhhh, I hate that! No way. There is no way to make that look good. I'm sorry but that's so cheesy and it makes a guy look like a cheesy mobster with a nugget ring. Call me judgmental, but if I see a man with a diamond, I don't trust him. If he has that bad of taste in that, then what else is wrong with him? I think, "What is wrong with this guy?" And like the man that sized my ring had on a diamond nugget thing, and I was like "Eeeeuuwwww, bless your heart, you poor thing. Don't you know how ugly that is?"

Tim also recalled Renee's point:

I think that I actually stereotypically associate men wearing diamonds with Italian American, "Sopranos"-type people. [6] Yeah, it's the Sopranos type of thing, like a pinky ring. Sorry [apologizing for his candor], but I work in Human Relations, so I am honest. If I saw a man with diamonds I wouldn't think much, but until I knew the person I would wonder what they were up to.

Rosetta's approach illustrates a slightly more tolerant perspective: "I don't think diamonds are for men. Men don't wear them, except for hip hop [artists] and the elderly or metrosexual types, so I think they are female-associated, but the engagement ring is really about heterosexual marriages, but earrings don't have that kind of association; women, hip hop guys, anyone, both men and women, can wear diamond earrings."

Regardless of their feminine associations, some men are willing, happy, and even proud to wear diamonds. Henry (not into hip hop nor a metrosexual) says he would wear a diamond, but only under extraordinary circumstances:

I don't wear jewelry. I mean I would if it were a gift from a loved one and I really respected their taste, then, and only out of respect for them,

I might wear one for special occasions, but I don't like that. I don't like to draw attention to myself. Diamonds do that, you know, even though I don't really tend to notice them. But guys wearing diamonds? It's relative. I may end up with one. But, I doubt it. It seems like a copout, but it's too Italian goombah, or Sammy Davis with the big rings.

Arnold told me that although the secrecy of the industry bothers him, he would still wear a diamond:

Not a big flashy ring, but perhaps something small and flush, or perhaps an earring, but only if it were of the best quality. For me I would only want a very good diamond, because I would know and that's what matters, it's like coffee or even tea, you experiment and try things and then you—well, for me, I like to buy the best, at least for me what seems to be the best, and it's the same with diamonds; even if I were to buy a cheap diamond that looked the same, if I thought it was somehow inferior, I wouldn't want that.

Diamonds in ads do symbolize heterosexual love, and indeed work to reproduce a kind of heteronormative marriage ritual. But against her views about the gendered/sexualized bent of engagement jewelry, Rosetta still wanted a diamond to celebrate engagement and, later, marriage, to her female partner. She has a few pieces of diamond jewelry from her parents, but this ring was one she chose herself:

There is a diamond in my engagement ring, just a tiny chip. You know, at first it fell out, it is small, it's only worth like fifty bucks, so it is discreet, it does not look like a big pointy thing, you know how engagement rings look. But I like this design, Grace and I bought it. Actually I picked it out. I wanted an engagement ring and this is similar, I mean it is a diamond ring, and I wanted a diamond, but I did not like the way they all looked. [Engagement rings are] all very heterosexual and loaded like that, but this ring does not really look like an engagement ring. It is a band and a diamond so some people will see it as an engagement ring, of course, but with this setting I think it is less legible. It has the elements, but in a new way, so it's not the uniform.

The uniform, I came to understand, is a gold band with a solitaire placed in a high setting.

Men and women both described looking for engagement jewelry that was different from what they viewed as "common," "ordinary," or, perhaps less pejoratively, "traditional," to set themselves apart from the "trend-following crowd." Exemplars of inconspicuous consumption, Frank and June both wear wedding bands, but the diamonds are placed on the side where a casual viewer cannot see them. June's friend, Suke, wears a ring in which the diamond is on the inside of the band, touching the skin. Only she and her husband know it is there; to others it looks like a plain band. Taking "inconspicuous consumption" to the limit, the Japanese Hitachi Corporation sells the world's smallest diamond ring: a diamond that is only one five-billionth of a carat is embedded in a 0.02 millimeter-diameter tungsten ring, and can be seen only under a microscope.[7] This product highlights how poorly these stones index gender, sexuality, class, or anything else in a reliable way.

Caught Up

Consumers are affected by marketing in convoluted ways. There is no simple correlation between consumption and an acceptance of the symbolic attributes seen in ads. An expressive example of the "messy" reading of ads is Sally's story:

> I have dreams. One day I would love to have a really big, fat, emerald-cut emerald, even as an engagement ring. Actually I would rather have that than a diamond, especially not a diamond solitaire. The emerald would be something different, but it can still represent what a diamond represents, and actually this is what is interesting to me. It upsets me that diamonds are so constructed and important, but I still want them! You

feel all this pressure to have a relationship, to get married, and get the ring, and we, my friends and I, say "until I have the rock"—as shorthand for saying that kind of relationship—"I am not going to live with a guy until I have the rock." So it's synonymous and that makes me angry. I mean, I am a sensitive and enlightened woman and I know enough to know that it should not be important, but it is! Why should it not be important? Because it's a material thing. It's a token. I mean don't get me wrong, I love nice things and gems, and stones are cool, I love rocks and stones that come from the earth, but diamonds come with a lot of baggage. Mainly status. I don't want to be that horrible woman in the De Beers commercial where they are in Italy and he is, like, yelling, "I love this woman," and then she is, like, "I love this man, I love this man," and it is so disgusting, and, I think it's for the three diamond thing, and the idea is that fifteen years of marriage have come down to a ring with a few rocks on it. It's so fake and socially constructed and I know that, and that's why it makes me really sad. But I am also part of society and, truthfully, I want those diamonds.

People like Sally do think of status, love, and romance when they think of diamonds, that is to say, diamonds in general. Tim explained why he purchased a diamond bracelet for his fiancée:

I picked diamonds because they are more rare as far as jewelry is concerned, and it goes with the ring and they tell me that all diamonds match. I mean I looked at a lot of other stuff like silver and I thought diamonds were the most, I don't know, special, I guess, and for me it's tied to the whole marriage thing. I mean, I don't know what other people do, but I hear "diamond" and "ring" and that means marriage.

Interestingly, his fiancée told me that, for her, the engagement ring is about Tim stepping away from his pragmatic side to do something he would normally consider frivolous because he thought it would make her happy. The "stepping away" is what is significant, she said, in addition to the "diamond is forever stuff. I don't really care about diamonds," but because "I know how important this was for him," partly because of the expense, she cherishes the stones.

And, of course, status is obliquely related to expense. Mary explained that she has not bought into the marketing, but she described one of her girlfriend's diamond purchases:

> [S]he is in her forties. She is not married, but she is really into diamonds and she started buying them. She calls them "starters" and she "trades up," as she calls it. She told me, "No man is going to do it for me so I have to do it myself," and for her it is a status symbol. Which I don't get, because you can go over to H&M and get the same thing for two dollars. And I defy anyone to tell the difference. I mean she overtly says that it is about status and power and she really cares a lot about it.

Like Mary, Allen notes that "a diamond is just a status symbol. Seeing it triggers you to say, 'Hey that's worth a lot of money.' If it's fake you could never tell the difference, but I think what most people think is, 'Wow! That's expensive.'"

So while consumers are ensnared in ad copy, at some level many remain cynical about the content, and try to distance themselves from the passive reception of corporate-sponsored symbolic meanings, particularly in terms of the troubled relationship that conspicuous consumption has with class or status.

This advertising, if you look at the level of the encouragement of purchases, does work; the retail market is worth more than $56 billion a year, while De Beers's advertising outlay is only just over $200 million, most of which is absorbed by the American market.[8] In our conversations, consumers constantly mentioned marketing phrases, but then welded them into new formulations in their own stories. Others denied the power of symbolism, but just by mentioning it, they shore up its authority: Mary Sue, a lawyer in her early forties, having inherited several diamonds, said that "in terms of the marketing, I haven't bought into it. I would never spend my own money on diamonds and if someone ever did want to buy me something like that I would rather have something besides a diamond because I like to be different and my birthstone is ruby. Maybe an onyx, yes, I prefer rubies and onyx." Others qualified their statements about meaning with explanations about how "other people buy into the myth"—they use diamonds as a tired symbol—but how for them, meaning is spun personally. So the dovetailing of industry-promoted significations and creative interpretations swings from person to person. Semiosis—the act of making meaning—is a complicated, context-bound activity; diamonds can operate as more than passive symbols to help people perform a social role, understand the world (their world), or say something singularly human. We explore this in the following chapters.

4

DIAMONDS AND EMOTIONS

I met Corinne, an educational psychologist in her early thirties, through a mutual friend. When she sat down for our interview she immediately said, "Oh, diamonds, humph. I think diamonds are strange." When asked to elaborate, she began talking about her husband, Brent, and her family in relation to diamonds. Later, when I complimented her large, emerald-cut diamond, she confided in me,

> I would never tell Brent, but frankly I am ashamed of it. And I don't always wear it. Sometimes I tell him that I'm not wearing it because I don't want it to get stolen, or that it's too flashy for the subway, but then whenever we go out together I always put it on and it's special and romantic and he thinks I am proud of it, and that makes him happy. And that makes me happy.

Corinne's husband Brent is a Wall Street stockbroker. She reported with some pride that "he makes a substantial salary," permitting them to live in a big apartment in Chelsea, a fashionable Manhattan neighborhood. Corinne's sisters-in-law, who live uptown, are "materialistic," as she put it, and "concerned about status and having things that show people how much money they have. And they have a lot of it. I mean they wear their diamonds and furs to eat at the greasiest diner in town. I have diamonds and furs too, but I would be embarrassed to be seen at a diner dressed like that."

"But you see, I have this other diamond," she said, becoming more animated.

"It is on a ring that came from my grandfather, and it has sapphires and rubies and—allegedly—diamonds. I mean, I have never had it appraised, so who knows if they are even real. But I don't always wear it. In fact, I never wear it." When I pressed her further about why she doesn't wear her grandfather's ring, she said, without pause, that it was because she was sure that miners were being mistreated:

> Truthfully, I have very negative associations with diamonds. I am sure somebody is being exploited, I mean—don't they come from Australia? I bet the Aborigines are the ones who have to go down into the mines to get the diamonds and they are probably treated so badly that I would not want to have any part of it. But it is from my grandfather, so I keep it and, well, he treasured it and so I do.

Corinne is sensitive to the issue of labor practices and what she sees as class-based materialism. She tries to avoid participating in an industry she believes to be unfair, but even so is drawn to maintaining the emotional bridges extended from one person to another when diamonds are gifted. Corinne experiences these ideals as countervailing sentiments, but her use of and emphasis on the phrase "but it is from my grandfather" make it plain that her familial attachments won out over her political awareness.

Contradictions like those embedded in Corinne's personal commitments and activities (including a moral position against exploitation) turned out to constitute a salient dimension of people's diamond narratives. As the interview proceeded, Corinne's relationship to diamonds was shown to be fraught with multiple ambiguities, which manifest as a mix-up of affection, pride, shame, love, and even contempt. How does this happen? What does this sentimental complexity tell us? How can we systematically explain such contradictions?

Contingency and Context

As previously detailed, diamonds are produced by a complex commodity chain, one that includes advertising. Some accept only selected elements of industry-sponsored symbolism while a few take it on wholesale. Most people, though, fashion meanings that are locally situated, flexible (changing over time and across circumstance), idiosyncratic, and creative. People tend to swallow ad meanings when it comes to thinking about other people's diamonds or about diamonds in the abstract, but they reject or transform publicly circulated meanings when confronted with their own individual gems.

People's interpretations of diamonds are often deliberately, intentionally opposed to marketing. Informants claimed that although other people are duped or brainwashed by advertising, they are "smarter than that," asserting that they operate independently of larger discursive structures. People regularly expressed—in more or less direct terms— that they are aware of and consciously working against the marketing that seeks to put ideas in their heads.

Mary Sue is a pretty, single, flamboyant lawyer who lives in Park Slope. I asked her how diamonds compare to other gems she has, and whether or not she believes them to be the most attractive or most desirable of all gems. She recited ideas promoted in marketing as a foil to her preference for rubies and onyx:

> Well, to me, diamonds have the most emotion attached to them because they are supposed to be tokens of love and used in engagements and things like that, so for that reason I attach a lot of emotion to them. But you know that baggage is just a huge marketing strategy and we have all bought into it, but it's not like that all over the world. I personally have not bought into it. Because well, you know my dad was sick last winter and he, I guess, knew that he didn't have much time left and so at that time he gave me a safe deposit box that contained my mom's ring—my biological mom, she had died, and her ring that he had given to her

was in there. She died when I was nineteen years old. And he also gave me his mother's—my grandmother's—diamonds. And I think they are real valuable and I've had them for almost a year, but I wouldn't even consider wearing them. I keep them in a cardboard box. They are not even insured, which is really stupid, because they are really big and expensive, but as far as how they actually look, they are not doing it for me. There is so much going on there that I can't even think about wearing them.

Mary Sue's stance toward ad symbolism as expressed in the phrase "I personally have not bought into it" is intriguing in that she tacitly acknowledges its power by striving to reject it. But more interesting is the fact that Mary Sue's diamonds are so saturated with emotion and personal history that she literally can't bear to wear them. As objects pregnant with meaning, they inhabit a category separate from all of the anonymous stones shown in ads. And that heavy emotional history is unique to Mary Sue, unshared, indexical of her circumstance, and attached only to her diamonds. Though there is a pervasive tendency to associate particular diamonds with the people to whom they once belonged, the set of meanings Mary Sue gives them is distinct, and in this sense idiosyncratic.

Icons and Indexes

To review, the sign as described by Saussurean structuralist theory is arbitrary and ahistorical; it does not specify any sense of real agency. The Peircean model, by contrast, does account for subjectivity, context, memory, and the creation of meaning with regard to material particularity, formal qualities, and temporal persistence by identifying three types of signs (symbol, icon, and index). Furthermore, as opposed to the binary Saussurean formula, Peircian signs are understood as triadic: a sign stands for something to somebody, so signification is more relational than code-like.

Icons are contingent upon the perception of likeness. For example, a portrait that resembles the person to whom it refers operates iconically. The key to the icon is structural similarity—think of metaphors and maps. In language, onomatopoeia has an iconic character; a word sounds like the thing it names, such as "snip" or "quack." Indexes operate by spatio-temporal contiguity—like a knock on the door heralding someone on the other side. Think of a souvenir, a weather vane, or a scar. In language, words like "this" or "that," or pronouns such as "I" are indexical signs whose meaning shifts according to context (see Crapanzano 2003). Indexes work symptomatically; they are caused by and tell us about something else, possibly remote in time and space, over there.

Saussurean signs are best subsumed within Peirce's rubric as symbols. In both models, meaning is arbitrary and conventional. A red octagon means "Stop!" But it could have been some other way—a green octagon, or a red square. There may be historical or cultural reasons behind the choice of the red octagon, but there is no identifiable causal or structural link between a red octagon and the command "Stop!" Most linguistic elements operate symbolically.

All three sign types—icon, index, and symbol—can work together to generate meaning. Instances of "pure" symbols, icons, and indexes are rare, if they even exist, but the interpretation of any sign generally privileges one mode over another. The "semiotic ideology" shapes what kind of sign someone takes it to be—a symbol, icon, or index (Keane 2003). Semiotic ideology tells us how a sign is thought to carry meaning. It tells us, for example, which of the many aspects of a sign require interpretation.

A crucial difference between these sign models has to do with how meaning is established in the first place. Meaning is processural for Peirce; it is context bound rather than static or defined by virtue of its relations to other signs within a larger universe, as in the Saussurean system. Meaning is generated through chains of associative signification—not by virtue of binary oppositions. Peirce's signs can, theoretically, mean anything in different given contexts and semiotic ideologies. And remember, diamonds can serve as symbols, icons, and indexes all at the same time, the potential result of which is a rich set of possibly conflicting meanings. Using a combination of interpretive strategies can produce a set of countervailing, cacophonic sentiments—such as "love" and "shame"—associated with the same diamond. Or, a single emotive note, say "pleasure," can be enriched when the outcome of all interpretations harmonize.

"Hey, I Pay My Power Bill on Time"

The term "motivation" describes the extent to which meaning determines or influences the form of the sign, sometimes called the "sign vehicle." The more the form of the sign is shaped by what it means, the more motivated the sign is said to be: icons and indexes are relatively motivated, while symbols are relatively unmotivated. The less motivated the sign, the more people must learn the agreed-upon meaning, as is the case with much language. For symbols, the form of the sign is neither caused nor linked to that which it represents. Icons and indexes are more motivated than symbols in the sense that the form of the sign is understood as influenced in part by that which it represents.

Because the symbol is not motivated—not attached to its meaning in any sustained way—the meaning is vulnerable to being reassigned. Advertisers exploit this slippage, tweaking or affixing new meanings to things through repetition, as they please. People, for example, acknowledge the symbolic pairing of diamonds with glamour or femininity. (Diamonds were once signs of masculinity and virility—but there is nothing intrinsically masculine or feminine about pressed carbon.) But as reflected in Corinne's narrative, these same people might go on to describe another set of (invented) symbolic meanings in addition to indexical and iconic ones they have developed. Corinne "gets" and recognizes that to some degree she is a participant in sustaining the ongoing construction of diamonds as a status symbol. Her conflicted interpretations and emotional responses to the diamonds she owns emerge in the tense space between the industry-promoted and socially accepted associations having to do with status, and those meanings that arise out of her biography. She values her diamond ring as a symbol of romance, glamour, and success, and appreciates its role as a meaningful index between herself and her grandfather and her husband, but she still simultaneously worries about it as an index of mistreatment, exploitation, "materialism," and "status-consciousness."

That diamonds are beautiful status symbols, and that there exists a relationship between potentially ugly labor practices and diamonds on the market (Corinne is "sure somebody is being exploited") exemplifies how one might read diamonds as a symbol but also as an index. Several themes popped up in the reading of diamonds as indexes. Some people interpreted them as symptomatic of, or as proof or evidence of, relatively distant circumstances of production or acquisition (with both positive and negative content). In much the same way that one can read backward through a souvenir to a trip taken, through a scar to an injury, or through a south-pointing weather vane to the fact that the wind is blowing southerly, people can, and they do, read (their own or others') diamonds as indexes of socioeconomic circumstance, global inequality, family ties, characteristics of the buyer, sacrifice, relationship, life events, and so forth, even though these things, as it turns out, are poor indicators of gender, sex, class, or anything else.

And individuals do sometimes expect and even work hard to use (unreliable) diamonds as straightforward indexes, as a (pale) reflection of the way they appear in larger discourses and pragmatic contexts in which race, class, sex, and so forth are defined and performed. What we learn from this paradox is that while diamonds do not map onto demographic categories in a Bourdieuian kind of way (in terms of straightforward indexicality), they still operate as vehicles for constructing class, race, sex, and so forth at a meta-level, in terms of semiotic ideologies and consumers' understandings of indexicality and how it works. But even these meta-level understandings can be highly individualized. Indexical ideologies and the subsequent readings they produce emerge from creative subjects interacting with signs whose meanings are then idiosyncratic, context specific, and entirely contingent, developing in concert and/or butting heads with industry-promoted meanings, a point nicely exemplified by Ian's story.

Ian, a science fiction writer, considers himself far removed from "the mainstream." When I asked him how he felt about the practice of giving, inheriting, or receiving diamonds from loved ones, he said,

> I have really started to appreciate Aileen, my ex, and our shared practicality because now I am finding that women want diamonds. They see a diamond as a symbol of "love" and "forever" and the rest of that bullshit, so, in a way—if I was thirty-five and getting married and my future wife was like, "OK, now let's go pick out a diamond," and I was actually participating in normal American society, which I don't really like to do, I know, I just know, that I would have a moment, a flash of darkness in which I would experience this feeling of "You are becoming one of them."

"One of who?" I asked. He responded,

> Well I am afraid to say this almost, but OK. You know, it's like Aileen and I didn't need anything. Anything material, that is, especially a twenty-thousand-dollar rock, to illustrate our love to one another. We liked to write poems on notebook paper and that was wonderful and important. So buying a diamond and all of that is slipping into this consumerism where money is equal to emotion and it's, for me, a moment of defeat. So "them" is the people who feel like they need to buy a diamond to prove their love, as opposed to those who do it more creatively, I guess, though, maybe a diamond can be creative.

Ian rejects the symbolic marketing association of diamonds with romance, love, and materialism, thinking instead of an imagined "them" with whom he does not (want to) identify. While believing that women want diamonds as a symbol, he reads them as proof of a lifestyle and a set of values he loathes. But his orientation to diamonds is contradictory, for he told me later that women, at least women in his family, women whom he loves and respects, value diamonds above all else "for remembering." This remembering quality is especially strong in the way they are handed down. If he had a girlfriend who really wanted a diamond, he would get her one. He would be "more than happy to give her something that would inspire good feelings" between them, regardless of his own prejudices. The function of the gift and the production of a relationship ultimately override his critiques of consumerism and materialism.

The tendency to treat family diamonds as indexes of kinship and life events showed up at another moment in our conversation. When I asked him whether he had any diamonds, he described his family's expectations about his inheritance:

> I will be asked to inherit some diamonds, because you see my family is very matriarchal and things get passed down and I am the only guy in the family in several generations and all across the board. But we pass things down, and they are very serious about it. Like, there is this painting—and I frankly find it scary—but when somebody died—my grandfather—my cousin was like, "Now you have to go and take that painting." And the painting is, well, there is this guy and he kind of looks like me, I think that's why I find it disturbing, but he is holding this thing that is a cross between a basketball and a goat bladder and I have the thing wrapped in brown paper—What am I going to do with that? I don't know. At least diamonds are small. But the most important thing for them, my mother and everybody, has to do with remembering, you know how it has been handed down, and for all the people in my family that is what those diamonds are all about. And they love to tell you about it. For hours. My mom will likely ask me to inherit the diamonds before she dies. I guess all her jewelry will be divided up and she will say, "Here take this for your girlfriend or wife," and then I will keep them in a box or something.

That Ian thinks of the family gems as markers of kinship and life events as his mother and sisters do is doubtful, but he knows that they interpret them in this way, and this shapes the way he might eventually understand them. These stones are, at the very least, perceived by Ian among other things as signs that can have an indexical significance related to family ties and life events, even if they are kept in a box under his bed or squirreled away in a closet, like Mary Sue's, although they would be stashed for very different reasons.

The opposite of Ian is Renee, a self-described diamond aficionado. She believes herself to be not particularly moneyed, yet she owns numerous diamonds (as do many women who are not wealthy), comfortably wears them on a daily basis, and appreciates the aesthetic of precious gems. We sat at my kitchen table talking and quickly found a friendly tone. She spoke freely, with a kind humor and in a style I would describe as straightforward, not self-conscious. I was struck by her insistence that while, "of course, some people associate diamonds with those ridiculous commercials on TV, with the lovers walking in the park about to overrun an elderly couple," she also said that, in examining others' diamonds, she can

see what kind of person someone is. Everyone looks at other people's diamonds and I think this is because people are inherently competitive. But I would say that much more than that, mainly, it is the curiosity element. Because when you see diamonds, you always wonder, or I do anyway, if they got it from family or what is the story behind the diamond—you know, "How did you get it and why?" That is really the interesting part and that's the part that gives diamonds their meaning. I don't think people care about all the other stuff, especially if it is someone young. When I see a young person with a big diamond, I wonder, "Where did you get that kind of money? Or did you get that from a family member, or what?" So it's really about the history behind the diamond that makes it worth having. I remember my friend Yvonne got diamonds when they had their first baby. And Eve got one when she had her second, Richard. To me it's interesting to get the story behind the diamond because it can be telling—like, I saw Yvonne at a party and she had one of these kind of horseshoe-shaped diamond earrings, and I commented on it, and it turns out they were part of a watch, the clasp actually, that belonged her mother-in-law, so her husband had them made into earrings for her and I thought that made it a lot more special.

We can see that Renee's first response to other people's diamonds is to try reading back through them, as indexes, to the scene of acquisition and the market value. It's not unusual to assume that others share in our own interpretive practices, and Renee clearly expects for others to back up her semiotic ideology.

Obviously, diamonds are symbols of wealth, which explains why Renee is attuned to their market value. Ian, in addition to identifying diamonds as indexes of family ties and life events, also pays attention to their market value, and, after discussing more sentimental issues, he turned to the issue of cost: "To me there are a couple of things going on with diamonds' meaning. There is the expense and value and rarity of the diamond, and that means that it is a sacrifice. When you buy a diamond, it is a financial sacrifice. Because they are expensive!" To acquire a diamond is to lay down money for it, "sacrificing" (hard-won) resources to do so. And we can point to an equivalence between diamonds and capital, an equivalence that is far from groundless. Diamonds are purchased at some point, and reading symptomatically into price not only informs Renee's and Ian's interpretations, but they may very well wish or expect others to do the same. Understanding diamonds in terms of cost is paramount for some, but this is troubled by the ease with which they are "faked," as Diana, a friend of Corinne's, pointed out.

Diana's husband works with Corinne's husband, Brent, and the four of them socialize frequently. Diana, a "stay-at-home mom" in her midthirties, explained to me that she loves diamonds and told me "I've done my research": she knows a lot about them. She "adores how they look," most especially a pair of earrings her husband gave her. Wearing them makes her feel "special and feminine." She explained,

What I really like is the glitter and sheen when it hits the sun, but this diamond is very important to me, I even have it insured, it's just worth a lot to me and to tell you the truth, I wanted stud earrings. I got them and I was ecstatic. I didn't think that I would be, but I was, and they were from Tiffany's, and I wanted to hang the tags on them so everybody would know where they came from and how expensive they were. I hated myself for thinking like that, but truthfully I was very pleased to have them.

Besides appreciating their aesthetic qualities, Diana hopes others will read the earrings as an index of that oh-so-special, oh-so-expensive purchase.

Tiffany & Co. is a high-end jewelry store, where a pair of round brilliant-cut earrings, having a total carat weight of .22 (so each weighs about .11, very much on the "small" side), with a color grade of I and a clarity grade of VS, and set in platinum can cost about $1,000 (in 2013). Earrings with total caratage of .95, color grade I, clarity grade VS, and set in platinum cost $8,850 (with prices partly inflated due to platinum's soaring value in the last decade). These are particularly costly diamonds because of the brand, not the size or quality, but by glance most people would not recognize them as Tiffany's diamonds. But for Diana, the brand is crucial in establishing how she feels about them. In fact, she mentioned only parenthetically that her husband had given them to her, but became most lively and eager when discussing Tiffany's, her pride in possessing such an item, and the fact that she wished others would recognize them as she did. Her interpretive work is strongly related to branding, luxury, price, status, and aesthetic overtones, as in, "what I really like is the glitter and sheen when it hits the sun." Her conflicted feelings of embarrassed self-condemnation ("I hated myself for thinking like that"), pride ("but truthfully I was very pleased"), and desire to show off her status ("I wanted to hang the tags on them"), along with her feeling feminine, special, and loved unfold from countervailing interpretations of meaning, both indexical and symbolic. The complex set of meaning-making strategies come together as she, consciously or unconsciously (probably a little bit of both), selects certain aspects of symbolic meanings in combination with others germane to her own situation.

In casting indexical value into relief, one might complain that we are right back to a discussion of diamonds in relation to economic status, which to some extent is true. But really, the relationship of meaning to material conditions, that is to say the kind of relationship that ties the diamond to status, is in this case indexical; it's not symbolic. There exists a real-world component to purchase and possession, and it is anything but arbitrary. Structuralist and poststructuralist readings of commodity meanings do not address this issue, since they focus on the social significations that symbolic objects, like diamonds, carry—and they do so without any sustained concern for the material or social circumstances surrounding a specific object. A straightforward political-economy approach would also link diamonds to class, aligning economic resources with status claims, but might miss crucial subjective renderings that are important to consumers themselves and discernible through a broader semiotic inquiry. While the consumption of Diana's diamonds is related to status (class), using the framework of the symbolic alongside the indexical provides a more nuanced view of commodity semioses. Because indexes are grounded in temporality and material circumstance, their meanings are often less flexible than their symbolic counterparts. Unlike symbols, indexes require spatio-temporal contiguity, or a causal relationship: one acquires and then exchanges cash to buy the Tiffany earrings. The issue of status or class remains in focus, but deliberately treating it as index rather than symbol highlights the mechanics of acquisition.

Zach describes an even more clear-cut example of interpreting diamonds as an index of money. A 38-year-old teacher, Zach occasionally wears diamond studs to snazz up an outfit. He only wears them on occasion because "it's not always appropriate." Wearing them is "about vanity. I mean they are not exactly expensive, but after all they are diamonds. It's like walking around with hundred-dollar bills taped to my ears. They are a low-level status symbol. It says, 'Hey, I pay my power bill on time!'" Having them indexes his "ability to produce." Zach's diamonds are understood as a direct exchange for money, indeed, very much like hundred-dollar bills taped to his ears, and his semiotic ideology can therefore be said to reflect indexical rather than symbolic interpretation. Interestingly, though people claim to interpret diamonds as indexes of cash, most admit that they cannot evaluate how much diamonds are worth, even their own, nor can they recognize simulants by sight. Taken together, these factors make the diamond a pretty strange status index or symbol.

Even experts, we know, cannot always tell a real from a simulant or synthetic (lab-produced) diamond, although some consumers insist that they can spot a fake when they see one. This ambiguity is worth exploring; it distinguishes diamonds even further, because using them for status purposes is risky since they may be taken for fakes. Brooke, a real-estate broker, asserted that "most people equate diamonds with wealth, which is wrong, because you can get a CZ [cubic zirconia] the size of your head and who will know? No one!" Diana said she would happily take a fake diamond if it were bigger than the real diamond that she already owns, because "the imitations are so easily taken for real that nobody can tell the difference, so, I mean, for all intents and purposes, the fake ones are real!"

The context of acquisition plays a principal role in interpretation. There is an implied distinction between a market diamond (one that is for sale or that is being bought) versus a gift diamond (one that has been received as a gift or through inheritance), which can be fruitfully interrogated using Annette Weiner's (1992) notion of "inalienability," and, in particular, the idea of "cosmological authentication," where wealth represents the objectification of identity (in this case, kinship). Inalienability in this context has to do with objects that should not be sold or given away except under special circumstances. There are relatively few types of these objects in the use-and-toss world of American consumerism, but some kinds of jewelry do carry these stipulations. Diamond engagement wear as well as other diamond gifts can come to inhabit this category (a fact supported by the normal commodity chain that does not encourage the repurposing of diamonds—in fact, "used" stones have an extremely low resale value). But thinking of meaning as pegged to acquisition can be risky, especially as kin relationships may change in unpredictable ways.

But a diamond can work like a powerful souvenir—Remember this? Remember when?—as a marker of events, relationships, or transactions; and as a site where emotions and memories are projected, so much so that it appears that the diamond itself is the actual repository of that significance. In this sense material culture becomes active—motivating people to do things—rather than working like a passive screen for interpretation. Tina, a young woman who had recently moved to New York, bases her interpretation on an acquisition that is largely absent status considerations, yet is firmly tied to a financial equivalence and to the general social sense of symbolic value nonetheless. Pointing to a small stone in a ring she was wearing, she said,

> This one, from my grandmother, is a diamond. I had it appraised once and the guy was like, "It's worth one hundred dollars." I was really disappointed. You see she had either been lying to me or maybe she was just mistaken, I don't know, but it was a real blow to me. Because you see she had given it to me before I came here and it was supposed to be for a last resort, I could sell it, she said. "If you get into trouble, you sell this." And so it was like having money in the bank, in a special savings account, but right here on my hand instead of in some dark vault. I really looked at this as an investment. And it ties me to her. We were really close. You know, many antiques are really just savings accounts, and the thing is that they become more valuable over time, just like interest, that is how I see this.

Tina's diamond is first and foremost an index of kinship, then a financial instrument. As conditions changed (when she discovered the stone was not worth much), so did her interpretation, and although one layer of her reading is contingent on agreed-upon social conventions, another connects her to family. The diamond is like a metaphorical cairn directing her to her grandmother.

But this economic aspect can take on a more sinister cast. For Deborah, a park ranger married to Jason, a music video producer, consuming diamonds is an index of ignorance and a lack of compassion. But her attitude is somewhat ambivalent. I had asked her about Jason giving her a big, expensive diamond. She responded with disdain, "Jason would, he knows—well, he better know!—not to ever come home with something like that for me." Still, she wears a diamond engagement ring, while she is aware of and rejects symbolic associations offered by the industry in favor of her own ideas. For diamonds she does not yet have, her interpretation is shaped by her knowledge of how they are produced:

> I saw a show on TV that was really horrible, showing how the mining industry takes advantage of children, and they don't pay anyone, and how they just fake the price. It's all artificial, like it's all a big fraud and the consumer is tricked. What came to my mind was: "Wow! It's all a myth!" Just a few companies and weird practices in place to keep up this myth about how rare they are and I bet they are real easy to come by. I don't know how they get them, but I know that they are not rare and that a lot of people get exploited. Personally I don't want to support the exploitation, or the myth. I wish everyone would find out about what those people do in Sierra Leone and then they would mean something different, something real: what they stand for is exploitation.

But Deborah was also adamant in saying that she wears her diamond because it belonged to Jason's mother, and is therefore acceptable. The difference for her is—a subtle point—that Jason cannot purchase a new diamond. As others suggested, those diamonds already in the family assume a special condition that new ones do not, cannot, possess. From Deborah's perspective, family diamonds are completely different from those on retail shelves that, as the fruit of a wretched market, indexically "stand for exploitation."

"Do You Have Anything to Skatell Me?"

The *icon* represents by resembling. By way of contrast, *symbols* work by habit: I am habituated to associating the (word/sound) symbol "tree" with ideas and images that correspond with really tall, barky plants. We are similarly habituated to thinking about diamonds in certain ways; that diamonds are a symbol of love or femininity is drilled into us over time. An *index* is grounded in temporal-spatial causality: the index has a direct existential connection with its object. For example, in Samuel Butler's sentence, "Her face . . . was a fair index to her disposition," the woman's disposition motivates her face to take on a smile. A smile indexes happiness.

An icon should not, however, be understood—as the word is ordinarily employed—to refer to things like the Christian cross, a painted representation of a sacred article or personage, a known and enduring symbol, or an idol. It is closer to the original Greek εἰκών, translated as *eikon*, from *eikenai*, which means "to be like" or "to seem." Diamonds are understood iconically when their qualities or features are taken as metaphors, as diagrammatic of some other idea, fact, value, or, perhaps, fantasy.

Though the matter is more involved than is necessary for our purposes here, it is worth mentioning how Peirce (1903, 4.447) conceptualizes the icon:

An icon is a representamen of what it represents and for the mind that interprets it as such, by virtue of its being an immediate image, that is to say by virtue of characters which belong to it in itself as a sensible object, and which it would possess just the same were there no object in nature that it resembled, and though it never were interpreted as a sign. It is of the nature of an appearance, and as such, strictly speaking, exists only in consciousness, although for convenience in ordinary parlance and when extreme precision is not called for, we extend the term icon to the outward objects which excite in consciousness the image itself. A geometrical diagram is a good example of an icon. A pure icon can convey no positive or factual information; for it affords no assurance that there is any such thing in nature. But it is of the utmost value for enabling its interpreter to study what would be the character of such an object in case any such did exist. Geometry sufficiently illustrates that.

Consumers treat diamonds less often as icons than they do as indexes or symbols. Of course, formal properties—brilliance, fire, clarity, size, hardness, and so forth—are understood metaphorically, standing for a range of ideas.[1]

Much to my surprise, after Ian ended his talk about memory, kinship, and romance, he launched into a rhapsodic detour into the topic of diamonds' brilliance—though that word is mine; he didn't use it himself. He said,

> To me there are a couple of things going on with the meaning of diamonds. First, there is the way that it reflects the light. But the light thing is, well, I mean, you look in there and the light is literally bouncing all around, and you get inspired. So, with the right cut and if it's a good diamond, I guess it's better. And it is sparkling, and you just feel like this thing is different from anything else. It's hard to describe because it's like describing the taste of tequila to someone who has no idea about it, or the flavor of a lime versus a lemon. I am not very poetic, I guess; it's hard to describe, but anyway, there is the visual, sensual aspect of diamonds, and it is a very pure experience. Looking into a diamond is stimulating to the eye. And I think that light is often associated with Christianity, and add to that the idea of the spirit or soul that is in there and people talk about when they die, there is the light and God has a big light around him, so I think the fact that it seems to have this really special intense light makes it a kind of spiritual object, and it makes it

perfect to use as a symbol for something that stands between, or brings together, two souls.

Here, Ian considers how to privilege the formal quality of refraction to think about the diamond as an object that bridges or binds: one that "stands between, or brings together, two souls." This is reminiscent of diamonds' symbolic association with romance, but the meaning here is motivated by the character of the diamond itself, and is, therefore, more properly understood as iconic. It's an important distinction. It reintroduces sensuality and materiality back into the consumption equation, showing that goods, after all, are not just empty containers to be filled with industry-produced ideas.

The play of light figured into other people's interpretations, but in different ways. Like Ian, Daphne saw the diamond as a brilliant entity, but she'd developed a darker constellation of iconic significations. A curious, intense, intelligent, efficient, and compassionate woman, Daphne is a visiting nurse, moving from hospital to hospital in temporary appointments. She thus has the opportunity to learn from each place, bringing what she has seen elsewhere to new environments peopled with new, same-but-different cases. We were talking about the diamond she inherited from her mother, and her engagement ring, which embraces a small diamond. Mostly we talked about her feelings about the inherited stone. She explained the circumstances under which she came to have it, beating out her manipulative brother, who "was trying his best to get it for himself." The stone suggests unpleasant memories of her mother's death, a lifetime of family strife, and discomfort with her mother's insistence on and pleasure in what Daphne described as wearing something showy and actually aggressive. Later our conversation turned to Daphne's job, and she described how she asks patients about their jewelry as a way to relax them and to while away the time.

A few days later, she called me to say that she had been thinking about why she dislikes diamonds: their "black-hole effect," she said. At first, I thought she was talking about a dark-centered diamond or the "fish-eye" effect that occurs when a diamond is not prepared close to "ideal cut" standards, so I started asking her about cut and light.

"No, no, no, I don't know anything about these things." The problem is that they "suck the life out of you. They pull you in. I mean you look in there and it's like a well that could suck you in, and you would never come back."

Of particular interest is the relationship between an (inanimate) object's personality and its anthropomorphized characteristics, like winking or blinking. Diamonds, whatever else they stand for, can act as a metaphor for character. For example, Renee combines diamonds as an index of kinship and finance with diamonds as an iconic representation of personality. We had stumbled onto the topic of big, fake diamonds when she told me about her friend whose diamonds mirror her character:

> I look at people's diamonds and sometimes I question if it is real or not, I mean you can't tell, but sometimes circumstances make me think. I have this one friend, Lissa, and she showed up one day with this really huge diamond ring and told me how her husband got it for her, and, I mean, she doesn't even have a dishwasher, but here she is with this big ring, and to tell you the truth I wondered about her priorities. I mean she had told me before that she doesn't like to cook because they don't have a dishwasher, and I was thinking to myself, "If you can afford to buy a ring like that, surely you can afford a dishwasher." Then she told me it was fake! I think it was Skatell.
>
> Skatell is a synthetic jeweler and they make quote diamonds, and Lissa is always joking, "Do you have anything to Skatell me?" Because she wears stuff like that and well, about that one ring, I was cracking up when she told me it was fake, but it doesn't change anything because it's funny. I mean the thing was so big and obnoxious and she is very gregarious and outgoing, and I thought it just fit her personality. It's too big for me, but it looked great on her. This thing was huge! I mean it was like the Star of India! No, not that big, but about I don't know, like five carats. I myself

wear fake diamonds all the time, and I have some great fake jewelry, and I love it because you don't have to worry about it and it looks just as pretty.

I heard again and again people discussing the extent to which this or that kind of cut or size or setting "fit" their personality. Renee's focus on size and the "wow factor" of Lissa's Skatell is a good example of a metaphorical, iconic rendering where such a "loud" object would not be in keeping with her self-image but would be for her friend. The "clean" or "pure" look of the diamond is also understood metaphorically.

Brooke told me that when she got engaged, she didn't want a diamond ring. Her fiancé gave her one anyway, and, in the end, she was thrilled. She drew a direct analogy between the diamond's "clean and pure beauty" and her own "clear thinking style" and "no-frills personality" in explaining why it is appropriate:

> As far as diamonds go, now that I have one—I never gave them a thought before this, but anyway, now that I have one—I recognize that they are just clean, pure beauty, and so I understand why they are so sought after. Other gems don't appeal to me and I think that's because I am a clean thinker, I am not an impressionistic thinker, I'm a black-and-white kind of person. Not frilly at all. So I think the clean lines of the diamond really suit me. It reflects my personality. "Simply elegant" is the way I like to think of it. And "clean" means that there is not a lot of room for interpretation. I am not a florally person. I wear black and white every day. I am not an impressionistic person; I am "what you see is what you get." So when I say diamonds are clean, that's what I mean, that you can see what you get and that's it.

The diamond's clarity is iconic of her own self-image.

Brooke focuses on aesthetic, material characteristics, but she's proud that the unusual cut and setting attract attention when she goes shopping or is out with friends. When her fiancé explained that he wanted her to have a diamond, insisting she have one, he said it was because other people would be paying attention and if she didn't have a diamond, or it was of poor quality, it would reflect poorly upon him. Convinced that peers might read her diamond as an index of her husband's ability, and even his willingness, to provide, she capitulated. The intertwining of indexicality, symbolism, and iconicity can bring about responses that are positive or negative, or somewhere in between. Brooke aligns herself, explains herself, and narrates herself in positive terms through an iconic reading, and a weaving of the diamond's indexical and symbolic characters.

I met Stephanie, an Iyengar instructor, at a yoga workshop. We found ourselves talking after the session. I told her about my project and asked if she would be willing to be interviewed. She excitedly agreed, saying that she had already thought a lot about this very topic. At a nearby coffee shop she explained that she likes diamonds and even has a few. Her mother had given her one diamond, plus she had previously married and divorced. Then she became engaged to someone else, but just before the wedding was supposed to take place, she "realized that it was all wrong" and canceled everything. Both her former husband and her former fiancé had given her a diamond. Partly because of these previous relationships, she and Charles, her current husband, "had discussed in depth whether or not to buy another diamond, and what it would mean within their relationship." Charles was surprised that Stephanie, who describes herself as unconventional and a "free-thinker," even wanted a diamond. But after lengthy talks, he came to see things as she did, and Stephanie now wears both a diamond engagement and a diamond wedding ring.

For her, a heightened sense of appreciation, love, and desire is reinforced by her interpretive strategy, which includes symbolic, iconic, and indexical modes. Stephanie reads diamonds as symbolic of romance and as a promise for a man "to be present" in the marriage. As icons, diamonds represent to her the intent to work to "make the marriage endure, like the diamond does." Indexes again have direct existential connections with their objects: for her, the outlay of money demonstrates a man's willingness to sacrifice for the sake of the marriage.

Stephanie's circumstances, behaviors, and memories, in addition to her knowledge and participation in American society, all shape her interpretation of her diamonds, which contains hybridized and braided combinations of iconicity, indexicality, and symbolism:

> I think that this diamond is symbolic of embracing the best union possible; it represents the ideal between a man and a woman. The diamond is the ideal gem in a lot of ways: it says, "We will strive to be the best for each other," and it reminds you of that when you look at it. Diamonds, I mean they have all these connections, and I am a woman in the modern age, and I just think that they are gorgeous so I have an emotional response, and maybe it is conditioned into my consciousness through advertising although it sure doesn't feel like that to me. [She paused to think about this for a moment.] No, it doesn't feel like that. But I do have a startling emotive response that just stops me whenever I see one. I can't even imagine other stones being able to create the same allure since, well, beauty is in the eye of the beholder, but the light and the translucence of diamonds do catch the eye whereas the darker stones or other kinds of stones just can't do that. They don't do that. So, it is the simplicity that is important. I don't know how to describe it, but a diamond is like the essence of something and this essence is reflected in the context.

After I asked her to explain what she meant by "essence," she responded, "Simplicity is part of the whole transaction of meaning because a diamond is pithy essence; it is beautiful and long lasting. It endures anything."

As an analytical method, relying on only the symbolic to interpret meaning fails to capture the fullness of Stephanie's meaning making. Meaning springs iconically from hardness, purity, and simplicity, but the presence of industry-marketed symbolism and notions of sacrifice (read indexically) are also at play. All three are braided together. The complexity of interpretation can be approached in a systematic fashion by considering it as a process that emerges from subjects who have individual histories, hopes, and imaginations but who are only naturally located in the social and political context in which they are exposed to—even bombarded at times by—marketing-speak. On the other hand, notions of gender, marriage, and family associated with diamonds are as culturally constructed as brand significance is—in fact, they are at least partly co-constituitive.

Icons, indexes, and symbols are not in reality discrete modes of interpretation; each really contains bits and pieces of the others. By getting down to the way consumers understand diamonds—or other things—as icon or index in addition to symbol, we can systematically investigate the way material culture mediates everyday experience in ways that are both like and unlike language. Contemporary material culture theory could do more to elucidate the subjectivity at the core of consuming by considering the idiosyncrasy there. As is currently under discussion in linguistics, the field of cultural studies benefits by recognizing idiosyncrasy (Johnstone 1996, 2001). We need the capacity to enter the matrix of time and space where individuals are positioned— there we can address the phenomenological aspect of consumerism while maintaining sensitivity to macro-scale issues of political economy and marketing. Analysis of consumers' meaning making with a Peircian semiotic helps achieve this goal. The following chapters explore what the poetic and the performative—predicated as they are on integrating symbolic, iconic, and indexical signage—say about us as creative agents.

5

DIAMONDS AND BLING

We do not experience the commonplace, we do not see it; rather, we recognize it. We do not see the walls of our room; and it is very difficult for us to see errors in proofreading, especially if the material is written in a language we know well, because we cannot force ourselves to see, to read, and not to "recognize" the familiar word. If we have to define specifically "poetic" perception and artistic perception in general, then we suggest this definition: "artistic" perception is that perception in which we experience form—perhaps not form alone, but certainly form.
—Viktor Shklovsky, 1914

This is a chapter about *ostranenie* (from the Russian остранение), or defamiliarization. Normally a poetic device associated with literature that forces us to see everyday, ordinary things from a new perspective, *ostranenie* makes them seem unfamiliar or strange, thus reframing our experience of them. It makes us see the world in a different and less automatic way. And while the wearing of "bling"—big, super-flashy diamonds—can be understood as a kind of creative poetic practice in its own right, as used by hip-hop performers and celebrities, it can also operate as *ostranenie* when it stands out from and against the standard use of diamonds within a national marketing aesthetic and thus casts these tastes (and the ideologies that power them) into relief.

Influenced by Saussure and two leading nineteenth-century literary and linguistic theoreticians, Alexander Veselovsky and Alexander Potebnya, the school of Russian Formalism arose during the second decade of the twentieth century and remained active until about 1930. The Russian Formalist circle was comprised of two groups: the Moscow Linguistic Circle, founded by Roman Jacobson, and the Petersburg Opojaz—or Society for the Study of Poetic Language—with Victor Shklovsky, Yuri Tynyanov, Boris Eichenbaum, Boris Tomashevsky, and Victor Vinogradov. As Lee Lemon and Marion Reis (1965) demonstrate, these scholars tried to do for literary theory what Saussure had done for linguistics: that is, redefine the object of study, emphasize synchrony, and identify how internal relationships generate meaning. For his part, Veselovsky argued that literary study should be bracketed off from scholarship in other disciplines, and that the literary device of motif is a cipher through which the structure of literary works is accessed. This disciplinary quarantine meant excluding sociohistorical considerations from "literariness" to focus instead on how literary devices help produce meaning.

Let me point out that the consumers I worked with showed me just how significant social and historical contexts are in "reading" diamonds, and so I appreciate that the Formalists eventually reconsidered the role of both historicity and context in the mechanics of signification. That said, I want to pick up the diamond again and handle it as through a literary lens. My—somewhat experimental—aim in this chapter is to consider bling as an example of the device *ostranenie*, as articulated by Shklovsky and his circle.

Formalists like Potebnya drew an analytic distinction between practical versus poetic language, and then, having literary mechanisms such as metaphor or parody as a starting point, they investigated how words are used. Potebnya, for example, began by making a distinction between poetry and prose (aesthetic and nonaesthetic language) as "separate approaches to the understanding of reality linked by their dependence upon language," so that the study of literature must be a study of language (Lemon and Reis 1965, xi). The idea here is that poetic language functions differently from practical, representational language in that it depends upon subjective, creative readers with critical facilities who can "get it." Understanding metaphor, for example, is a process of transitive thinking (where if A = B and B = C, then A = C) requiring readers' active effort to identify the relevant, sometimes contextual, criteria. But for "practical" language, readers need not be as creative, engaged, or critical; they are at more ease, the passive recipients of sounds matched to an overarching lexicon or code. Each type of language has its ideal reader, particularly with respect to bringing idiosyncrasy, agency, context, and play to bear.

In their attempt to understand literary devices, Formalists realized that a referential theory of meaning—where the meaning of words or phrases is set in a lexicon-like code—was too narrow and failed to adequately explain all the layered, playful, ambiguous, or critical meanings that are at the core of good literature. This might function well for some language, like "the window is open" (glass panes are raised to let in a breeze), but does not completely explain the nuanced operations of metaphor, parody, irony, or insinuation. What about times when "the window is open" means that an opportunity has presented itself? No dictionary will help you with that. You can see how interpretive strategies, and the kind of reader required for a literal versus a poetic reading of the phrase "the window is open" differ markedly.

Shklovsky's general point about the perception, or interpretation, of nonpoetic language in *Art as Technique* is crucial to his overall treatise on the literary, and aligns nicely with Peirce's ideas about habit: "If we start to examine the general laws of perception, we see that as perception becomes habitual, it becomes automatic" (qtd. in Kolocotroni et al. 1999, 218). Interpretation can become so habitual that attention to the form of the signifier erodes and the sign seems to vanish. Another passage by Shklovsky on habituation is worth quoting at length:

> We apprehend objects only as shapes with imprecise extensions; we do not see them in their entirety but rather recognize them by their main characteristics. We see them as if they were enveloped in a sack. We know what it is by its configuration, but we see only its silhouette. The object, perceived thus in the manner of prose perception, fades and does not even leave a first impression; ultimately even the essence of what was is forgotten. (qtd. in Kolocotroni et al. 1999, 218)

When meaning becomes habitually attached to an object, we barely pay attention to the object itself. We "skip" straight to what it means. In practical language, we ignore the sound, or the form, of the words—and for good reason. If, for example, you pay attention to the shapes of letters, doing so makes reading, a practice predicated on habituation, slow and very tedious. In fact, for practical language, the form of the words should not draw particular notice. Conversely, in poetic language, even the shapes of the letters or words are front and center. We are invited to linger, to take notice, to savor, to explore the language itself—what does it sound like? How does it feel in your mouth? What else does it bring to mind? Shklovsky writes,

> Habituation devours works, clothes, furniture, one's wife, and the fear of war. If the whole complex lives of many people go on unconsciously, then such lives are is if they had never been. And art exists that one may recover the sensation of life; it exists to make one feel things, to make the stone stony. The purpose of art is to impart the sensation of things as they are perceived and not as they are known. The technique of art is to make objects "unfamiliar," to make forms difficult, to increase the difficulty and length of perception because the process of perception is an aesthetic end in itself and must be prolonged. (qtd. in Kolocotroni et al. 1999, 219)

Ostranenie to the rescue, saving us from the deadening effects of habit!

Not unlike the way that Fredric Jameson (1972, 51) writes in *The Prison House of Language* that art "is a way of restoring conscious experience, of breaking through deadening and mechanical habits of conduct . . . and allowing us to be reborn to the world in its existential freshness and horror," Shklovsky in his 1917 essay *Art as Technique* explores how art and artfulness move us away from unconscious, rote interpretation, regardless of the medium. He writes, "*Art is a way of experiencing the artfulness of an object, the object is not important*" (Shklovsky 1965, 12; italics in original). In this way, words, actions, and diamonds can all be artful in having a potential to dehabitualize. As a device, *ostranenie* makes strange, denaturalizing the normal way we understand language by calling attention to itself as poetic. It asks for a creative, reformist, if not revolutionary, meaning. Through *ostranenie*, art divorces signs from their habit-driven meanings. *Ostranenie* is, in this sense, playful, metaphorical, and evocative. A thing we've become accustomed to—an omnipresent, domestic, plain old thing—may suddenly step into the light as an untried, neoteric, and Martian Other. So while *ostranenie* is part of a theory of art developed for literary criticism, it can help us understand how people interpret bling.[1]

Bling Bling

Now a part of mainstream American discourse, "bling" was added to the Oxford English Dictionary in 2003. The term "bling bling," generally shortened to "bling," describing big diamonds, jewelry, and all forms of flashy style, was popularized by the New Orleans rap group Cash Money Millionaires. It gained national awareness in the late 1990s with the song "Bling Bling" by Cash Money artist BG (Baby Gangsta). "I'm so surprised that the word has spread like it has," BG told MTV, "but I knew it was serious when I saw that the N.B.A. championship ring for the Los Angeles Lakers had the word 'bling-bling' written in diamonds on it" (Oh 2003). The term appears in the song's chorus:

Bling bling
Every time I come around yo city
Bling bling
Pinky ring worth about fifty
Bling bling
Every time I buy a new ride
Bling bling
Lorenzos on Yokahama tires
Bling bling

Hip-hop is a multimillion dollar enterprise, revolving around music, personalities, and style, that—far from occupying the obscure spaces of South Bronx schoolyards and streets (as it once did)—has gone global (see Mitchell 2001; Condry 2006). Bling is a striking element in rap lyrics and rapper ensembles everywhere. And while it can be interpreted as a straight status symbol, there are more complex possibilities. Having been co-opted by mainstream media and culture (and by the time you read this, capitalism will have even further neutralized bling's potential for dissent), it will eventually lose all of its ability to jar. But still, with its roots in a marginalized subculture, it can be politically and poetically brandished.

This chapter explores how white middle-class consumers interpret bling. I do not claim authoritative knowledge regarding the intentions of rap stars, film stars, or athletes with respect to diamond wear. I chose not to interview hip-hop artists since I was more interested in knowing how consumers' ideas about these celebrities informed what they were doing with diamonds than in knowing how those ideas might diverge from rappers' own reflections on diamond wear, perhaps in some cases as a subcultural form of symbolic resistance of the kind that Dick Hebdige (1979) outlines in *Subculture: The Meaning of Style*. Here my aim is to illustrate how diamond consumption is read as a poetic practice, in which an extraordinary form of diamond wear is treated as a foil by those most directly targeted by diamond marketing. Since poetic devices always come into view within historical context, bling must be situated in a cultural landscape, in a valley nested between two competing mountains of discourse, the one promoted by De Beers, the other by hip-hop stars.

"Ice"

The "A Diamond Is Forever" campaign largely promotes consumption to demure, white, family-oriented, middle-class women who receive diamonds as gifts from husbands or husbands-to-be. Ads almost never feature diamonds in ways that could be construed as aggressive, status seeking, or ostentatious. But they appear in the vocabulary of the world of hip-hop in a different way. *The Source*, a self-stylized "magazine of Hip-Hop Music, Culture and Politics," has in every issue in recent years published thousands of photographs of young, single, (mostly) African

Figure 5.1. Icey rapper. (Illustration by Kay Wolfersperger, used by permission.)

American men, wearing "ice": huge diamonds in flashy platinum and gold necklaces, pendants, earrings, rings, pimp cups (diamond-encrusted platinum chalices), fronts (worn over the teeth), and other custom-made objects. Below these images are captions that discuss the jewelry in detail, often including the price. Rappers, in contrast to the ideal of heterosexual monogamy—but in keeping with a kind of machismo promoted in De Beers ads—often perform "pimp," "gangsta," or "playa'" personae by buying diamonds for themselves as indexes of prowess and success.

Rappers' "ice" overtly challenges traditional, commonplace diamond practices in terms of race, gender, personality, setting, and size. Of the commonplace, Shklovsky (1914) wrote that it is right there in front of us and we know about it, but we do not see it. Consumers like Kate, a middle-class mother of three, echoed Shklovsky's notion of the commonplace, saying, "I do not really notice other people's diamonds, I mean unless it is unusual in some way—then I notice it." Implicitly, there is a "usual" way to wear diamonds, and it's partly for this reason that bling calls attention to itself. That we even notice bling is in itself an index that, yes, normalized wear exists.

In the beginning, hip-hop was a performance-oriented activity, only occasionally and informally recorded. Most accounts place it on the mainstream radar when Sugar Hill Gangs' studio recording of "Rapper's Delight" hit the Top 40 charts in 1979—I know this was my own introduction to it. "Rapper's Delight" opens with the now well-known words,

> I said a hip hop the hippie the hippie
> to the hip hip hop, a you don't stop
> the rock it to the bang bang boogie say up jumped the boogie
> to the rhythm of the boogie, the beat[2]

These first lines foreshadow the song's overall apolitical, PG-rated content that accounts for its broad appeal. The lyrics contain no mention of killing, fucking, pimping, pissing, stealing, raping, smoking, or gangbanging, in contrast with lyrics in "The Message," which was released later by Grand Master Flash and the Furious Five. The first lines in "The Message," one of the most important songs in the history of the genre because of its overt realism and social commentary, suggest a much more politically aggressive content:

> Broken glass everywhere
> People pissing on the stairs, you know they just don't care
> I can't take the smell, I can't take the noise
> Got no money to move out, I guess I got no choice
> Rats in the front room, roaches in the back
> Junkie's in the alley with a baseball bat
> I tried to get away, but I couldn't get far
> Cause a man with the tow-truck repossessed my car.[3]

Hip-hop diversified and spread out of New York in the 1980s. Groups like Public Enemy, with Chuck D and Flavor Flav, assumed a radical stance; urban whites such as the Beastie Boys mixed a somewhat punk sensibility with rap, groups like De La Soul produced sampled, more "palatable" messages, while the popularity of other East Coast groups such as Run DMC and LL Cool J swept across the country and into increasingly greater (and whiter) segments of the market. On the West Coast, particularly in inner-city Los Angeles, groups like N.W.A. (Niggas With Attitude), with front men Ice-T and Dr. Dre, and Tupac Shakur celebrated a culture of guns, drugs, sex, and violence.

During the 1990s, hip-hop evolved into a huge industry, managed by celebrities like Russell Simmons, Sean Coombs (P. Diddy, formerly known as Puff Daddy, or Puffy), and Suge Knight. Moral outcry surged—still surges—particularly from conservative politicians and their wives, academics, parents, and cultural critics who, in recognizing a challenge to the status quo, denounced rap on the grounds of profanity, violence, sexism, and bigotry. The anti-rap hysteria reached a crescendo in the mid-1990s when Robert Bork (1996, 125), a conservative political commentator and Supreme Court nominee, wrote that rap is a monolithic genre of crude "noise with a beat" in which the "obscenity of word and thought is staggering," little more than a "knuckle-dragging sub-pidgin of grunts and snarls, capable of fully expressing only the more pointless forms of violence and the more brutal forms of sex."

Obviously, efforts by anti-rap critics to quell enthusiasm failed, and in creating so much free publicity, may have even had the opposite effect. Snoop Doggy Dogg (now Snoop Lion), Jay-Z, P. Diddy, Missy "Misdemeanor" Elliot, Tupac Shakur, OutKast, 50 Cent, Biggie Smalls, Lil' Kim, Dr. Dre, and many others articulated underreported aspects of the American experience: poverty, racism, sexism, crime, violence, death, prostitution, imprisonment, venereal disease, murder, despair, rage, political oppression, alcohol and drug (ab)use, and other aspects of "ghetto life" constitute lyrical themes. But another prominent theme is consumerism. While some songs brag about having, others issue warnings that aspiring to consume luxury goods (cars, clothes, and jewels) can lead to death, jail, or destitution—even as many rappers contradictorily glorified their own commercial success through overt, Dionysian excess, including the consumption of jumbo diamonds set, winking and blinking, in platinum nests.

The two genres most relevant to this discussion are hard-core rap and gangsta rap. On the one hand, hard-core rappers like Run DMC, LL Cool J, Mos Def, the Roots, and Talib Kweli promote social and political awareness. Committed to a racialized identity, they work to develop a political aesthetic that forges a fruitful path toward what Todd Boyd (2003b) argues is an authentic existence for black Americans. Opposing any diversion from the social task at hand, they make "a class-specific argument that wants the negative imagery of lower-class gangsterism to disappear" (Boyd 2003b, 52).

Conversely, gangsta rap, associated most prominently with Tupac Shakur, Suge Knight, Ice-T, and Dr. Dre, and its offshoot, gangsta riche, associated with Jay-Z, Nas, Notorious B.I.G. (a.k.a. Biggie Smalls), Snoop Doggy Dogg, DMX, and Mobb Deep, promote capital pursuit as a means to authentic existence. As opposed to those who see a concerted political aesthetic as the best path for improving black life, Boyd (2003a, 20–21) writes that they promote "the accumulation of wealth and material possession as significant to the articulation of their own sense of identity. Considering the odds of success for poor urban black youth in a hostile society, they see a triumph over these obstacles to be a political journey in and of itself." Gangsta style melds several lines of media influence. For example, the documentary film "Biggie and Tupac" (Broomfield 2002), covering the career trajectories, rivalries, and assassinations of Tupac Shakur and Biggie Smalls, notes that Tupac and Suge Knight (of California Death Row records) were aficionados of the movie *The Godfather* and its sequels. The documentary even contains scenes of Tupac acting out scenes from *Scarface*. Filmic influences on gangsta rap also include blaxploitation classic films such as *Superfly* and *The Mack*, but the emphasis and play on gangster culture became most elaborate during heightened gang wars in Los Angeles, a phenomenon made visible in films such as *Boyz n the Hood* and *The Wood*. In the development of the extreme gangsta character, thug life and extreme menace tend to be more commonly associated with the West Coast/Los Angeles, whereas the politically radical "hard core" style is loosely linked to the East Coast/New York, where gang wars were somewhat less elaborate. In terms of style, gangsta personae mimic Hollywood presentations of organized crime bosses and drug kingpins, some of whom bedeck themselves with bling.

"Grillz"

"Bling" refers to diamonds of exaggerated size, unusual color, or striking placement, and includes encrusting personalized designs with diamonds or adding sparkle to customized tooth-covers (called "fronts," and also known as "grillz," "snatch-outs," or "caps"), pendants, and nameplates.

Relocating a commonplace thing to a new semantic setting, or tampering with and playing against conventional expectations, norms, and

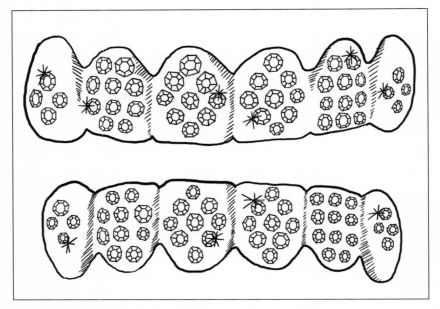

Figure 5.2. Grillz. (Illustration by Kay Wolfersperger, used by permission.)

habits causes people to turn their heads and notice—and that's how bling works. Since it is highly stylized, exaggerated, and set against the norm, bling works as poesy, requiring, in turn, special interpretative engagement.

That bling has seeped out of its role in the hip-hop community is reflected in commentaries on ice in mainstream media, from fashion magazines to NBA pregame shows to the *New York Times Magazine*. The association of diamonds with the culture of hip-hop is what gives it its tone. The object of vigorous academic attention (see Mitchell 2001; George 2005; Ogbar 1999; Perkins 1996; Rose 1994), Russell Simmons's (2001, 4) claim that "hip-hop is . . . the new American cultural mainstream. We don't change for you, you adapt to us" seems to have some truth to it. That the once local, esoteric phenomenon created by and for urban black youth is known to New Yorkers who are only tenuously dialed in to contemporary popular culture was striking. My informants (many of whom are members of the relatively well-educated, white middle class) introduced bling into the discussion without any prompting from me. Bling, however, is "different from," as one woman put it, "you know, regular diamonds." Now, what can we make of this? Shklovsky's *ostranenie* can help explain these constructions.

Remember, the use of language as a communicative device depends upon the habituation of signification. It follows that in mundane communication, the formal qualities of the language (the sounds of the words, for example) are subordinated, if not erased, by attention to the message; we rarely notice the form of language at all. But not all language is practical. Poetic language, where the form of the language is essential, disrupts habituated reading on purpose. *Ostranenie*—making strange— takes an image or object (a sign) into a new orbit of perception. The effect is a semantic shift. It pulls us away from rote recognition because of a heightened awareness of things and their sensory nature in an act of, as Victor Erlich (1980, 177) puts it, "creative deformation" that "restores sharpness to our perceptions, giving 'density' to the world around us." But of course, this dynamic depends upon the reader and whether or not he or she apprehends the object as special. Reading diamonds as a status symbol can be a habitualized act reflecting social norms that link generic diamonds to femininity or wealth, but with bling, the social-norm reading falls rather short.

People can interpret diamond display by others as a poetic device, rather than a gesture meant to be taken at a habit-driven face value. In literature, a device is a writing technique in which practical language is embellished, enhanced, extended, or reversed. Literary language shouldn't always be taken "literally"; a device signals when a nonliteral interpretive strategy is called for. The meaning is often outside of, even in contradiction to, literalness. And bling is often interpreted as explicitly literary, or, let's say, artful. Taking it as metaphor, parody, or exaggeration throws a bright light on naturalized, unconscious diamond consumption. We may not actively experience—notice—commonplace diamonds, but one that is very large or worn in an unusual way calls attention to itself. And then, as Shklovsky suggests, we see the diamond.

Diamond conventions regarding size and setting were underscored by those discussing big diamonds in the context of "old ladies on the Upper East Side [neighborhood of Manhattan]," or "women in their fur coats and giant jewels," but also in the context of rappers, as examples of what they considered (in)appropriate. People described large diamonds as "vulgar," "showy," or "flashy," as a way to obliquely explain their own values. They became animated, expressing strong opinions while talking about rappers' "huge diamonds."

There is a lot going on when someone talks about bling as emblematic of "their culture," as "self-serving," as "like, but not the same as, nouveau riche," as a "gesture of one-upsmanship," as "calling attention to their background," as "exaggerated, just like their sexuality," as "eye-catching—it's a way to get you to wonder 'how did they get that?'" Some see it positively—as an ironic gesture, a critique of consumerism, or a parody. Reflecting more progressive politics, those discussing bling as tantamount to a literary device were also likely to extend a rich, complex interpretation to songs, rather than just taking lyrics at their (sur)face value. On the other hand, bling is understood as a flat-footed play for status that reflects an unsophisticated, if not skewed, notion of how the "real [authentically] wealthy" behave.

Setting and Context

Rosetta and Sally, educated, white, middle-class women between the ages of twenty-five and thirty-five, both described bling. Rosetta told me that diamonds are gendered: "Diamonds are not for men, they are female associated." Sally said she wanted a big diamond, "but only a good one—it's got to be a big one," in her engagement ring "because the diamond becomes something that tells others—and I am embarrassed to say this but you are an anthropologist so I can tell you what I really think—that someone loves me and is committed to me and there is just no getting around it." Both women project onto others—strangers "out there"—ideas that aren't congruent with what they reported a particular diamond means to them. But those projected, intended readings are not necessarily shared by others. This, for example: the diamond Rosetta imagines to be a sexualized, gendered marker as far as others are concerned is, to Rosetta, mainly embedded in kinship ties with her mother, from whom she received it as a gift. A stranger, particularly in a large urban center such as New York City, does not, and will likely never, have this information. Strangers are left to read her diamond on the basis of their own experiences or according to a generic set of notions—if the diamond is even noticed.

"Diamonds," Rosetta further explained, are "conservative," "suburban," and "snooty, if they are big," but they can also be "sparkly" and "pretty." She describes the tennis bracelet, a fad started by tennis player Chris Everett when she dropped a diamond bracelet during the 1987 U.S. Open Tennis Tournament, as "obnoxious. My mother is really into that shit, and maybe I am reacting to that, but I mean, why is it called that? Are you supposed to wear it when you play tennis? Who would do that? It's so over the top—waaaaay too ostentatious. By that I mean: 'showy.'" So for Rosetta, setting emerges as a salient issue in what and how diamonds signify. This issue is compounded by her attitude toward her mother, and her mother's values and beliefs.

By way of contrast, Sally argues that ostentatious diamonds are showy and can signify status, but for all of her concern and worry about what they say to the world, she still finds them sexy and glamorous. Both her mother and grandmother are "gem aficionados, owning big, gorgeous diamonds" that she "would like very much to have and wear," to "make [her] feel beautiful—as long as they are not so big as to create the impression that they are fake. You know, the bigger they are the more people assume that they are fake." Chunky jewelry has positive associations for Sally, whose affectionate relationships with kin and their jewels provide a partial template for her interpretation of "showy" diamonds.

Rosetta explained that showy diamonds are about wanting to be seen and admired, but with the whole rap thing and ghetto fab and hip-hop, it's different—I don't really get that whole thing, but to me it's not as offensive as a tennis bracelet. It's all about the overexaggeration or the performance of wealth and, yes, its visible exaggeration, and I don't know if it's intentional or not, but they are playing with images and being self-conscious about it. They know it's over-the-top and showy—that is why they are doing it! There's a difference between bling and tennis bracelets: tennis bracelets are oppressive and stupid, bling is more ironic and witty.

Rosetta, pointing out the "overexaggeration," "performance," "irony," and "play with images," illustrates that bling requires conscious interpretation.

Sally, plying her idea that "big diamonds argue for status," straightforwardly interprets bling as part of the overall style of "ghetto chic" that works, in the end, ironically with respect to what she believes the wearer's intention to be. Bling is a classed and raced marker oppositional to the status and glamour she attaches to diamonds for herself:

Bling is for blacks and the Hispanic lower, working-class. I guess that might sound racist, but I can own that. They are just people trying to be showy, saying "I have arisen! I have transcended the race, place, and class that I am singing about." But then they haven't. It's just a sign of a lower-class lifestyle with an upper-class price tag.[4]

So although Rosetta and Sally view big diamonds as signifying class and status, and even race, when setting and context come into play (which they inevitably do), the impact of individual experiences is likewise worthy of our attention. Rosetta demonstrated the significance of her biography when she stated,

My family aspired to tennis bracelets, but if they were to aspire to bling bling, well, I don't know, I can't even imagine that, I studied rap music in college and so I think that I have a more detached response than most people. For me, it's a cultural phenomenon. To me it's interesting to think about what is going on—I mean it's such an exaggeration.

Sally's reflections are work related. She's proud of her work with "inner-city teens in a New York public school improvement project," where she has sustained contact with urban youth of color.

We don't allow do-rags or any of that crap at work—I mean, it's supposed to be a work day, but sometimes they do show up, you know, with the teeth, or diamond earrings or those name plates and, you know, they are blingin', and like little Axle showed up the other day with the big diamond earrings, and I just assumed they were fake. Definitely bling bling, but definitely fake. Maybe it's racist or classist on my part, but how could he get the real thing? Unless he is a drug dealer. Which he might be.

But she finds it "strange and discomforting that her kids have to be about bling to feel proud or cool. Everybody needs something. When I was coming along it was these Calvin Klein sweatshirts, but with diamonds, it takes it to another level. It should be easier to fit in." While she loves and covets diamonds, she hates that she's buying into "a fake construct," but far from being an interesting or self-conscious, playful phenomena, Sally stated that, "bling basically sucks." It is an inauthentic claim to status, and as a practice, results in undue pressure on urban youth, perhaps even reproducing their marginalization.

Diamonds' size, settings, and her overall knowledge of hip-hop culture inform Rosetta's interpretive work. Rosetta, like Sally, doesn't interpret bling as "real" class, or as status marking, but for her, it's exactly because diamonds are being used as a device, demanding special attention, that she reads the entire practice through a special set of considerations. Given that she admits "she does not really get the whole thing," her encounter is unfinished and ongoing, prolonged in just the way that Shklovsky describes reader encounters with literary *ostranenie*. The (habitual) legibility of diamonds is transformed by the context of display, ripped from the commonplace to effect a rejuvenated hermeneutic.

The generic model of language, and of the meaning of commodities, where ads come to define the meanings of signs, does plain, some might say flat-footed, work on a gross level (as in Sally's statement that "nothing says money like a diamond"), much in the same way that a dictionary carries legitimate information about what words mean. But generic definitions are only provisional: creative uses—of language and material signs—generate brand-new meanings. In the "dictionary" version, big diamonds do mean "status," but this is neither predictive nor authoritative, and in terms of individual encounters with specific diamonds, it is far from universal.

Challenging the Cliché: Ian, Luke, and David

Ian, the writer, said diamonds are "silly," part of a consumerist society in which people use impersonal things to signify love, the most personal of emotions. Finding this highly contradictory and "weird," he went on:

> I know that some people criticize the whole hip-hop culture and wearing those huge diamonds for its materialism, but to me, I think it is just a game of materialism to the nth degree and bling bling is its logical conclusion. You know, it's like big pendants on a huge chain with giant gold letters filled with diamonds. Guys like Cobain and other white rockers tried to hide their money, whereas blacks want to show it off because, I mean, they don't come from there, and there is a whole history that explains why. Rappers are multimillionaires and showing it off. So while the white guys romanticize poverty, bling is part of the romanticizing of wealth. I mean they certainly do not come from that world. I look at it in those terms. Not only that, but supposedly it's a good way to get a lot of pussy. I hear 50 Cent and all those diamond-wearin' rap stars get a lot of pussy so, I guess, bling, that's a chick magnet.

Ostentatious diamond display by rap stars is not, for Ian, reflective of "normal American society," nor does it have anything to do with romantic love (versus "getting pussy") or status (of the kind that he equates with "super-wealthy people"—even though he talks about rap stars as multimillionaires), so it must be read through a different lens. And though Ian is loath to participate in the diamond consumption he views as an index of submission to a consumerist ethic, he will happily align himself with bling, in a spirit more reminiscent of the way that Hebdige (1979) analyzes punk and ska music as oppositional or revolutionary. Ian explained,

> If I ever had a diamond I would, well, there is this book by J. G. Ballard called *Cocaine Nights* where there is this utopian place, and there is this tennis coach and he keeps inserting bits of violence into the whole thing. One night he just like goes on this crime spree, you know crashing into cars and robbing and stuff and he comes out of this one place and he has this diamond on his finger and it's real flashy and that I do like, that's more rock and roll. So it's like an affront. That's bling.

Rosetta and Ian positively identify bling's challenge to the cliché through form and context. Some, however, see the claims of diamonds as a ruse. Luke, a computer technician, considers himself an average consumerist who "likes to have nice things, you know, the 27-inch TV, the diamond ring I gave my wife, and I would like to have a nicer car." He says he is in favor of

> having functional things that have a purpose—but this bling bling thing is just a distraction. It's part of the consumerism and commercialization of hip-hop in the past, say, ten years that has stymied creative development. These guys just use bling to cover up a lack of talent. Maybe it's their way of distracting you into just thinking about what you don't have versus what they do have, and that is how they are trying to earn respect, based on the

diamonds that they have instead of what they can do. And it is distracting. I mean you can't help but to look right at it.

The term *"Differenzqualitat,"* or quality of divergence, developed by German aesthetician B. Christensen, became of one the key terms of Formalist aesthetics (Erlich 1980, 178). Here, poetic language is perceived against the background of ordinary speech, against "practical" speech, so that a true explication of the deformation or deviation from the norm must also include within it some articulation of how the norm is constructed—in this sense, *ostranenie* is both historically situated and revolutionary, and the pleasure of the aesthetic encounter is contingent upon recognizing a tension between the two. This idea comes to life when we consider how Luke is not looking at bling as he would his wife's diamond. There is what amounts to a "quality of divergence" between diamond consumption by "your average guy" who "just wants to have nice things" and its "obscene" use by rappers. When asked to explain what he meant by "obscene," he urged me to consider "that guy 'Jacob the Jeweler.'" Jacob the Jeweler, Uzbecki Jacob Arabo, who has a shop on Diamond Row (Fifty-seventh Street, Manhattan), is known for making commissioned pieces for rappers. Jacob is himself something of an idol, featured in hip-hop magazines and newspapers, and in rap lyrics ("I took you outta Jacob's / Busters, they wanna rush us / Love the way you sparkle when the sun touch ya" raps Jay-Z in "Girl's Best Friend," an ode to his diamonds). Luke noted with unconcealed scorn, "Man, one of those watches can cost like $50,000 or earrings that are like $100,000!" He continued,

> People talk about the politics of hip-hop when it's not really about that a lot of the time. It certainly is not a consistent progressive politics, if you listen to the lyrics you see that it is very inconsistent—in terms of race, in terms of violence, in terms of the objectification of women, and things like that—they are all over the place, and I mean how can you talk about progressive politics when you are sitting there wearing these

obscene diamonds and still have the gall to be silent about the realities of the South African diamond trade? That just doesn't make any sense, so to me hip-hop and blinging and all that can't be said to be about politics, but about the manufacture of personas, and I mean it is hard to characterize because there are regional variations. It would be interesting to see how different regions play into the whole bling bling thing, or underground versus above-ground rappers talking about bling. Mostly what I hear is the above-ground stuff and that whole bling thing, it's just a huge turnoff.

But Luke found his own telling unsatisfactory, too sweeping, and he immediately began qualifying his own comments:

But wait, generally, it's all about vanity and covering up a lack of talent but then you start really thinking about it and looking at individuals. Like there is Kanye West, he is produced by Jay-Z, and he just released a new album, "College Drop-out," and he is talking about blingin' but it's different from guys like Master-P, who took it to another level, where it really is all vanity. And Jay-Z uses "ice" to create this pimp persona, but I mean he is partners with Ratner in the Jersey Nets deal so he is also using bling bling to create a player persona when he is in real life a player too. So he is a pimp and a playa and diamonds help him to achieve the look. So that's different, that's more about a performance.

The creation of ever more discrete categories of signification is ambivalent, based not only on size and setting but also on who is involved, when, and why.

"I Wish I Had More Bling!" Jane and Zach

Informant narratives were often studded with complex, internally contradictory interpretations. Signs often take on multiple meanings, so this is no surprise, but it is nevertheless worth noting that a single consumer often engages in several narratives and value systems with none assuming any obvious privilege. People maintain multiple layers of beliefs that are not necessarily in coherence with one another. For example, Jane, an English teacher, remarked,

> I wish I had more bling! I have this necklace here [pointing to a gold diamond-studded pendant nameplate of her nickname, "Squirrel"], see? But I want a big ol' canary yellow diamond. A few months ago in *Source* there was a thing on Puff and the hottest jewelry, which is how I know about the canary diamond thing. There is a lot that is very playful and theatrical about it. I love it. I love the bling bling thing. But I have problems with it too—it's about misogyny. There is section in *Source* called "The Dime Piece," which is a centerfold and it's total objectification. Like this month the pin-up is there and then it says "Destined to Blow" underneath it, and there is a Q & A where she tells people who write in about how much they loved the Dime Piece—and it's always the same boring letter—how she "keeps it together," and it's so stupid. I hate it. It's totally gross, but that's bling too.

Like Jane, others play with a bling lens for their own diamonds. Zach, wearing small, diamond stud earrings, told me that he had received them as a gift from an ex-wife, but then he lost one of the studs, and so had purchased a new pair to replace the set. "With these earrings," he explained,

> There is an element of affectation. I was never a gold man and I was never one to wear silver hoops or rubies—I mean I'm not a pirate walking around with a peg leg, like "Aarrrrgggggghhhh!" I like diamonds because of the bling factor, the sparkle, but in the early eighties when I started wearing this, not many guys were doing it so I was being different, but big status symbols, like in the hip-hop world, are big diamonds, big-ass rings, Cristal champagne, mansions, big cars. These are not things I indulge in. But I do it to dress up. It's fashion. It's a nice thing. But these are like blip blip—in bling bling it's all about size—and blinging is

like the light, you know, blinging! Glowing, bouncing off of the thing. Anything can be encrusted with diamonds so it can be blinging. But me? I'm blippin'.

Far from making a legible statement about class, race, or gender, Zack is clearly toying. Meaning has changed over time, and with the emergence of diamond wear in the hip-hop community, he can link his practices with theirs, albeit in a teasing manner. He acquired this pair to replace a loss—it had nothing to do with copying rappers—but underscoring the historical and contingent nature of interpretation, he puts them in the context of bling. History and context are crucial aspects of *ostranenie* since the device operates against contestable routinized practices.[5] Today we can talk about diamonds in relation to hip-hop; in 1984, before bling, this wasn't possible.[6]

Class as Style

There seems to be a fairly radical (and probably mutual) incommensurability when it comes down to signification practices between people. Resorting to a stereotypical script to explain strangers' behavior isn't unusual, and consumers frequently, when shifting to discuss a single person, had more nuanced and, at times, elaborate things to say. People projected narratives onto others that were vastly different from what they said about themselves—and the more socially distant the other, the more this tended to be the case.

Liza, told me,

If I saw JLo [Jennifer Lopez] wearing her big-ass, pink, bling ring versus if I saw Paris Hilton wearing it, I would think Paris got it from her dad whereas I know JLo is working the system, and she is just part of a machine—doing the movie thing and getting with Ben Affleck and P. [Diddy] so she is in the spotlight where people want to market stuff through her. Like Harry Winston will lend her something to wear and she will have a photo taken in his store on Fifth Avenue or mention it on *Access Hollywood*, and she is probably getting a deal because it's marketing for Harry Winston. But Paris grew up with stuff like that, and JLo, she is just "from the block,"[7] so I mean it's not really about status, it's about making money and revenue.

In saying so, Liza makes Jennifer Lopez into a billboard, relieving her of the kind of subjectivity, complexity, or agency she might allow Paris Hilton. Here, Lopez's diamond is a failed emulation of the ones Hilton wears as a legitimate index of her place in society.

Liza was not the only one to see bling as a failed bid to identify with "high society." JLo is, after all, "just from the block." People are willing to read diamonds as a status claim, but in reflecting American stratification, class is as much about style, race, and ethnicity as it is a function of socioeconomics. So for Liza, wearing a big pink diamond or rapper bling is "not really a convincing act to me—and I believe it is an act." The way she told it, bling is a naive, ultimately vain attempt on the part of lower-class people to claim a social position based on mimicry of the way they think—mistakenly—wealthy people behave: "Their culture is removed from the reality of how it is supposed to be when you have money. These people just seem to want to better themselves in the sense that they are always on the market, and the whole thing is just a shallow attempt at self-promotion rather than a bettering of your neighbor."

Perceiving bling as *ostranenie*, Liza explicitly explores irony:

Aesthetically I don't necessarily have anything against it—as a matter of fact, if Conrad [her husband] gave me a plaque with my name on it and some huge diamonds, I would definitely wear that—but because it would be funny. Hilarious actually! But they are not trying to be funny. For me to do it, it would be funny because I am not in that scene and so I have a certain distance, and it's an ironic distance. For them, it's just a normal way to behave.

The "normal way to behave" has to do not just with possessions but also with how one acquires money and presents oneself, especially with regard to gender, sexuality, and style. For Liza, in the end, these issues are bound up with authenticity:

The whole persona is entirely exaggerated—like the advent of *MTV Cribs* where they show rappers' houses and it's like "Oh my God!" Everything is so exaggerated and totally overt—overt sexuality, overt consumption, overt violence, everything. And whereas twenty years ago, or today, other people who could have those things, they might still wear an ostentatious diamond, but they certainly wouldn't be caught humpin' on television, or feeling themselves up and down like they are fucking. So I think it's also about sexuality and their bodies in some ways. They are so exaggerated and they want to prove that they can do what has been done by others. I mean, as a culture they have been held back in so many obvious ways and they have found a way to express themselves, so that elevates them, in a sense, and they are putting it in your face. It's almost like "Fuck you," but it's sad because they will just spend it [money] all. I don't think people find, well, look—it's just not real.

Bling is a foil against which people can talk about "class" (and race), where membership is about behavior, style, and even, to a certain degree, morality, alongside economic and occupational considerations. These constructions of class were quite varied, including the designation "gangsta riche" (likened to nouveau riche but "more interesting and less tacky") and "gangsta chic" (like heroin chic but racialized, less East Village, and more macho). In this sense, diamond consumption is part of a constellation of activities that can reflect class as an aesthetic phenomenon in addition to its better-known, but not always useful, association with socioeconomics. As Henry put it,

A diamond can be too much if it's all about size. You know, if it's just bling bling. Ostentatious diamonds. That shows a real lack of subtlety to me. It says, "Hey! I have poor taste, bad taste," because it should be worn as if it's not there, with subtle grace, and when it's too big or the shape is jarring or juttering, you know if it has too many angles and refracts the light incessantly. That's just: "Look at me!" People that do the bling thing are nouveau riche, you know, poorly educated, but it's not that they are not good and nice people, I have cousins like that. You go to their house and there are leopard prints everywhere and the whole thing is in really poor taste. Like Donald Trump–style buildings. Terrible. To me, it's all gilded lilies, taking a perfectly good and beautiful lily, and then spray-painting it with gold paint and just ruining everything.

Henry continued: "They are claiming a kind of wealth through the diamonds, but half the time it is not really true." Here, money and class are decoupled: class is not just about having money but also about knowing how to spend, or display, it "correctly."

Now, there are shelves of rich ethnographic literature that focuses on race, gender, ethnicity, and class in the United States (see examples in Susser and Patterson 2001; Goode and Mascovsky 2002). Class is often treated as an economic and occupational variable situated within dynamic global or national political economies. Subcultures are identified where categories of race, class, gender, and ethnicity intersect in particular places—for example, Filipino transnationals in Los Angeles (Bonus 2000) or junkies in San Francisco (Bourgois and Shonberg 2009). Many such studies track the way neoliberal policies at national and international scales impact local communities, particularly those most vulnerable to structural violence. Practical considerations such as geography and the labor market do shape the way communities are formed and the way they can be identified, but there is also a small body of work seeking to understand commonalities of experience in large, sometimes geographically dispersed, noncommunities that can be identified on the basis of practices, such as reading strategies (Crapanzano 2001) or the consumption of particular brands (Muniz and O'Guinn 2001), and that may have little congruency with other ways of identifying informants for study. I find these kinds of approaches to be extremely illuminating because they allow for a set of details to emerge that may be obscured if one starts with class, or race, or other more commonly studied vectors of identity. Class can, for example, show up as style rather than as a function of economics.

The construction of a white middle-classness in ads and in "normalized" diamond wear is indexed and reproduced by the (sometimes sharp) way consumers perceive and distance themselves from rappers and bling, often avoiding the use of overtly racialized language (in keeping with taboos against identifying people by race, they used euphemisms like "guys from the ghetto" instead). By transgressing the race, class, and gender norms in marketing, bling makes these norms seem explicit. Henry, for example, said rappers are showing "their people" that they have succeeded:

> You don't need a 1950-style culture of conformity to understand that it is a form of showing the neighbors that they can keep up [with what success means in white society], even though in reality they can't, but they won't sell that diamond for anything. I bet they would sell the house, the car, everything, before the diamond would go because of what it represents to them.

Tom was more unequivocal in his discussion of race, "Now, I do not associate diamonds with wealthy people or with glamour because they have been co-opted by black people so that they can call attention to themselves. They are saying, 'I have arrived, I am rich, I am valuable.'" When I asked him why "rap guys" do this, he explained, "They want to show white people what they have. They want to show that they are louder, faster, bigger, and better." Here, wearing diamonds is a showy public act, a reverse image of how the legitimately moneyed—and presumably white—behave.

Clearly consumption is implicated in the construction of identity, including ethnicity, class, and race, but talk about consumption is also itself, as a social practice, part of this dynamic. Informants talking about bling often invoked phrases—like "those people" or "they want to show white people"—that reflect a larger, sustained practice of reproducing whiteness through insinuation and oppositionality. The lesson is that talk about diamonds—like other things—uncloaks the way race, class, gender, and ethnicity can be understood and reproduced.

Emulation

When we encounter language or goods artistically or poetically, we disregard automatized perceptions and instead make new connections. The idea is that roughened forms of language, disorderly rhythms, strange and fantastic phraseology, unpredictability, writing against convention, and rhetorical devices—such as repetition or exaggeration, as we see in rap lyrics—can catapult a reader into a heightened state of interpretation that brings about brightened understandings. *Ostranenie* reconfigures habituated takes, much in the way that some anthropology seeks, through a rhetoric of denaturalization, to reconfigure the way we perceive our own realities or, through remediation, those of other peoples.[8]

Bling consumed as a kaleidoscopic aesthetic phenomenon, as entertainment, works as a basis upon which individual practices are modeled, as failed or successful status claims, or as class or racial reifiers, all of which are mediated, enabled, and maintained by marketing. Bling makes strange what is usually not an object of particularly conscious interpretation. Consumers interpret the diamond as if it were a poetic device in these exhibitions that argue, quote, hide, pan, parody, and sometimes (though more rarely) critique the status quo. Reading bling as *ostranenie* means bringing a whole set of unique experiences, values, and beliefs to bear such that meanings are at once highly local (idiosyncratic) and socially constrained (structured).

This tension between the local and the socially constrained is particularly evident in the fact that although I have foregrounded variation, informants' voices echo with references to culturally salient identity categories like class, race, and gender.[9] People's perceptions of others that reference ideas about physical appearance or other identity markers are refracted in the ways they talked about diamonds. So, a diamond received through inheritance, even a gaudily large one, might become acceptable if worn for the "right" reasons while people who are "not really" middle class—even if they are very wealthy—because they do not "come from" money might be read as flashy and pathetic, especially if they (are assumed to have) purchased the diamonds for themselves in a ploy to claim status. But when people talk about their own, specific diamonds, they tend to highlight what makes them special and appropriate, often linking them to individual life histories or relationships. Of course, sometimes people judge the material and performative qualities of stones according to rather classist understandings about modes of acquisition and authenticity, which are perhaps best understood in terms of Veblenesque pecuniary emulation, which I cover in the next chapter.

6

DIAMONDS AND PERFORMANCE

Carla and Gene, successful thirty-somethings, live uptown. Carla writes children's books. Gene is a novelist. Carla and I scheduled a meeting to talk in a bar in downtown Manhattan. She arrived wearing a suit and lugging a briefcase overflowing with papers. After some small talk, Carla told me that when she and Gene were first married, five or six years ago, she had refused to wear a ring, much less a diamond. Then her aunt, seeing that she was without, gave her one to wear. Her aunt was very excited and proud to be able to give Carla a diamond. Because it was a gift from a close family member, and because she didn't want to seem ungrateful, Carla felt obliged not only to accept it but to wear it. As previewed in the introduction, she told me,

> I could not have cared less about wearing a diamond, really, but I have been surprised, because what turns out to be the most important thing, or the thing I notice the most I should say, is the way people react—and that's why I want Gene to wear a ring, I insist that he wear one, now. I mean when people see this they back off. My aunt gave me this and I really didn't even want to wear it or even have it. But it's growing on me. Actually, I had to get it reset because it had this really high setting and it looked like a rocket that was about to be launched, and I didn't like that, so this is better. But you cannot believe the way people, men actually, just automatically look at a diamond. And men were always hitting on me, at

the gas station, at bars, wherever they are, but they take one look at this and they are gone. Usually.

Carla thinks wearing a diamond causes men to behave differently than they might otherwise. She counts on the fact that men who would venture to approach her are themselves aware of, and accept, a convention that "will keep them from hitting on [her]." She uses her diamond to control her social environment, and in this sense, it has a forceful, performative potential. Her diamonds says, "I'm taken. Don't get any ideas!"

Diamond performances take place in a social landscape, but their insertion in this landscape is varied because agency and creativity loom large. The presence of performative elements in the diamond narratives I collected suggests that a focus on the individual—who is embedded in a social group, discursive universe, and commodity chain—will help clarify how diamonds are used in the everyday making of life. Rather than thinking of these elements of commodity-hood as embedded one inside another, in the fashion of Russian nesting dolls, an entanglement metaphor is more apt, as individuals draw on ideas, memories, and relationships in the direct presence of diamonds. These emerge with greater vigor in people's narratives of interpreting diamonds than do the more distant marketing images or norms of identity production, though the impact resulting from those factors is significant and cannot be ignored.

Doing Things

We experience, know, react, and enact our will via material culture. The meanings that objects carry can be produced through social discourse, like advertising, but we have seen that when it comes to particular objects, meaning is also local and downright personal. And the space between the socially shared and the locally personal can be exploited for performative usage.

Combining insights garnered from Austin's (1962) *How to Do Things with Words* with the growing attention to idiosyncrasy in linguistics, this chapter examines how diamonds are wielded. Consumers reported that they, and others, use diamonds in ways that suggest "performance," but they do so contextually, with intended outcomes shifting over time and place. By "performance," I mean that diamonds, rather than merely describing, or constating, actually impact circumstances; they, in other words, have consequences. Wearing a diamond can be part a performative action meant to change the world in some observable way. Diamonds do things.

Austin's taxonomy of linguistic elements distinguishes *performatives*, words that "do things," from *constantives*, which are descriptive. Performatives are utterances that do not describe, report, or merely refer but are actually part of an action with consequences that follow. Working with first-person utterances, Austin identifies several types of performative language acts, including the "declaratory" (as in "I declare war" or "I dub thee knight") and the "contractual" (as in "I bet" or "I promise"), in which saying something makes it so.[1] Performatives are neither true nor false, but they are more or less successful depending upon the conditions under which they are uttered. Austin describes how the context must be felicitous for success—if and only if the conditions and intention are appropriate will the performative action succeed. In Austin's example, to declare war, you must both be in a position to declare war and be sincere. So, when "I declare war!" is uttered, war is actually declared, setting off a series of events.

The diamond, like ordinary language, can also be understood as performative á la Austin. They can be deployed as a performative prop, a necessary but not quite sufficient ingredient in elbowing circumstances in a given direction. And here, felicitous conditions may be conventional and/or idiosyncratic.

Homo Performans

As a cipher or prop, diamonds allow people to inhabit a kind of stage upon which to present, imagine, or act out plays about themselves (and sometimes others). These stages and plays may be reserved for the self alone, or for those real or imagined others. Given that, a theatrical metaphor supports the use of the Austinian concept of performative in clarifying how material culture is used for particular ends.

Erving Goffman (1958), focusing on impression management through controlled, sometimes negotiated behavior, developed a dramaturgical paradigm to examine the dynamics of social relationships. My use of the term "performative" draws from Goffman a sensitivity to the impact of context and circumstance on meaning making outside of the realm of plays, concerts, and lectures, in what Milton Singer (1984) calls publicly communicative "cultural performances." And because these plays can be directed at the self, a strongly reflexive dimension should be added to the notion of cultural performance, as in Victor Turner's (1986, 81) formulation:

> If man is a sapient animal, a tool-making animal, a symbol-using animal, he is, no less, a performing animal, Homo performans, not in the sense, perhaps that a circus animal may be a performing animal, but in the sense that a man is a self-performing animal—his performances are, in a way, reflexive, in performing he reveals himself to himself. This occurs in two ways: the actor may come to know himself better through acting or enactment; or one set of human beings may come to know themselves better through observing and/or participating in performances generated and presented by another set of human beings.

Material culture too can be used to (culturally) perform the self to the self (reflexively) or to others, but it isn't always certain how these performances are received. An example: one woman suggested that people who wear diamonds are ostentatious but that she wears them differently. In fact, she would love to have a large, emerald-cut stone, but does not consider herself a showy person:

> Mostly I see diamond jewelry as frivolous and a real marker of excess and also status seeking. I mean in earrings there are even two of them! So it's

diamonds times two! That's showy. I might want something like that, but it would be special and I would probably feel self-conscious at first. But I would also feel beautiful. Special.

Throughout our interview she described people who wear diamonds as flashy and concerned with creating an impression of money or status, but for her, she sees them as a way to make herself feel a certain way: beautiful and special.

Felicitous Performance

As part of a semiotic ideology, social convention informs the way we approach material culture and what roles it can play in performative acts. For instance, we habitually break a bottle of champagne over the bow of a ship upon its maiden voyage, not a bottle of soda or a vase filled with flowers. Convention dictates that we use champagne. Diamonds are also called for in conventionally defined cultural performances, a point forcefully made by Allen. He had recently proposed to his girlfriend, but said that he knew almost nothing about diamonds beforehand and that he had done a lot of internet research and talking with his female friends and colleagues before making a purchase. When "I asked for her hand, I knew that I had to present her with a diamond," he explained. In an aside, he confided that truthfully he did not want to buy one: "You can put me down as anti-diamond. As far as being a requirement, I think it's pretty much just silly. But," he continued, "I didn't even think about getting another stone because, you know, the diamond is a requirement, I could not imagine proposing without a diamond because then it [the proposal] would not be real." Two felicity conditions—(a) the sincerity of Allen's proposal and (b) the diamond—are ingredients that are necessary, but each standing alone is insufficient to make an authentic proposal. From Allen's point of view a diamond's presence is necessary to the successful execution of the proposal. Conversely, it is the proposal that makes this particular diamond a symbol of a promise to marry.

The "requirement" of a diamond in legitimizing a proposal is an American social convention, a tradition, we recall, so strongly promoted by De Beers marketers. In highlighting the historical conventionality of the engagement stone, it is instructive to compare American practices to those in Europe, where De Beers tried but failed to promote the same tradition. Shared ideas about legitimizing props— felicity conditions—can also develop locally, so a working theory of commodity performativity needs to account for both socially shared and locally devised felicity conditions (which may not reflect the industry-engineered tradition at all).

Illustrating just how short industry discourse falls from achieving hegemony is the perspective of Margaret, Allen's fiancée. Margaret works at a TV station, and when I went to visit her in her midtown Manhattan office, we sat at her large desk overlooking the Hudson River. She calmly explained that she really didn't care about receiving a diamond from Allen, but beseeched me, "Don't ever tell him that!" To her, a sincere proposal alone would have been felicitous enough to take seriously.

More obviously idiosyncratic interpretations popped up in interviews, especially when diamonds are used to stage narratives. Some women said that they use jewelry to mark status, but diamonds can also create and maintain specific narratives. Particular stones sometimes become fetishized, taking on special meanings and becoming stewed in memories, fantasies, or plots, overthrowing "A Diamond Is Forever." Here, meaning becomes naturalized to the extent that people think of it as part of the diamond itself, as if emanating from it, or even embedded in it, rather than seeing the stone as something upon which a set of meanings is imputed.

When treated as a repository for memories, diamonds become sites of condensation—like a souvenir or touchstone—for private imaginaries that can be made public through talk. Semiotically, their use as props often involves indexicalization, where people read a causal history into acquisition, for example, and then take the diamond as a stand-in for those circumstances. In this way, it is a cairn, marking the way to an internal landscape that can be translated into a public story while simultaneously representing indexical "proof" of those circumstances.

Over and above their use as touchstone, diamonds are sometimes implicated in producing outcomes, and then used to represent that outcome. They can, for instance, be acquired or redistributed in association with rites of passage such as births, graduations, weddings, and deaths. Mary Sue explained that a diamond, given to her when she graduated from high school, marked an entrance into the world of adults for her and her family, and that wearing this diamond, which she thought was "incredibly valuable and glamorous," not only worked to recall a rite of passage but actually carried her over from adolescence to full personhood. Because a similar gift had been given to her sister, local family tradition had rendered the diamond a necessary—"felicitous," in Austin's terms—element in making the rite of passage happen. From where she stood, donning this "valuable pendant" literally helped metamorphose her into a woman. The diamond is performative, perhaps magical in the force it exerts, in addition to carrying culturally shared symbolic meanings such as glamour. Mary Sue's semiosis can be understood as a foil against the idea that meaning resides in a code, a priori and external to the individual and his or her context. The significance of her "passage diamond" is a family activity that is accurately, though not unrelatedly, understood as an event in a restricted context rather than as an object cohering to a social code produced by industry discourse. Of course, the latter is partially entangled with the former.

The Declaratory: Is That Real?

Commodity studies tracking relationships between social groups and consumption—especially those linking political economy to social practices, and consumption patterns to social structures—tend to focus on class, usually understood as a socioeconomic category. The idea that commodity preference is correlated to class has been most elaborately explicated in the work on taste by Pierre Bourdieu (1984). Much, much less has been done on consumerism from the perspective of individual consumers, and neither subjectivity nor agency have received due attention (see Daniel Miller 1998 as an exception). This focus on the analysis of consumption at the level of social organization begins as far back as Thorstein Veblen's 1899 classic, *A Theory of the Leisure Class*.

Veblen linked consumerism to declarations of class. In approaching consumption from a perspective grounded in time, emulation, and material experience, his attention to conspicuous consumption has been influential in academia and in mainstream public discourse (even shaping advertising strategy), although clearly the relationship between consumption and class is far more complex than Veblen suggests. He did, however, explicitly explore the relationship between class and consumption using a semiotic model amenable to a Peircian symbol-index-icon framework, in that conspicuous consumption includes consuming goods that are symbols (which Veblen called the "insignia" or "badge" [1899, 46]), as well as those cast as indexes, where goods are understood as tangible results of productive labor (having certain goods is "proof" of financial success), and as icons, the consumption of which is to be emulated. Conspicuous consumption is a performance in which commodities and other entities (such as having a wife who is a woman of leisure) are wielded in symbolic and status claims, but having these things is itself an index of a person's wealth. The idea of "pecuniary emulation," where consumption of class insignias or indexes is practiced by those of a lesser status, can best be understood under the rubric of Peircian iconicity in which resemblance motivates acquisition and consumption of goods.

The relationship of status to emulated—or fake—diamonds is troubled by the ease with which they are simulated. A closer look at the semiotics of emulation shows why simulants can be a powerful status symbol (that is, one that powerfully marks status), and why a "knock-off" lacks a declaratory punch. Fake diamonds are icons, having abstracted from diamond certain qualities to emulate: Moissanite, for example, is a simulant that "refers" to diamond in clarity, hardness, and dispersion through similitude, but not in "rarity," which is part of the discourse that maintains its market and symbolic value and creates the possibility for interpreting diamond as indexical of financial standing or status. Cheap cubic zirconia, even softer (and less expensive) than Moissanite, gives off a bright fire and has even less semantic force than Moissanite. Its similarity to the real thing is degraded, more visibly fake, and, because its artifice is revealed, it calls attention to itself as what it is: an icon. Through the lens of conspicuous consumption, wearing cubic zirconia may mark one—powerfully—as an emulator, occupying a "lesser" status than the bearer of a diamond.

While the issue of authenticity is challenged by the relative ease of simulating diamond, any purported correlation between display and socioeconomic class is problematic because of the wide spectrum of ideas Americans entertain about wealth and conspicuous display. Even though some people I interviewed reported that diamonds are for the elite, others characterized inverse relationships between alleged wealth and/or status and conspicuous consumption, which can render one "tacky." Tom told me that in terms of wearing larger, more expensive diamonds, "Wealthy people do not engage in such behavior." A number of consumers said things like, "People with money do not wear big diamonds," while others stated that diamonds are used as declarations in an "attempt to convince people that they have status when they really don't." Large diamonds are sometimes associated with wealth, but wearing them was also deemed a "vulgar display" or "obnoxious." Wearing big diamonds was also associated with the nouveau riche, a group described as the economic equals of the upper class, but constituting a separate category because of their failed emulation. Applying authenticity as a mode of evaluation in both cases, for diamonds and for class, points to (actually is itself an index of) the existence of a normative state of affairs where real diamonds and real wealth are the legitimate, unmarked, and semantically powerful cases standing in contrast to degraded, inauthentic fakes ("zirconia" and the nouveau riche).

In what way do these pieces of polished gravel act as status markers? Allen, who had done "extensive research" about bigger diamonds, explained,

> When I see bigger diamonds I am—now especially that I know how much they cost— am like "Oh my God, look at that thing! That's too flashy!" or "It's fake!" It's too superficial to be like that, and I think there is an inverse relationship to an extent—I mean that is how I think of it, and it's all just appearance and probably nothing underneath.

Like Allen, Tim, a 35-year-old human relations officer, explained that he doesn't "like to see people wearing large diamonds," since he is "more impressed by a small, simple stone with a lot of personal meaning, because to be otherwise is a sign of superficiality." Allen's use of "superficial" suggests that he thinks others believe wearing flashy diamonds is a convincing performance of wealth but that their efforts are doomed—authentic wealth does not employ such loud performances. Tim's use of the term also points to inauthenticity, though of a personal rather than of a material sort. Similar beliefs that big diamonds create an impression of tastelessness and indicate a probable absence of class or "real wealth," variously constructed, were shared by more than a few. But size is relative: there was virtually no agreement on what counts as "too big" or the value at which a diamond becomes vulgar. A convincing declaratory performance of wealth with diamonds is evidently pretty tricky business.

Still, people do associate diamonds with class. I spoke with women who overtly strategize to achieve financial success (or help their husbands to do so), so that they can "acquire bigger diamonds so other people will know that we have arrived"—very much a Veblenesque scenario. Some people plan to "trade up" as soon as possible, exchanging what they currently own for larger stones (for a price, of course), while others celebrate the "sweetness" or "special attachment" to even very small diamonds—professing they "would never want any other stone."

Tommy, a young professional, bought a diamond for his wife. He thought it was an extravagant expense, but she really wanted a particular shape and size. "I decided to go ahead and make the investment," he said, but still he worries about the future expense involved in trading up, something for which his wife has already expressed a desire. He continued,

> The older you are, the bigger jewelry you can get away with wearing, and that's why they have this trade-up program where I got the stone. This is really geared toward more materialistic people when really it should just have sentimental value, but my wife wanted it so I enrolled and now in the future we can turn in that stone and get a bigger one. The only thing is that the next one has to cost twice as much as the first one did so it's like I have to buy it all over again!

Trading up is an arrangement for the future that retailers now offer: consumers can exchange their purchase for a larger stone, usually at a slightly discounted price, but the arrangement may contain caveats, such as that the new one must be twice as large as the old one.

Molly, who "definitely plans to upgrade," is interested in status performance. She knew more than most about grading and prices, confidently explaining that her diamond "is a brilliant cut, a little over two carats, and its color is G." She told me that she had forgotten the clarity characteristics, but given her self-assured and expansive knowledge about grading, it was odd that she would "forget" such crucial information. Molly hopes to acquire "something around three or four carats in an emerald or radiant cut. . . . It's like a princess cut only better."

Now, the strategic use of synthetic or imitation diamonds is, in some cases, a successful iconic ploy; the appearance so resembles a diamond as to be taken for the real McCoy. Given Molly's aficionado-like attitude toward diamonds, I was surprised to hear her say that "in up-grading, you know, I would take Moissanite instead. It is man-made but nobody can tell and it's a third of the price so to me that's fine and I'd rather have a big Moissanite than this smaller real one." Molly imagines that in terms of effect, Moissanite is, for all intents and purposes, identical to diamond on the basis of what others think they are seeing. The performative value of diamond and Moissanite are one and the same.

Molly's attitude here speaks to the nonessentiality of diamonds' meaning—meaning comes from us rather than from our things. For her, big diamonds, whether real or simulated, satisfy her aims. While deftly sidestepping questions that dealt directly with why she wanted a larger stone and what she hoped wearing big diamonds would say about her to others, she explained that she "feels good" when she wears diamonds: "I truly appreciate the beauty of the diamond, more so than other people. They make me feel very special, very feminine and powerful." The stones have a palpable impact on the way she experiences herself. In the midst of exploring her subjective experience, she changed the topic to branded stones, but her message was the same:

Have you heard of all the branded stones? Like the Yehuda diamond?[2] They can actually laser a signature on there. But to me this is just a waste of money because no one else can see the brand—if it showed, I might feel differently, but you have to have a loupe to see it, so who's even going to know?

I pressed her to say why she cared, but she would only say, "Well, bigger is better." This exact phrase actually appears on Yehuda advertisements.

Molly is explicitly concerned with the interpretations of others in addition to the feelings she enjoys while wearing diamonds or their look-alikes. Not everyone shares this open-mindedness—one's own knowledge of quality may be paramount over others' impressions. Ahmed said, "Even if I were to buy a cheap diamond that looked the same (as a quality, expensive one), if I knew that it was somehow inferior, then, I would not want that." For him, the consequences of wearing a cheap stone or a fake one are different from those of wearing an expensive, high-quality stone; they are not "the same" as they are for Molly, and therefore the performative effects are different. Ahmed's felicity conditions have to do with what he believes about the quality of the stone; for him to feel good about wearing it, he needs to know that it is "the best," whereas for Molly, the way the stone appears to others is what matters: "I mean people can tell if you are wearing low-quality, cheap zircs, but not with the good Moissanite." Her easy use of slang such as "zircs"—for cubic zirconia—belies a certain level of comfort with looking at, evaluating, and talking about diamonds and their simulants that most people do not have.

People had varied feelings about simulants—fakes. Some worried about aesthetics (for example, too much "sparkle") or feeling disingenuous or ashamed to be engaged in deception. People were divided about whether they would consider wearing a fake or inexpensive stone. Shannon, in her late twenties, told me that her parents don't have a lot of money and that when they got married her father could not afford a diamond, but "last Christmas my mom opened her gift from him"—and then, in an preemptive defense, she interrupted herself:

> I mean, I have never seen my mom act like this; she is really the most gracious and polite woman you will ever meet. But anyway, so she opened the present and there was a diamond ring and she took one look at it and handed it back over to my father and said, "This is fake." And that was the end of it. I don't know how she knew, maybe the size, but she didn't want it and was not about to take it. So anyway, he finally did on their last anniversary give her a real one. It's small, but real.

Besides the fact that her father may have been trying to trick his wife, the ability of a stone to carry appropriate meaning hinged on its honest-to-goodness authenticity.

The relative construction of "authenticity" is highlighted by the story of Sandra and her husband, Ron, both magazine editors whom I met at a dinner party. Ron had given Sandra a "paste" (glass) diamond when they were engaged. Many years later, he confiscated it when she took it off to work in the garden one day, had the paste replaced with a diamond, and gave it to her again. She was very pleased that he had done this for her, but told me while he was away from the table, "in strictest confidence," that she didn't really care if the diamond was real or fake: "To me, the only thing that matters is that it is from his heart." For Sandra, the paste is as "authentic" as the real.

Related to the success of declaration is the person to whom a declaration is being made, which reminds us that, as Peirce points out, a sign means something to someone, leaving the door open for alterity and contingency. Some men, concerned with the way others might perceive them, argued that even though their girlfriends claimed not to have any preference about size, they wouldn't buy a small gem because it would reflect badly upon them. I heard many men saying things like, "I don't want anyone to think I'm cheap" or "You have to go for something that is big enough so people don't think I am a cheap guy but not so big as to be over the top." These statements reflect the way men imagine others will read diamonds, rather than the way they themselves see them, let alone the way others actually do read them, which in some ways is one of the most salient cornerstones of outwardly directed performance.

But will others even notice? Jenny believes diamonds are popular primarily for aesthetic reasons, which complicates their use by men as a status claim. She elaborated that diamonds are

> so popular because they are not colored and so they go with everything— they are the most versatile fashion accessory and I guess that they have some status but that is really more important for the guy who is like, "See what I got for my wife." But I don't think that women care. Men are the ones who really think about it but it's weird because they don't ever notice other people's diamonds.

So the conspicuous consumption of a large "real" diamond can be simultaneously a claim and a demonstration of status and wealth.

The Contractual: I Promise

Signs are employed in contractual performances. In Austin's model, "I'll bet you five dollars that the Tarheels take the Devils," is a contractual illocution resulting in a relationship with contingencies and obligations. Some see diamonds as part of a contract, for example, as a promise of sexual availability. The following excerpt from my interview with Stephanie shows how diamonds can be perceived as a contract:

> I mean there are all those symbolic associations like trust and love and stuff but to me when a man gives a woman a diamond it is like he is making a promise to hold up his end of the bargain, a bargain that takes place on several levels—on the one hand if there is a family involved then it is the man's role to be both a provider on a material basis and also to be secure and committed and so it's about money and other material provisions, but even more than that he is promising his presence, his interested presence, his protective presence, and that he will be there to protect the vulnerable family unit. He promises to create a situation in which the mother can devote herself to the care of the children and so to me this is all gelled in the diamond. The diamond is an example of his ability and willingness to be a good provider.

A woman, in accepting the promise-as-diamond, is responsible "for being nurturing and supportive and honoring what the man is giving up, namely, his freedom." While admitting that in having such a thing, there is an "aura of conservative-ness," and that she is conflicted by the guilt she feels when confronted with the realities of diamond production, which "siphons off some of the pleasure," Kristen's interpretation is nuanced and personalized, the result of protracted conversations between her and her husband.

Into the Past

I met Liza, an articulate, artistic woman in her thirties, at a coffee shop for a formal interview. In discussing how her family thinks about jewelry handed down from her grandparents, she explained how they are used as props on a stage or cairns on a path. Props suggest, authenticate, or identify a setting. A cairn is a pile of stones heaped up, a pyramid of twigs, perhaps a specially tied frond, that is used as a landmark meant to catch your attention and mark a particular spot; hikers leave cairns at places where they change directions, or a cairn may be left to identify a site at which something can be seen or found. Diamonds as cairns direct one's attention toward memories, or imaginaries, and then act as props within those very landscapes. Objects can literally set the stage for stories because they are attached to memories or fantasies. We use them to convey a particular stance, mood, or spirit. Our consciousness can be transported, projected back into the past, or the past may be "brought forward" to the present when we're confronted with these meaningful things.

The following excerpt is about a collection of jewelry that belongs to Liza's family, currently in the possession of her aunt Mariana. We had been discussing "bling," the "deplorable" use of diamonds for self-promotion by rappers, and the social responsibilities that accompany wealth. Liza used the term "prop" to describe how diamonds help set a mood for others:

> Talking about all of this, it all makes me think about my Aunt Mariana. She is, and has been for as long as I can remember, so consumed by the diamond jewelry that is in our family. My father's family once had a good deal of money—now they don't, but they did before, and the last pieces to go are always the jewelry and the silver—and why? Because she hangs onto her ideals and memories through them and she doesn't want to let go. I have watched how Mariana has clinged [sic] to those diamonds, like with her life. Like she possesses them and now actually they possess her. She is literally out of her mind. And that has given me such a different view on diamonds than I otherwise would have had. I would rather be happy and be with my husband and my friends and family and have good relationships than have some diamond if it came down to that, which in

this case it has. She uses them to create a fantasy world, she clings to every remnant of the past through those things. And she and all her siblings, they don't even talk over it.

And I think for her it is all about being owed something. Maybe by birthright, but she won't even share with her brothers and sister! I mean people do have a responsibility when they have money, to look after their neighbors and also to be careful with that money so that their children can benefit from it. But Mariana has never had any responsibility in that way, she has frittered away everything, you know, except for the diamonds, and she is not even sharing that. Like the hip-hop community putting diamonds in their teeth is absurd, especially, you know, knowing where they came from, it's all so selfish and irresponsible, why don't they use that money for people who really don't have anything?

But Mariana, she is addicted to diamonds, some people actually get addicted to them, and it's like the diamonds are her greatest happiness and getting a new one is the only thing that she looks forward to. Because she has run off all her brothers and sisters over them so there is no family happiness, really, to speak of.

And she will hang onto them at any cost. And I have thought about this a lot. You see, to her it represents what she once had, and what she could have had, what she should have had, and she really did have it in some ways—I mean the family had more money than anyone else in town— so she had that feeling of status and importance and security, so it's like living in the past. And she has ironically lost the irreplaceable things like her family over these things, but she, well, she did kind of ruin her life. Her mother died when she was very young, and granddaddy remarried this woman that frankly wasn't very nurturing. And so Mariana, she got in with a wild crowd, and was being rebellious, and got pregnant, and granddaddy wanted to send her to a convent in Europe to have the baby and put it up for adoption, but she wouldn't have any of that. And so she eloped when she was sixteen with Tim, this redneck, and she stayed with him for a long time. Too long. And she even went to college but she was the only one to graduate that already had kids.

So she was more nontraditional in those days but then she started clinging—I don't know when this happened—but anyway there she is— these diamonds are part of a past that is partly true, I mean they are like characters in her memory, but she has built them up in her mind so that they are props in this fantasy that she has about what could have been, what the possibilities were, what she should have been, and things like that. But these are dreams that don't exist in any way. These are false realities and having the diamonds make it all seem real to her. She is willing to give up the here-and-now to keep those diamonds that allow her to live in a fantasy world of I don't know what.

This story exemplifies the extent to which historical and local as well as imaginary factors enter into the signification process, and it underscores the need to theorize commodity performativity at a fine level. Here, diamonds operate like characters in a past; they represent alternative realities and perhaps even have personality. Others perform themselves into scenarios, past, present, and future, taking diamonds as felicitous props with which to "do things" such as become engaged, become an adult, or place themselves into an imagined (better) landscape. But, after all, these events also take place within a social milieu rife with media and production ideologies. Advertising and marketing spectacles inform personal dramas that unfurl in shared society as well as in fantasy. The unique nature of personal meanings, colored by experience and imagination, participates both with and against discourse centering on romance, glamour, and wealth.

Into the Future and Other Imaginary Spaces

In the same way that diamonds serve as props to support imagined or remembered pasts, people use them to launch projections of themselves into the future or spatially distant places. I was talking with Mary Sue in her Brooklyn office when she introduced her inherited diamonds—she acquired several large diamonds from her mother—and, thinking about them, slowly conjured them up. When she described what her mind's eye saw, she told me of their presence in a cardboard box along with other valuable jewelry that she doesn't like to wear. As she was talking, we were both transported to her apartment, to the top of her dark closet, inside a box lying just under a pile of sweaters and other wintry clothes, to an unassuming "cardboard crypt" holding several loose stones. She describes the stones in as much detail as she can revive. The stones contain, she explains tentatively, emotions they absorbed from her mother. She rehearsed the memory of their close, loving relationship and her mother's untimely death, and then spoke about the future, when she will pass them on to her nephews.

Because the diamonds have for Mary Sue "absorbed emotional content from the wearer," these particular diamonds operate legitimately (felicitously) in this setting. Meaning is generated indexically in space where familial relationships are remembered, reenacted, and performed. Passing these objects to her nephews will "do things," namely, reinforce kinship between her nephews and her mother, and between herself and her nephews' fiancées. These diamonds provoke memories of the past and hopes for the future, whose content emerges in concert with, but is far from determined by, marketing campaigns. Mary Sue recognizes the association of diamonds with glamour, and that they can be used to legitimize a proposal, but for her, they first and foremost provide a link to her mother; they are a means by which to underscore existing relations and participate in the formation of new ones. Because she believes that they absorb emotions from the wearer, these particular stones, and no other, are the authentic repositories of memory and enactors of kinship. The authenticity of the stone, as she defines it, is a felicity condition allowing the stone to act performatively.

Shifting Performances

Diamonds operate in imaginaries of future generations, as glamorous accessories or as rainy-day savings accounts, but these imaginaries are dynamic: they respond to changing circumstance. Narratives of acquisition and dispossession are negotiated, renegotiated, and then rehearsed as visions of the future become honed, or transform, over time. For example, during a casual conversation with Valerie, she told me that her engagement stone was reset in a necklace when she divorced; now it's a fashion accessory rather than a performance of marital commitment.

In another example of the way meaning changes with circumstances, a pair of large diamond earrings, a former souvenir of Renee's marriage to her ex-husband, Howard, has been aestheticized. The diamonds' former significance has given way to one revolving around looking special and fashionable:

> I reset the diamonds in a ring with a sapphire and I wear it to parties and on other dressy occasions. Howard always hated to get dressed up and do anything social, so now I use this diamond when I want to look special. You see, I had a friend who was wearing a sapphire and diamond combination—now, hers were huge and the sapphire was about as big as my head, and mine is much smaller—but I love the colors together and I wear it a lot. It goes with a lot of things and it always looks nice and crisp.

It's through the possession, display, and imputation of meaning—in response to the change of circumstance upon specific commodities—that people like Renee successfully perform themselves into the play of todays, yesterdays, or tomorrows.

Foundational Status

As a paradigm for examining the role of material culture in social relationships, a linguistic model such as that outlined by Austin can be augmented by considering the individual as a producer of meaning. Austin explores language as a consequence-generating phenomenon, but the model doesn't really problematize the mechanics of meaning. Identifying the production of meaning as emergent from individual agents who interact with but are not wholly determined by known social codes, as Barbara Johnstone (2001) has done, manages to capture both idiosyncrasy and convention in language use. Consumption is similarly idiosyncratic and conventional. Meaning production cannot be predicted by reference to at-large social codes, nor to people's identification with categories such as race, class, gender, or ethnicity, although ideas and commentary about these categories (which are sometimes quite sharp) are certainly implicated.

By taking the individual as the locus of investigation and allowing for subjectivity, ambiguity, and negotiation in the performance of, for instance, gender or kinship rather than in the construction or reflection of it, we maintain a space for the impact of knowledge, memory, and agency on consumption activities. Performative consumption takes place within individuated circumstance. It means calling for a reversal from theory that starts with the society or group and then arrives at the individual to one that gives foundational status to the individual and individual differences (Hymes 1979).

Looking at daily activity from a more rarified perspective, Michel de Certeau, using a metaphor of wandering the city, posits that individual practices are private meanderings within an overarching structure that provides a matrix, but does not determine its subjects' pathways or experience. While de Certeau casts the individual as creative and agentive, this individual creativity is not productive. Analysis of consumer narratives in this chapter suggests that individual actors generate performances that are both productive and creative. Paying attention to the way people think of signs as productive, as performative, as "doing things," helps us understand how material culture is used to exert change or to create circumstances.

CONCLUSION: THE FULLNESS OF DIAMONDS

When I started doing research for this project, I was surprised by the variety of ideas, images, and metaphors in consumers' stories that diverged from the ad-based associations with class and romance that I had expected. Going far beyond those symbolic associations, people treat diamonds as if they have personalities, give them sacred histories, see them in terms that are primarily metaphorical or poetic, or deploy them performatively. Noting the variety of consumers' engagements with diamonds, I began looking for social theory that would embrace such idiosyncrasy, since accounting for variation, difference, and the unexpected is a prerequisite to making the world intelligible. I have presented one idea for integrating idiosyncrasy here in a study of the commodity.

"Consumption" is understood as the set of practices, including meaning making, that people undertake with things—commodities—they buy. I have used the term "commodity" to mean objects (though of course, services and experiences might be included too) that are usually mass produced, are often highly marketed and/or branded, and are sold in exchange for cash or its equivalent on the open market. Commodities usually have conventional, socially sanctioned—but not overdetermined—uses and meanings. The presence of commodities in contemporary American society can hardly be overstated. They acquire meaning, and it is by, through, and with commodities that we negotiate our lives. But how do things come to mean anything at all? This book has examined people's stories to uncover the range of semiotic ideologies, or the kinds of signs diamonds are taken to be, but what can such a study suggest about consumption in general? Looking at some of the particular issues that shape the meaning of diamonds—authenticity, sensuality, luxury, and symbolic load—can help us open up the study of consumption to incorporate idiosyncratic meanings.

On a meta-level, fakes index the power of real diamonds. Many commodities engender fakes or replicas: "Gucci" watches, "leather" handbags, and gemstone jewelry can all be bought on the streets of New York for a fraction of the price one pays for the "real" things in a retail store where "authentic" goods are sold. Diamond owners frequently remarked upon the fact that diamonds are "easily faked" or that there are "lots of fakes out there." And some people are comfortable with wearing fakes, or even prefer fakes or knock-offs. The existence of simulated diamonds attests to the power of real diamonds' meaning, though they do have an ambiguous relationship. Fakes, for example, encode a set of commentaries on "real" diamonds through iconic resemblance; they may operate as a play for status, but the ease with which they are faked speaks to an uneasy relationship with their utility as a status marker.

Industry as well as consumer concern with authenticity is reflected in the professionalization and growth of grading and certification bodies such as GIA. In addition to the common "4 Cs" of diamond quality, retailers now urge consumers to pay attention to a fifth "C," which stands for "Certificates" that define, map, and legitimize the evaluation of diamonds using the first four "Cs." The trend toward certification reflects the threat presented to the industry by "good" fakes: to remain in power, the industry must construct and maintain a belief that the difference between a carbon gem and a paste is relevant and worth paying for. The industry has even developed responses to synthetic goods by promoting the idea that natural diamonds, with their irregularities and flaws, are more legitimate than lab-produced stones with their regular chemistry and lack of mineral inclusions. By calling flaws and inclusions "nature's signature" at the point of sale, retailers intimate that stones are one-of-a-kind, "signed" pieces, akin to great works of art. (In fact, it was this analogy of a diamond to a great [and unique] work of art that led to an ad campaign that featured paintings by well-known artists such as Pablo Picasso and Salvador Dali.) Laser branding, though virtually invisible, further adds to the sense that each diamond is special, not just one among millions of nearly identical stones.

It is through such efforts that mass-produced diamonds are orchestrated into having greater uniqueness and thus value. These activities—in combination with meaning making by individuals—generate an aura that cannot be replaced with a fake, a synthetic, or even another real diamond. On the other hand, when used purely for status marking, a less expensive but large fake diamond may be preferred to an expensive but small real diamond. The extent to which, and how, this aura of distinctiveness is construed varies depending on the combination of semiotic tactics the consumer deploys.

The issue of authenticity affects the study of commodities in general on several counts. Certain kinds of goods motivate the production of fakes. Works of art, or antiques, inspire reproductions and imitations, while branded goods are similarly "reproduced," often in ways that are playful and obvious (e.g., giant cubic zirconia jewelry), or in more subtle ways where there is a real effort, sometimes to the point of criminality, to imitate "real" things. Emulatory, iconic, and fake goods can mark or index the established presence of an authentic good, and can even challenge the authority of those goods whose value may be, ironically, further enhanced by emulation. This emulation often takes place in the visual arena but may work on other senses as well.

Furniture, chocolates, handbags, frying pans, stereos, shoes, and diamonds are all examples of material culture that address the senses. But sometimes in studies of consumerism, the sensual materiality of the object goes underappreciated. Material goods serve as a useful lens through which to investigate the labor, political, economic, and social relationships within which they are produced and of which they are symptomatic. But, materiality is not inconsequential when it comes to the way we use commodities every day. Consumers "read" objects' formal qualities: the way something feels, smells, sounds, looks, or tastes can contribute to what it means.

With diamonds, several material variables tend to fuel interpretation. For instance, diamonds are durable; they are easily maintained and can last over many generations. This imperishability enables their conceptualization as heirlooms thought to carry memories and generational histories within them. And since diamonds are small and portable, they can be worn every day over the course of a lifetime. This makes diamonds a good candidate for what Jane Schneider (2006) has called "self-enhancement," the use of material culture to build the self both personally and interactively. The same could be said of clothes or cosmetics, or other materials that generate feelings of potentiality and self-confidence. People use objects to encode memory or experience, and as protective amulets draped on the body, hovering in that liminal space and incorporated into the person: consumer and commodity become one entity greater than the sum of its parts.

Moving away from direct, physical sensation, the notion of luxuriousness is more abstract. Luxury items sometimes serve as indexes of class, and diamonds are portrayed in the media, and characterized in consumer narratives, as very expensive things the wealthy or upper classes have. But demand has been democratized: cheap labor and increased extraction means larger and better-quality stones on the market. While price has remained relatively stable, the greater availability of inexpensive stones has meant that ever more people can afford to have some kind of diamond. So, while there is some truth to the idea that only the elite can afford to have large, high-quality diamonds (which are rare and pricey), the combined availability and fakeability of diamonds make it somewhat tricky to regard them as a luxury item that marks class, or anything at all, in a reliable way.

Though marketing sometimes uses celebrity endorsements, people in most advertisements for diamonds appear to be members of the (mainly white) "wholesome" middle class. The category of "middle class" in the United States is itself problematic, however, since there is so much differentiation within it, and those differences are variably understood and negotiated regionally, economically, behaviorally, and stylistically (Rudd and Descartes 2008). But insofar as "luxury" cars, branded clothing, and the like are part of the set of highly marketed commodities that the middle class consumes, diamond jewelry fits right in, reflected in the fact that most American women own at least one diamond.

With a long history of tightly managed marketing, diamonds do have an especially high symbolic load. The industry spends inordinate amounts of money to maintain the appearance of diamonds in public discourse and is unrelenting in its efforts to fix meaning. Many commodities do not fit this profile, at least in degree (it's hard to imagine similar campaigns for sweet potatoes or dental braces, for example), though the symbolic load attached to "status" items may receive more similar treatment.

Because of the impact of these four features (authenticity, materiality, luxury, and symbolic load) in using diamond as an example, extrapolating how semiosis takes place is most justified when one is considering similar entities. Commodities that are faked or imitated, are used in personal adornment or drama, are considered luxurious even in a mild way, and carry a high symbolic load will probably be treated with similar modalities. Examples of such things include art, branded shoes and clothing, housewares, cars, and precious metals or gems such as gold or pearls.

Language Is to Culture

Interpretive strategies are complex, rife with incoherencies and irrationalities. People use an individualized mélange of semiotic strategies, combining cultural ideas with their own particular experiences and attitudes. Meanings are indeterminate and can change over time. Some diamond consumers struggle with contradictory values, such as "wanting a big, gorgeous stone" but simultaneously rejecting the conventionality or materiality they associate with diamonds. Diamond consumption is idiosyncratic, historically and locally situated, and sensitive to context. Methods used to study it must be able to discern and make sense of these factors.

Anthropology has used a "culture as text" model for analyzing cultural phenomena, and insofar as culture does share some traits with language, this has been a productive strategy. The model of language this metaphor uses is drawn from Saussure, and contains a theory of meaning that can be described as referential. Following Saussure's dictum that analysts see only what their model allows, we expect the use of such a model to reveal those aspects of cultural communiqué that are referential (only). The lack of attention to subjectivity, history, and situatedness that is characteristic of consumer studies working from a "culture as text" position is a logical result of using this structuralist-based notion of the sign. That result is caused by three crucial features within Saussurean thought: the lack of speakers in favor of an idealized speaker, ahistorical systematicity, and a code of meaning that exists prior to individuals. Saussure argued that to study language, it was necessary to reconfigure the way that we understand it, having realized that "you can see only as far as your model permits you to see; that the methodological starting point does much more than simply reveal—it actually creates, the object under study" (Jameson 1972, 14).

But there are aspects of language left uncaptured by a structural (referential) paradigm. For example, explaining the context-specific use of pronouns requires expansion of the model. Other nonreferential modes of language include metaphors and performatives. Becoming more sensitive to different kinds of modalities enhances our understanding of language, and the same theoretical developments that capture nonreferential aspects of language can be mobilized to help us understand our dealings with material culture.

Using a lens open to both referentiality and nonreferentiality to examine diamond narratives, I have aimed to show that the language-as-text model is fruitful, but it can be executed with a model of language that accounts for many more mechanisms of meaning. Reconfiguring the object under study—approaching commodities as various types of signs, rather than treating commodities only as symbols—we discern a fuller range of cultural practices.

An important aspect of cultural practice has to do with ideologies that direct or shape the semiotic strategies that we routinely deploy. "Linguistic ideology" is broadly defined as "shared bodies of commonsense notions about the nature of language in the world" (Rumsey 1990, 346). What we think language is and how we think it works informs our ideology of language, and is even one of the factors that shapes meta-theories of language. Ideologies of language are contingent upon some theory of how meaning works. A referential linguistic ideology contains a referential theory of meaning. Here, language is thought to refer to, point to, and call out entities or events in our experience, real or imaginary— proper names are perhaps the clearest example. A referential theory of meaning, again, traced to the sign concept as defined by Saussure, posits that words have meaning purely by virtue of their naming—or directly referring to—some entity. The linguistic term "Jorge Luis Borges" refers to a specific writer of some renown and wit. "Easter Bunny" refers to a more imaginary being, but one that inhabits our experience nonetheless.

In his work on linguistic ideology, Michael Silverstein (1979, 1995) has expressed concerns over the tendency to view propositionality as the essence of language and to confuse indexical functions with referential ones (see also Rumsey 1990; Schieffelin and Wollard 1994). Webb Keane (2003) has illustrated that language cannot generally be abstracted from context and cultural presuppositions and that, in addition to reference, language has indexical, performative, and poetic dimensions that make interaction richly meaningful. While some language is plainly referential, the various understandings of how language works as a social process, and to what ends, are culturally variable and need to be discovered rather than simply assumed (Bauman 1983, 16). And as some linguistic utterances are not comfortably contained under a conception of linguistic referentiality—for example, articles ("the," "an"), imperatives and declaratives ("Go!" "ma'am," "I promise"), and indexes (pronouns, including "this" and "that") in standard American English—it has been necessary for linguistics to weave theoretical nets that catch nonreferential functions. The referential paradigm, with its code-like framework, suffers from a kind of literalism, eclipsing space for the combination of literal information with desire, struggle, critique, humor, and play that characterize natural discourse at the crux of real human interaction. And while material culture, like language, can be code-like or representational at times, it, like language, can mediate, enhance, motivate, and produce social realities. Focusing on the relationship between language and social dynamics, both within and between social groups, shows us that language is an important mediator of identity formation and social relationships. Language has practical consequences that are underexplained by reference alone. Nevertheless, a referential paradigm is often mobilized as the metaphor used in cultural analysis.

The tendency to view language as solely propositional rather than as some combination of propositionality, indexicality, and/or iconicity has been transported into the social sciences, via the metaphor of culture-as-text, to produce an ideology of consumption in which commodities are thought to function essentially referentially. If a referentially wrought linguistic ideology, which works to occlude nonreferential signing functions, is applied in commodity studies, it becomes difficult to appreciate the various nonreferential functions of commodities that emerge in narratives, at both the theoretical and empirical levels.

Referential theories of language do not easily account for poetic communication, such as irony, parody, or *ostranenie*, that subvert standard codes of meaning. We have seen just how "bling" partly operates as a symbol of glamour and status but also calls attention to itself and its signmanship, and how this can incite a critical, questioning, hermeneutic engagement in contrast to normative diamond display. In this sense bling acts as a poetic device, as a provocation, and instead of reflecting, or even pretending to reflect, a preexisting circumstance, it has the potential to create new knowledges and relationships.

Diamond consumers described rappers wearing diamonds as, for example, "ironic," or "witty." Because *ostranenie* operates as part of a larger theory of artfulness defined as a mode of readerly engagement, we are not required to take the intention of the industry or even the wearer as the final authority on meaning. Meaning exists as the product of an artful relationship between the reader and the (art/literary/poetic) sign—in this case between a person and another person's diamond. As part of a larger exploration of nonreferentiality in commodity meanings, the concept of *ostranenie* helps us understand diamond consumption. Rather than taking diamonds solely as signs deployed in claims about identity or socioeconomic status, they become unfamiliar carriers of the emotive, the political, and the ironic, and provocateurs of feeling, desire, and aesthetic sensibility. Commodities are more than containers of conventionally agreed-upon information; working with an openness toward sign types, and finding poesy, we identify meaning making that is invisible using only a Saussurean lens.

When analyzing cultural activity through a referential theory, "meaning" is located in a shared lexicon. Consumers clearly knew the lexicon of diamonds, but did not accept it wholesale. They routinely told me that diamonds are associated with power, status, and wealth for "your average Joe," but tended to see this as a social code that others, but not they themselves, accept and follow. Many people argued that their own diamonds have a different, more personalized meaning, and that they neither read nor use their own stones in accordance with the lexicon they view as a combined product of advertising and "the Hollywood thing."

In structural linguistics, individuals come to know a "code" in a more or less "competent" way, but the focus of study is on the code itself, not individuals or variations among individuals. Instead, there is an imagined ideal speaker who has perfect mastery of the code. This vocabulary of competence, and the consequential methodological step to put aside the individual and variations among individuals in favor of an underlying or generative grammar comes out of Noam Chomsky's work on linguistics. That an ideal code, which is the supposed object of study, has been abstracted from a compendium of individual utterances, none of which is in and of itself representative or ideal, presents a fascinating paradox. And, while there is a tacit acknowledgment that differences among individuals exist, variation has been most insistently trivialized, although investigations of variation and change is an area currently benefiting from the supplementation of the "linguistics of systems" with a "linguistics of speakers" (Johnstone 2000). Currently, more linguists are paying attention to the individual and idiolects, and to the relationships among variations, within overarching abstracted systems, in attempts to understanding how language works in various contexts. Similarly, individuals use material culture in ways that are idiosyncratic; this idiosyncrasy must be cast into relief instead of smoothed into homogeneity if we are to understand the role objects have in creating, mediating, and reproducing social realities.

Fullness

Diamond meanings do refract ad discourse, but gaining a wider and more nuanced understanding of consumerism requires a methodological expansion in three ways. First, refocusing the gaze from the use of diamonds by social groups or as defined in marketing discourse to individual interpretations foregrounds everyday subjective perspectives without sacrificing a necessary and dedicated awareness of the political, cultural, and economic processes in which consumerism is inevitably and dialectically involved.

Second, there has been surprisingly little comprehensive work based on empirical observations of the practical relationships between consumers and commodities, particularly once these objects are acquired and integrated into everyday lives (Dant 1996, 2000). I have tried to demonstrate some of the ways in which commodities operate in postacquisition life, where they become meaningful and impact the everyday. And, third, a methodological focus on the interaction between individuals and objects illustrates how things are encountered. People

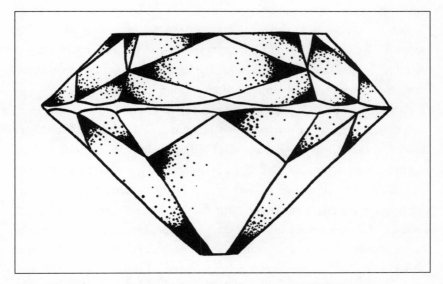

Figure C.1. Diamond. (Illustration by Kay Wolfersperger, used by permission.)

report surprising and contradictory interpretations and attendant emotional responses. In this book, I have examined how people consume objects by analyzing the types of meanings generated.

Work in the anthropology of commodities commonly reflects the idea that commodities function referentially, where commodities refer to cultural codes. And commodities do work like this, but pushing referentiality to its logical limits in the context of consumption can erase the very important local and contingent aspects of commodity interpretation. This erasure can result in overlooking the unpredictable mix of indexical, iconic, poetic, and performative semioses that constitute consumers' semiotic ideologies.

The existence of this unpredictability suggests that we ought to take a keener interest in idiosyncrasy: far from trivial, and without lauding individualism as a political project or social position, idiosyncrasy makes living in society not just bearable, but comprehensible. Its presence must, therefore, be integrated into cultural theory. But there is an even more vital point: material culture is not a blank slate for unconstrained meaning making; it refracts, rejects, motivates, and expresses cultural patterns. By casting individual interpretative variations against these patterns, we pry open a theoretical space for creative agency, recognizing that alternative ways of being are often hidden in plain sight.

And finally, by peering into the subjective domain of consumption, we can expand in new directions our understanding of life under advanced capitalism. Inspired by exciting work done in phenomenology (Lingis 2004), affect (Berlant 1991; Stewart 2007), and individual voice (Johnstone 2000), I argue that recognizing creativity in everyday experience is crucial to theorizing human experience; it makes the landscape comprehensible, our days memorable, and the mundane extraordinary. The funny, strange, sad, heroic, and boring, but always idiosyncratic, diamond stories people shared with me, and that I share in this book, illustrate just how hard we work, not always with success, to ground our experience within personalized horizons of intelligibility.

NOTES

NOTE TO THE PREFACE

1. See "The Diamond Cutter Sutra," a well-known Mahayana teachings on the concept of emptiness.

NOTES TO THE INTRODUCTION

1. Diamondeers must trust their employees, and as a result, almost every aspect of the industry is organized around kinship or close friendships. Cutting diamonds has sustained families for generations, and cutting families such as the Tolkowskys are well known. Maurice Tolkowsky, arriving in Antwerp in 1880, worked in a thriving factory where cutters relied on experience, intuition, and luck to polish facets. Using new technologies for cleaving, "bruting" (also known as "girdling," this process forms a flat belt around the widest diameter of the stone), polishing, and sawing, Tolkowsky's grandson, Marcel Tolkowsky, a mathematician and experienced cutter, developed the 58-sided "brilliant" cut in 1919. The brilliant remains the standard round cut today.

2. Efforts to market diamonds in Brazil and Europe have been far less effective. Reflecting the vagaries of the global political economy, China is the new emerging diamond market.

3. Henri Moissan discovered silicon carbide in an Arizona meteorite in 1904. It was later named "moissanite" to commemorate Moissan's many scientific contributions. Despite industry concerns, synthetic Moissanite was eventually developed and is now sold as a diamond substitute. For a history of the discovery of moissanite up through the production and sale of synthetic silicon carbide, see Nassau 1999.

4. Efforts to develop more nuanced approaches to understanding commodities have looked to the movement and temporary social constructedness of commodities, commodity-hood, and the relationship of commodity-hood to alienability (see Kopytoff 1986; Gell 1992; Thomas 1991).

5. The term "luxury" is derived from the Latin "luxuria," for "lust," "frolicsomeness," and "frivolous." The want/need distinction within sociological literature on

consumption is predicated on concepts such as consumer rationality, as argued by Applbaum (1998) and by Doyal and Gough (1991); the construction of desire and its naturalization via metaphor (see Belk et al. 1996); consumer imagination and consumption as an aesthetic reflex (DeNora 2000); and the persistence of aesthetic judgment versus "need" concepts over time (see Lehtonen 1999). And, when it implies want and a hedonistic notion of need or desire, luxury can be implicated in the spectacular constitution of social categories such as gender and class (see Pointon 1999).

6. To track ongoing themes in academic debates on advertising, see also Barthes 1957; Berger 2000; Ewen1988; Gailbraith 1977; and Williamson 1978.

7. Consumers use other modes of interpretation; I have chosen to focus on the four most prevalent in my interviews.

NOTES TO CHAPTER 1

1. For autobiographical accounts by industry insiders, see Wharton-Tiger and Wilson (1987) and Joris (1986).

2. See also Tavernier (1676); Burton (1869); Mawe (1812); Pearson (1926); One Who Has Visited the Fields (1872); and Omeara (1926).

3. See also Capt. J. H. Du Plessis (1960).

4. See Frolick (1999) and Hart (2002).

5. Some scholarship on the intersection of industry with global politics and violence walks a thin line between criticizing and mythologizing the De Beers empire (for example, Kanfer 1993), while others are flatly derogatory (see Roberts 2004). See also Turrell (1987), Worger (1987), Wheatcroft (1987), and Westwood (2000) for descriptions of capital and labor. See Szenberg (1973) for a depiction of the economics of the Israeli diamond industry.

6. De Beers developed the "Forever Mark" logo for advertising and marketing rough, freeing the De Beers name for flagship stores in London, Tokyo, and Paris through the luxury-item conglomeration LVMH. Capital leveraged from consumers, partly from the "Bigger Is Better" campaign, helped fund a store on Fifth Avenue near Fifty-seventh Street in New York, which opened in 2005 to great fanfare. When I visited the store, I was not surprised to find it decorated like other high-end shops with subtle colors, halogen lights, sound-absorbing carpet, a plush video room, and semiprivate desks where customers are wooed.

7. The discovery of the volcanic tuff, or pipes, by a German geologist in 1872 was the first step in rationalizing the search for diamonds by looking for geological markers, a process that has turned out to be extremely productive.

8. Nicky Oppenheimer (and family) was ranked #182 on *Forbes Magazine*'s list of billionaires in 2013. But Oppenheimer isn't the only diamond-industry executive listed there. Reflecting a loosening of De Beers's hegemony, competing diamond mogul Lev Leviev was ranked at #974. Incidentally, Bernard Arbault, chairman of LVMH, is ranked #10. (See http://www.forbes.com/billionaires.)

9. Diamond simulants—fakes—do not possess all of the properties of natural diamond. (Simulants include Moissanite, cubic zirconia, colorless synthetic Corundum [sapphire], spinel, Strontium titanate, Gadolinium gallium garnet, and glass.) It is hard to tell the difference between Moissanite and diamond since Moissanite is hard, has a high refractive index, and is thermally conductive; however, as I learned at GIA, the edges of cut Moissanite look doubled, its color tends toward green, and rather than containing small inclusions like most natural diamonds, it has milky ribboning inside from the growth process.

10. Earth is comprised of concentric layers: the core, the mantle, and the crust. The core consists of iron-nickel alloy and is dense, hot, and stable. The mantle, made of magnesium and iron silicate minerals, lies between the crust and the core; it is convecting, and circulates slowly. The moving crust plates are mineral-rich and less dense than the underlying mantle. The thickest areas of the crust host the continents, while thinner layers form the ocean bed. The crust is continually reinvented as plates slide one over another: as one plate is subsumed under another (in a process known as "subduction"), plate material is forced downward, and eventually reintegrated into the magma. On the ocean floor, melted magma squeezes up though vents, thickening ocean floors, as other plates are subducting. The thickest, oldest plates that form the continents have a particular shape and form a kind of keel. Known as a cratons, they are least 2.5 billion years old. It is within diamondiferous kimberlite pipes found on archons, the oldest type of cratons, where gem-quality diamonds can be found.

11. Diamondiferous harzburgite typically contains chromium- and magnesium-rich garnets, and is known as "garnet harzburgite." Inclusions made of harzburgitic minerals within diamond can be dated to determine the diamond's age. Diamonds from harzburgitic rock were created during the early formation of the earth's crust, three billion years ago. Diamondiferous ecologite can yield a higher concentration of diamond, but is usually associated with processes related to subduction of crust plates or to seafloor spreading in which carbon debris is reabsorbed into the mantle, becoming available for crystallization into diamond. Dated at three billion years or younger, ecologitic diamond is younger than harzburgitic.

12. Even though it faced technical problems and a strike in 2004, Debswana remains a top producer. Unfortunately, indigenous Botswanans have also been compulsorily removed from diamond-rich lands by the state, instigating calls for a boycott by NGOs that oppose forcible relocation. Debswana, however, benefits De Beers as well as the Botswanan government and people: a serious global boycott on diamonds would have deleterious consequences on the lives of many Botswanans.

13. BHP Billiton's diamond mine in Vancouver has been described as an excellent workplace. Canadian Ekati mineworkers have a recreation center, internet access, golf simulators, saunas, yoga classes, and gourmet meals (Macqueen 2004). This article must, however, be considered against reports of racism, exploitation, and miner deaths and injuries in the industry at large (see Roberts 2004).

NOTE TO CHAPTER 2

1. Available at http://www.diamondsourceva.com/Education/BrandedDiamonds/branded-diamond-shapes.asp (accessed June 7, 2013).

NOTES TO CHAPTER 3

1. In 1999, De Beers spent $67 million on advertising (Bittar 2000).

2. The average amount spent on new diamond jewelry is about $600, not truly prohibitive for most American families. This challenges popular ideas about scarcity and value.

3. While this book does not focus on conflict diamonds, or "blood diamonds," the specter of violence along the commodity chain haunts contemporary diamond consumption. As defined by the UN, conflict diamonds "originate from areas controlled by forces or factions opposed to legitimate and internationally recognized governments, and are used to fund military action in opposition to those governments, or in contravention of the decisions of the Security Council" (United Nations 2001). The term "blood diamonds" is particularly associated with late-1990s Sierra Leone, where diamonds, many of excellent color and quality, were being traded on black markets in Liberia. Proceeds were used to fund a brutal civil war. Later, these same stones were integrated into the licit trade. Blood diamonds were at one time thought to make up anywhere from 3 to 15 percent of all gems sold on the retail market (see Campbell 2002; Hart 2001; Hirsch 2001; Levy 2003). After 2005, blood diamonds became more visible than ever (see Falls 2011). There is now a rather large body of both scholarly and popular literature on the topic (see Gberie 2006 for an excellent treatment), but, in 2004, consumers I worked with generally had little awareness of them.

4. Lewis Malka, n.d., "Celebrity Diamonds Seen at the Oscars, Bafta's, and Golden Globes," *Pinterest*, available at http://pinterest.com/lewismalka/celebrity-diamonds-seen-at-the-oscars-bafta-s-and (accessed August 15, 2013).

5. According to a no-longer-available LMVH website, well-known African model Iman, married to rock superstar David Bowie, was hired to promote De Beers because her "international, committed lifestyle and her African roots both perfectly match the values of the De Beers brand." She has since relinquished her position in solidarity with the Gana and Gwi Bushmen in Botswana's Central Kalahari Game Reserve, who have lost land to mining. De Beers denies any role in the governmental decision to relocate people. NGOs like Survival International have tried, without success, to arbitrate land disputes among Botswana, De Beers, and aboriginal peoples through petition and ad-buster campaigning. An ad-buster campaign at the London De Beers flagship store said, "The Bushmen Aren't Forever." Iman, bringing great embarrassment to De Beers, quit just days before the store was set to open. In 2005, Lily Cole, a supermodel who became the new face of De Beers, having been alerted to allegations that Bushmen were being evicted from homes in Botswana to make way for diamond mines, began refusing to work.

6. *The Sopranos* was a popular television series centered upon an Italian American Mafia family operating in New Jersey.

7. The tiny diamonds come from the powder recovered from polishing large stones.

8. For comparison, Gucci spends about 15 percent of profits on advertising while De Beers spends 1 percent (see Lyden and Ardalan 2001).

NOTE TO CHAPTER 4

1. "Brilliance" is the fraction of the light that upon hitting a diamond is returned to the eyes of an observer. The more light returned, the more brilliance a stone is said to have. "Fire" results from the splitting of white light into a colorful prism so that the greater the separation of color, the greater the fire.

NOTES TO CHAPTER 5

1. Poetics and performatives both have an indexical dimension; they are embedded within a discursive universe where industry-sponsored symbolism reigns, and in a material universe in which iconic imitation of diamonds and styles of wielding them is mundane. Consumption, and talk about commodities, takes place in a social milieu threaded through with multiply layered social indexicals, where objects and words are read, and perhaps meant, as markers of both the vague and the concrete. In fact, during interviews, people's statements about diamonds can be taken as indexical signs about a person's (real or imagined) identity, class, educational level, interests, values, or attitudes in general, which then beg, request, or suggest a certain response. Diamond narratives, like other species of conversation, communicate at multiple levels—for example, in chapter 5, the use of derogatory terms and phrases like "those guys from the ghetto" contains a semantic message that refers to African American rappers but also sets the speaker apart from them. The phrase flags a forbidden racialized discourse. This kind of talk also marks the speaker's identification with—and to a certain extent reproduces—a certain kind of middle-class whiteness. Other narratives indexed social position, attitudes about aesthetics and style, cosmopolitanism, and/or views about ethnicity. Interviews contained semantic messages about how people interpret diamonds, but also about the consumers themselves.

2. Lyrics found at http://www.lyricsondemand.com/onehitwonders/ rappersdelightlyrics.html (accessed May 12, 2013).

3. Lyrics found at http://www.lyricsfreak.com/g/grandmaster-flash/62225.html (accessed March 12, 2013).

4. Terms such as "ghetto chic" and "gangsta' chic" are part of a cluster of high-fashion terms that describe styles that are in vogue but set against mainstream norms. Other "chics" include "nerd chic," "geek chic," and the controversial "heroin chic," in which models appear as drug addicts in sets that look like sleazy

bathroom shooting galleries. A bit outré by now, "ghetto fabulous" was a related style in which rappers use couture as part of their appearance, and, of course, hip-hop fashions continue to inform couture.

5. Formalists were responding to a limitation in existing theories that constructed language as a means of referential communication. By dividing language into practical and poetic components, they were recognizing and then highlighting extra-referential aspects, at least in literature. Although in their attempt to develop a science of literature formalists initially cleaved historical and social contexts from their object of study, after they saw that literary devices are only created and recognized as a result of historical situatedness, historical contextualization was brought back into the fold. As Eichenbaum explained in his "Theory of Formal Method," "Our moving into the area of history of literature was no simple expansion of our study; it resulted from the evolution of our concept of form. We found that we could not see the literary work in isolation, that we had to see its form against a background of other works rather than by itself," and then he continued, actually the original attempt of the Formalists to take a particular structural device and to establish its identity in diverse materials became an attempt to differentiate, to understand, the function of a device in each given case. The idea of functional significance was gradually pushed to the foreground and the original idea of the device pushed to the background. . . . [W]ork on specific materials compelled us to speak of functions and thus to revise our idea of the device. The theory itself demanded that we turn to history. (Lemon and Reis 1965 119, 132)

6. Finally, the artistic device cannot be systematized—should a disordering device or practice that defamiliarizes become conventional or routine, its reading will become habituated: the art falls into the mundane. What is implied in this formula is a temporal and contextual embeddedness. Devices operate against that which has come before, that which is habitual and conventional—the poetic device is unexpected, jarring, startling! It demands, "Who am I now?" It is this quality that interpolates the reader, provoking him or her to explore, to play. Because a poetic device operates against habituated knowledge, it is useful to excavate the origins and facts of the conventions against which a device is working. So, although formalist theory had in one breath sworn off "history," their work mandates attention to history.

7. "Jenny from the Block" was a hit song by Jennifer Lopez in 2002. In it, she claims that fame hasn't changed her; she is still the same girl from the neighborhood, "just Jenny from the Block." She makes multiple references to her diamonds: "Everybody mad about the rocks I wear," and "Don't be fooled by the rocks that I got / I'm still, I'm still Jenny from the block / Used to have a little, now I have a lot / No matter where I go / I know where I came from." Lyrics found at http://www.lyricsfreak.com/j/jennifer+lopez/jenny+from+the+block_20070484.html (accessed June 25, 2013).

8. See the example of anthropology making the familiar strange in Miner's famous essay on the Nacirema (1956).

9. I thank one of my reviewers for this insightful comment.

NOTES TO CHAPTER 6

1. Austin's *How to Do Things with Words* deals with first-person utterances. I am using his terms to describe diamond interpretation/use that falls outside of first-person cases.

2. Yehuda diamonds are treated to improve clarity grades, rather problematically for the gem industry, by removing inclusions, the appearance of cleavages, and "bearded" girdles. Diamonds are cleaned, then filled with a molten glass formula (the procedure and material composition is a company secret).

BIBLIOGRAPHY

Adorno, T., and M. Horkheimer. 1944. "Dialectic of Enlightenment." In *The Culture Industry: Enlightenment as Mass Deception*, edited by T. Adorno and M. Horkheimer, 120–68. New York: Herder and Herder.

Antwerp Facets Online. 2011. "After De Beers, What's Next for the Oppenheimers?" Antwerp, Belgium: World Diamond Centre, http://www.antwerpfacetsonline.be/nc/articles/single/article/after-de-beers-whats-next-for-the-oppenheimers (link now defunct).

Appadurai, Arjun. 1986. "Introduction: Commodities and the Politics of Value." In *The Social Life of Things: Commodities in Cultural Perspective*, edited by Arjun Appadurai, 3–63. Cambridge: Cambridge University Press.

Applbaum, K. 1998. "The Sweetness of Salvation: Consumer Marketing and the Liberal-Bourgeois Theory of Needs." *Current Anthropology* 39, no. 3: 323–49.

Ariovich, G. 1985. "The Economics of Diamond Price Movements." *Managerial and Decision Economics* 6, no. 4: 234–40.

Arkansas Diamond Company. 1908. *Diamonds in Arkansas: A Brief Account of the Discovery and Investigation and the Official Reports of Geologist and Mining Engineer on the Occurrence of Diamonds in Pike County, Arkansas*. Arkansas: Arkansas Diamond Company.

Austin, J. L. 1962. *How to Do Things with Words*. Cambridge, MA: Harvard University Press.

Bain & Company, Inc. 2012a. "The Global Diamond Industry; Portrait of Growth," http://www.bain.com/Images/BAIN_REPORT_Global_diamond_industry_portrait_of_growth_.pdf (file no longer available).

———. 2012b. "Worldwide Diamond Consumption to Surge by More Than 60 Percent by End of Decade," http://www.bain.com/about/press/press-releases/bain-2012-global-diamond-report.aspx.

Bally, Charles, Albert Sechehaye, and Albert Riedlinger, eds. 1986. *Ferdinand De Saussure: Course in General Linguistics*. La Salle, IL: Open Court.

Banerjee, Mukulika, and Daniel Miller. 2008. *The Sari*. Oxford: Berg.

Barthes, Roland. 1957. *Mythologies*. Paris: Editions du Seuil.

———. 1974. *S/Z: An Essay*. Translated by Richard Miller. New York: Hill and Wang.

Baudrillard, Jean. 1972 (1981). *For a Critique of the Political Economy of the Sign*. St. Louis, MO: Telos.

———.1975. *The Mirror of Production*. St. Louis, MO: Telos.

Bauman, Richard. 1983. *Let Your Words Be Few: Symbolism of Speaking and Silence among Seventeenth-Century Quakers*. New York: Cambridge University Press.

Belk, Russell W., Gnliz Ger, and Soren Askegaard. 1996. "Metaphors of Consumer Desire." *Advances in Consumer Research* 23: 369–73.

Benjamin, Walter. 1969. "Art in the Age of Mechanical Reproduction." In *Illuminations*, edited by Hannah Arendt, 217–52. New York: Schocken.

Beres, G. 2002. *Something Old, Something New*. New York: New York Diamonds.

Bergenstock, Donna J., and James M. Maskulka. 2001. "The De Beers Story: Are Diamonds Forever?" *Business Horizons* 44, no. 3: 37–44.

Berger, Arthur Asa. 2000. *Ads, Fads, and the Consumer Culture: Advertising's Impact on American Character and Society*. Oxford: Rowman and Littlefield.

Berlant, Lauren. 1991. *The Anatomy of National Fantasy: Hawthorne, Utopia, and Everyday Life*. Chicago: University of Chicago Press.

Berman, Phyllis, and Lea Goldman. 2003. "Cracked De Beers." *Forbes Magazine*, August 15, http://www.forbes.com/forbes/2003/0915/108.html.

Bernstein, Harry. 1986. *The Brazilian Diamond in Contracts, Contraband, and Capital*. Lanham, MD: University Press of America.

Birch, Ian H., and Henry Davenport Northrop. 1899. *History of the War in South Africa, Containing a Thrilling Account of the Great Struggle between the British and the Boers*. Halifax, Nova Scotia: Globe.

Bittar, Christine. 2000. "De Beers Plays up Details, Diamond in Ad Push." *Brandweek* no. 10.

Bonus, Rick. 2000. *Locating Filipino Americans: Ethnicity and the Cultural Politics of Space*. Philadelphia: Temple University Press.

Bork, Robert. 1996. *Slouching towards Gomorrah: Modern Liberalism and American Decline*. New York: Regan Books, HarperCollins.

Bourdieu, Pierre. 1984. *Distinction: A Social Judgement of Class*. Cambridge, MA: Harvard University Press.

Bourgois, Philippe, and Jeffrey Schonberg. 2009. *Righteous Dopefiend*, California Series in Public Anthropology. Berkeley: University of California Press.

Boyd, Todd. 2003a. *The New H.N.I.C. (Head Niggas in Charge)*. New York: New York University Press.

———. 2003b. *Young, Black, Rich, and Famous: The Rise of the NBA, the Hip Hop Invasion, and the Transformation of American Culture*. New York: Doubleday.

Bratton, Lisa Mardelle. 2001. "African American Attitude and Behavior Change toward Purchasing Diamonds: The South African Diamond Industry and Its Impact on South African Economic Independence." MA thesis. Temple University.

Brazeal, Brian. 2012. "Indian Religions in the Global Emerald Trade: A Photo Essay." *Visual Anthropology Review* 28, no. 2: 120–32.

Broomfield, Nick, dir. 2002. "Biggie and Tupac." 108. USA: Roxy Releasing.

Buchli, Victor. 2002. "Introduction." In *The Material Culture Reader*, edited by Victor Buchli, 1–22. Oxford: Berg.

Burton, Captain Richard Francis, Sr. 1869. *Explorations of the Highlands of the Brazil, with a Full Account of the Gold and Diamond Mines.* London: Tinsley Brothers.

Campbell, Greg. 2002. *Blood Diamonds: Tracing the Deadly Path of the World's Most Precious Stones.* Boulder, CO: Westview.

Carstens, Peter. 2001. *In the Company of Diamonds: De Beers, Kleinzee, and the Control of a Town.* Canton: Ohio University Press.

Carter, Kelly. 2002. "On the Other Hand, Diamonds Still Have Nice Ring." *USA Today*, June 7, http://search.epnet.com/login.aspx?direct=true&AuthType=cookie,ip,url,uid &db=aph&an=J0E397080336902 (accessed July 7, 2003).

Chang, So-Young, A. Heron, J. Kwon, G. Maxwell, and L. Rocca. 2000. "The Global Diamond Industry" (electronic version), http://www4.gsb.columbia.edu/chazen/journal/article/14252/The+Global+Diamond+Industry.

Chaudhuri, Maitrayee. 2001. "Gender and Advertisements: The Rhetoric of Globalization." *Women's Studies International Forum*, 24, no. 3/4: 373–86.

Chin, Elizabeth. 2001. *Purchasing Power: Black Kids and the American Consumer Culture* Minneapolis: University of Minnesota Press.

Condry, Ian. 2006. *Hip-Hop Japan: Rap and the Paths of Cultural Globalization.* Durham, NC: Duke University Press.

Crane, William H. 1965. "Alienation in the New African Society." *Social Compass* 12, no. 6: 367–77.

Crapanzano, Vincent. 1985. *Tuhami: Portrait of a Moroccan.* Chicago: University of Chicago Press.

———. 2001. *Serving the Word: Literalism in America from the Pulpit to the Bench.* New York: New Press.

———. 2003. *Imaginative Horizons: An Essay in Literary-Philosophical Anthropology.* Chicago: University of Chicago Press.

Daniel, E. Valentine. 1984. *Fluid Signs: Being a Person the Tamil Way.* Berkeley: University of California Press.

———. 1996. *Charred Lullabies: Chapters in an Anthropography of Violence.* Princeton, NJ: Princeton University Press.

Dant, Tim. 1996. Fetishism and the Social Value of Objects. *Sociological Review* 44, no. 3: 495–515.

———. 1999. *Material Culture in the Social World.* Berkshire, UK: Open University Press.

———. 2000. "Consumption Caught in the Cash Nexus." *Sociology* 34, no. 4: 655–70.

Davila, Arlene. 2001. *Latinos Inc.: Marketing and the Making of a People.* Berkeley: University of California Press.

De Boeck, Filip. 1998. "Domesticating Diamonds and Dollars: Identity, Expenditure, and Sharing in Southwestern Zaire (1984–1997)." *Development & Change* 29, no. 4: 777–811.

De Certeau, Michel. 2002. *The Practice of Everyday Life*. Translated by Steven F. Rendall. Berkeley: University of California Press.

DeNora, Tia. 2000. "When You're Trying Something On You Picture Yourself in a Place Where They Are Playing This Kind of Music." *Sociological Review* 48, no. 1: 80–101.

"Diamond Jewelry Report/National Jewelry Study 2003." 2003. *2 Degrees Freedom*, no. 1.

Diamond Source. N.d. "Branded Diamond Shapes." Diamond Source website, http://www.diamondsourceva.com/Education/BrandedDiamonds/branded-diamond-shapes.asp.

Dickinson, Joan Younger. 1965. *The Book of Diamonds*. New York: Avenel Books.

Doherty, Dermot. 2007. "Largest Red Diamond Ever Auctioned Sets Record at Christie's." *Bloomberg News*, November 15, http://www.bloomberg.com/apps/news?pid=newsarchive&sid=aVvzZhLZ2Tro.

Doyal, Len, and Ian Gough. 1991. *A Theory of Human Needs*. London: Macmillan.

Du Plessis, Capt. J. H. 1960. *Diamonds Are Dangerous: The Adventures of an Agent of the International Diamond Security Organization*. London: Cassell.

Eiss, Paul, and David Pedersen. 2008. "Introduction: Values of Value." *Cultural Anthropology* 17, no. 3: 283–90.

Epstein, Edward J. 1982a. "Have You Ever Tried to Sell a Diamond?" *Atlantic Monthly*, February 1, http://www.theatlantic.com/magazine/archive/1982/02/have-you-ever-tried-to-sell-a-diamond/304575.

———. 1982b. *The Diamond Invention*. London: Hutchinson.

———. 1982c. *The Rise and Fall of Diamonds: The Shattering of a Brilliant Illusion*. New York: Simon & Schuster.

Erlich, Victor. 1980. *Russian Formalism*, 5th ed. Hague, Netherlands: Mouton.

Evans, Martin. 2010. "World's Most Expensive Diamond Goes under the Hammer." Telegraph Media Group, November 15, http://www.telegraph.co.uk/culture/art/artsales/8140090/Worlds-most-expensive-diamond-goes-under-the-hammer.html.

Ewen, Stuart. 1988. *All-Consuming Images*. New York: Basic Books.

Falls, Susan. 2008. "Diamond Signs: Generic Stones and Particular Gems." *Social Semiotics* 18, no. 4: 449–65.

———. 2011. "Picturing Blood Diamonds." *Critical Arts: South-North Cultural and Media Studies* 25, no. 3: 441–66.

Faudree, Paja L. 2012. "Music, Language, and Texts: Sound and Semiotic Ethnography." *Annual Review of Anthropology* 41: 519–36.

Fischer, Olga, and Max Nänny, eds. 2001. *The Motivated Sign: Iconicity in Language and Literature*, volume 2. Amsterdam: University of Amsterdam.

Fiske, John. 1994. "Radical Shopping in Los Angeles: Race, Media, and the Sphere of Consumption." *Media, Culture & Society* 16, no. 3: 469–87.

Fleming, Ian. 1956. *Diamonds Are Forever*. London: Johnathan Cape.

———. 1957. *The Diamond Smugglers*. London: Johnathan Cape.

Foster, Robert. 1999. "The Commercial Construction of 'New Nations.'" *Journal of Material Culture* 4, no. 3: 263–83.

————. 2007. "The Work of the New Economy: Consumers, Brands, and Value Creation." *Cultural Anthropology* 22, no. 4: 707–31.

Friedan, Betty. 1963. *The Feminine Mystique*. New York: Norton.

Friedman, Jonathan, ed. 1994. *Consumption and Identity*. London: Harwood Academic.

Frolick, Vernon. 1999. *Fire into Ice: Charles Fipke and the Great Diamond Hunt*. Vancouver: Raincoast Books.

Gadamer, Hans-Georg. 1975. *Truth and Method*. New York: Seabury.

Gailbraith, John Kenneth. 1977. "The Dependence Effect." In *The Consumer Society Reader*, edited by J. Schor and D. Holt, 20–25. New York: New Press.

Gberie, Lansana. 2006. *A Dirty War in West Africa: The RUF and the Destruction of Sierra Leone*. Bloomington: Indiana University Press.

Geertz, Clifford. 1977. *The Interpretation of Cultures*. New York: Basic Books.

Gell, Alfred. 1992. "Inter-Tribal Commodity Barter and Reproductive Gift Exchange in Old Melanesia." In *Barter, Exchange, and Value: An Anthropological Approach*, edited by Caroline Humphrey and Stephen Hugh-Jones, 142–68. Cambridge: Cambridge University Press.

George, Nelson. 2005. *Hip Hop America*. New York: Penguin.

Gereffi, Gay, and Miguel Korzeniewicz. 1994. *Commodity Chains and Global Capitalism*. Westport, CT: Praeger.

Goffman, Erving. 1958. *The Presentation of Self in Everyday Life*. New York: Doubleday Anchor.

Goldman, Robert, and Stephen Papson. 1991. *Sign Wars: The Cluttered Landscape of Advertising*. New York: Guilford.

Goode, Judith, and Jeff Mascovsky, eds. 2002. *The New Poverty Studies: The Ethnography of Power, Politics, and Impoverished People in the United States*. New York: New York University Press.

Gottdeiner, Mark. 1995. *Postmodern Semiotics: Material Culture and the Forms of Postmodern Life*. Hoboken, NJ: Blackwell.

Graeber, David. 1996. "Beads and Money: Notes toward a Theory of Wealth and Power." *American Ethnologist* 23, no. 1: 4–24.

————. 2001. *Toward an Anthropological Theory of Value: The False Coin of Our Own Dreams*. New York: Palgrave.

Hall, Stuart, and Tony Jefferson, eds. 1975. *Resistance through Rituals: Youth Subcultures in Post-War Britain*. London: Hutchinson.

Halle, David. 1996. *Inside Culture: Art and Class in the American Home*. Chicago: University of Chicago Press.

Harlow, George.1998. "What Is Diamond?" In *The Nature of Diamonds*, edited by George Harlow, 5-22. Cambridge: Cambridge University Press, 1998.

Harlow, George, Vladislav Shatsky, and Nikolai Sobolev. 1998. "Natural Sources of Diamond Other Than the Earth's Mantle." In *The Nature of Diamonds*, edited by George Harlow, 66–71. Cambridge: Cambridge University Press.

Harris, Harvey. 1994. *Fancy-Color Diamonds*. Liechtenstein: Fancoldi Reg. Trust.

Hart, Matthew. 2001. *Diamond: Journey to the Heart of an Obsession*. New York: Walker.

———. 2002. *Diamond: The History of a Cold-Blooded Love Affair*. New York: Plume.

Hartshorne, Charles, and Paul Weiss, eds. 1931–1935. *The Collected Papers of Charles Sanders Peirce*, vols. 1–6. Cambridge, MA: Harvard University Press.

Hay, Carla. 2004. "Diamond Girls: Ladies Flaunt Their Own Right-Hand Rings." *Billboard*, August 21, 46–48, 3c.

Hazen, Robert M. 1999. *The Diamond Makers*. New York: Cambridge University Press.

Hearts on Fire. N.d. " Home Page." http://www.heartsonfire.com/Shop-Jewelry/Rings/Engagement-Rings.aspx.

Hebdige, Dick. 1979. *Subculture: The Meaning of Style*. London: Methuen.

Hendrickson, Carol. 1995. *Weaving Identities: Construction of Dress and Self in a Highland Guatemala Town*. Austin: University of Texas Press.

Hicks, Dan, and Mary Beaudry, eds. 2010. *The Oxford Handbook of Material Culture Studies*. Oxford: Oxford Handbooks, Oxford University Press.

Hirsch, John. 2001. *Sierra Leone: Diamonds and the Struggle for Democracy*. Boulder, CO: Reinner.

Hoskins, Janet. 1998. *Biographical Objects: How Things Tell the Stories of People's Lives*. New York: Routledge.

Howes, David. 1996. *Cross-Cultural Consumption: Global Markets, Local Realities*. London: Routledge.

Hymes, Dell. 1979. "Sapir, Competence, Voices." In *Individual Differences in Language Ability and Language Behavior*, edited by C. J. Fillmore, D. Kempler, and W. S-Y. Want, 33–45. New York: Academic.

Ingold, Tim. 2012. "Toward an Ecology of Materials." *Annual Review of Anthropology* 41: 427–42.

Jameson, Fredric. 1972. *The Prison House of Language*. Princeton, NJ: Princeton University Press.

Janse, A. J. A. (Bram). 2007. "Global Rough Diamond Production since 1870." *Gems & Gemology* 43, no. 2: 98–119.

Johnstone, Barbara. 1996. *The Linguistic Individual: Self-Expression in Language and Linguistics*. New York: Oxford University Press.

———. 2000. "The Individual Voice in Language." *Annual Review of Anthropology* 29: 405–24.

———. 2001. "The Individual." *Journal of Linguistic Anthropology,* special issue on Language Matters in Anthropology: A Lexicon for the New Millennium, edited by Alessandro Duranti 9: 123–26.

Joris, Albert. 1986. *A Destiny in Diamonds*. Queensland, Australia: Boolarong.

Journal of Material Culture. 1996. "Editorial, Introduction of New Journal." *Journal of Material Culture* 1, no. 1: 5–14.

Kanfer, Stefan. 1993. *The Last Empire: De Beers, Diamonds, and the World*. New York: Farrar, Straus, Giroux.

Keane, Webb. 2003. "Semiotics and the Social Analysis of Material Things." *Language & Communication* 23: 409–25.

Kirn, Walter. 2007. "Here, There, and Everywhere." *New York Times*, February 11, http://www.nytimes.com/2007/02/11/magazine/11wwlnlede.t.html.

Klein, Naomi. 2000. *No Logo: Taking Aim at the Brand Bullies*. New York: Picador.

Kockelman, Paul. 2006. "A Semiotic Ontology of the Commodity." *Journal of Linguistic Anthropology* 16, no. 1: 76–102.

Kolocotroni, Vassiliki, Jane Goldman, and Olga Taxidou, eds. 1999. *Modernism: An Anthology of Sources and Documents*, 1st ed. Chicago: University of Chicago Press.

Kopytoff, Igor. 1986. "The Cultural Biography of Things: Commoditization as Process." In *The Social Life of Things*, edited by Arjun Appadurai, 66–94. Cambridge: Cambridge University Press.

Krawitz, Avi. 2012. "DTC June Sight Estimated at $540m: Tight Liquidity Brings Weak Rough Trading." *Rapaport News*, June 13.

Kurin, Richard. 2006. *Hope Diamond: The Legendary History of a Cursed Gem*. Washington, DC: Smithsonian Books.

Le Billon, Philippe. 2001. "Angola's Political-Economy of War: The Role of Oil and Diamonds, 1975–2000." *African Affairs* 100, no. 398: 55–81.

Lehtonen, Turo-Kimmo. 1999. "Any Room for Aesthetics? Shopping Practices of Heavily Indebted Consumers." *Journal of Material Culture* 4, no. 3: 243–63.

Lemon, Lee T., and Marion J. Reis. 1965. *Russian Formalist Criticism: Four Essays*. Lincoln: University of Nebraska.

Lenzen, Godfrey. 1970. *The History of Diamond Production and the Diamond Trade*. London: Barrie Books.

Levy, Arthur V., ed. 2003. *Diamonds and Conflict: Problems and Solutions*. Hauppauge, NY: Novinka Books.

Lindquist, Galina. 2001. "Transforming Signs: Typologies of Affliction in Contemporary Russian Magic and Healing." *Ethos* 66, no. 2: 181–206.

Lingis, Alfonso. 2004. *Trust (Theory out of Bounds)*. Minneapolis: University of Minnesota Press.

Lunt, Peter, and Sonia M. Livingstone. 1992. *Mass Consumption and Personal Identity: Everyday Economic Experience*. Philadelphia: Open University Press.

Lyden, Jacki, and Davar Ardalan. 2001. "The Democratic Diamond," http://american radioworks.publicradio.org/features/diamonds/nyprint.html.

Macqueen, Ken. 2004. "Top 10 Physical Workplaces." *Macleans*, Oct. 11, 25.

Marx, Karl. 1990 (1867). *Capital, Volume 1*, 26th ed. Translated by Ben Fowkes. New York: Penguin Books.

Mauss, Marcel. 1990 (1922). *The Gift: Forms and Functions of Exchange in Archaic Societies*. London: Routledge.

Mawe, John. 1812. *Travels in the Interior of Brazil, Particularly in the Gold and Diamond Districts of That Country: Including a Voyage to the Rio De La Plata, and an Historical Sketch of the Revolution of Buenos Ayres*. London: Longman, Hurst, Rees, Orme, and Brown.

McCracken, Grant. 1990. *Culture and Consumption: New Approaches to the Symbolic Character of Consumer Goods and Activities.* Bloomington: Indiana University Press.

Meneley, Anne. 2008. "Oleo-Signs and Quali-Signs: The Qualities of Olive Oil." *Ethnos* 73, no. 3: 303–26.

Mertz, Elizabeth. 2007. "Semiotic Anthropology." *Annual Review of Anthropology* 36: 337–53.

Myers, Fred, ed. 2002. *The Empire of Things: Regimes of Value and Material Culture.* School of American Research Advanced Seminar Series, edited by Joan K. O'Donnell and Jane Kepp. Santa Fe, NM: SAR Press.

Miller, Daniel. 1995. "Consumption Studies as the Transformation of Anthropology." In *Acknowledging Consumption*, edited by Daniel Miller, 264–95. New York: Routledge.

———. 1998. *A Theory of Shopping.* Ithaca, NY: Cornell University Press.

———. 2001. *The Dialectics of Shopping.* Chicago: University of Chicago Press.

———. 2009a. *Stuff.* Cambridge: Polity.

———. 2009b. *The Comfort of Things.* London: Polity.

Miller, Daniel, ed. 2005. *Materiality.* Durham, NC: Duke University Press.

Miner, Horace. 1956. "Body Ritual among the Nacirema." *American Anthropologist* 58, no. 3: 503–7.

Mitchell, Tony, ed. 2001. *Global Noise: Rap and Hip Hop outside the USA.* Middletown, CT: Wesleyan University Press.

Muniz, Albert M., and Thomas C. O'Guinn. 2001. "Brand Community." *Journal of Consumer Research* 27, no. 4: 412–33.

Munn, Nancy. 1962. "Walbiri Graphic Signs: An Analysis." *American Anthropologist* 64, no. 5: 972–84.

Murray, Barbara. 2004. "Sarin to Launch Diamond Analyzers at JCK." In *Rapaport Report*, edited by Martin Rapaport, June 1, http://www.diamonds.net/News/NewsItem.aspx?ArticleID=9676&ArticleTitle=Sarin+to+Launch+Diamond+Analyzers+at+JCK.

Nassau, Kurt. 1999. "Moissanite: A New Synthetic Gemstone Material." *Journal of Gemmology* 26, no. 7: 425–38.

Nixon, Sean. 2003. *Advertising Cultures: Gender, Commerce, and Creativity.* London: Sage.

Ogbar, Jeffrey O. G. 1999. "Slouching toward Bork: The Culture Wars and Self-Criticism in Hip-Hop Music." *Journal of Black Studies* 30, no. 2: 164–83.

Oh, Minya. 2003. "'Bling Bling' Added to Oxford English Dictionary: Term Joins Words like 'Jiggy,' 'Dope,' and 'Phat' in the Definitions Resource." *MTV News*, April 30, http://www.mtv.com/news/articles/1471629/bling-bling-added-dictionary.jhtml.

Omeara, Walter Alfred John Kekewich. 1926. *Walter Alfred John Kekewich Omeara in Kimberley, Being an Account of the Defence of the Diamond Fields, October 14th, 1890–February 15th, 1900.* London: Medici Society.

One Who Has Visited the Fields. 1872. *The Diamond Fields of South Africa, with Notes of Journeys There and Homeward.* New York: American News Company.

Oppenheimer, Nicky. 2002. "Chairman's Statement." De Beers Annual Report, http://
www.diamonds.net/news/newsitem.asp?num=5199&type=all&topic=De%Beers.

Parmentier, Richard. 2009. "Troubles with Trichotomies: Reflections on the Utility of
Peirce's Sign Trichotomies for Social Analysis." *Semiotica* 177, no. 1: 139–55.

Paterson, Mark. 2005. *Consumption and Everyday Life*. London: Routledge.

Pearson, Hugh. 1926. *The Diamond Trail, an Account of Travel among the Little-Known
Bahian Diamond Fields of Brazil, with Photographs and a Map*. London: Witherby.

Peirce, Charles S. 1903. "Logical Tracts, No. 2, 4:447. " In *Collected Papers of Charles
Sanders Peirce*, edited by Charles Hartshorne and Paul Weiss. Cambridge, MA:
Harvard University Press.

Perkins, William Eric, ed. 1996. *Droppin' Science: Critical Essays on Rap Music and Hip
Hop Culture*. Philadelphia: Temple University Press.

Pointon, Marsha. 1999. "Jewelry in Eighteenth-Century England." In *Consumers and
Jewelry*, edited by Maxine Berg and Helen Clifford, 120–46. Manchester, UK:
Manchester University Press.

Preucel, Robert W. 2010. *Archaeological Semiotics, Social Archaeology*. Malden, MA:
Wiley-Blackwell.

Prown, Jules D. 1996. "Material Culture: Can the Farmer and the Cowman Still Be
Friends?" In *Learning from Things: Method and Theory in Material Culture Studies*,
edited by W. D. Kingery, 19–30. Washington, DC: Smithsonian Instutute.

Qureshi, Karen, and Shaun Moore. 1999. "Identity Remix: Tradition and Translation
in the Lives of Young Pakistani Scots." *European Journal of Cultural Studies* 2, no. 3:
311–30.

Rapaport, Martin. 1998. "Buddha Cut" (electronic version). *Rapaport Diamond Report*
21, no. 45: 101.

———. 2003. "Out of Sight." *Rapaport News*, September 4, http://www.diamonds.net/
News/NewsItem.aspx?ArticleID=8491&ArticleTitle=Out+of+Sight.

———. 2004. "De Beers Says SoC Strategy Boosts Retailers' Ad Outlays." *Rapaport
TradeWire*, June 18.

Riggins, Stephen, ed. 1994. *The Socialness of Things: Essays on the Socio-Semiotics of
Objects*. New York: de Gruyter.

Ritzer, George. 1996. *The McDonaldization of Society*. Thousand Oaks, CA: Pine Forge.

Roberts, Janine. 2004. *Glitter and Greed: The Secret World of the Diamond Cartel*. New
York: Disinformation Company.

Rose, Tricia. 1994. *Black Noise: Rap Music and Black Culture in Contemporary America*.
Middletown, CT: Wesleyan University Press.

Rudd, Elizabeth, and Lara Descartes, eds. 2008. *The Changing Landscape of Work and
Family in the American Middle Class*. Lanham, MD: Lexington Books.

Rumsey, Alan. 1990. "Wording, Meaning, and Linguistic Ideology." *American
Anthropologist* 92, no. 2: 346–61.

Saatchi & Saatchi. 2013. "Lovemarks: The Future beyond Brands," http://www.
lovemarks.com/index.php?pageID=20020.

Scheld, Suzanne. 2003. "The City in a Shoe: Redefining Urban Africa through Sebago Footwear Consumption." *City & Society* 15, no. 1: 109–30.

Schieffelin, Bambi, and Katherine Wollard. 1994. "Language Ideology." *Annual Review of Anthropology* 23: 55–82.

Schneider, Jane. 2006. "Cloth and Clothing." In *Handbook of Material Culture*, edited by Christopher Tilly, Webb Keane, Susanne Kuechler, Michael Rowlands, and Patricia Spyer, 203–20. New York: Sage.

Schor, Juliet, and Douglas Holt, eds. 2000. *The Consumer Society Reader*. New York: New Press.

Sennet, Richard. 2008. *The Craftsman*. New Haven, CT: Yale University Press.

Shenk, David. 1997. *Data Smog: Surviving the Information Glut*. New York: Harper Edge.

Shield, Renée Rose. 2002. *Diamond Stories: Enduring Change on 47th Street*. Ithaca, NY: Cornell University Press.

Shklovsky, Victor. 1914. *Voskresheniye Slova* (The Resurrection of the Word). Petersburg.

———. 1965 (1917). "Art as Technique." In *Russian Formalist Criticism: Four Essays*, edited by L. T. Lemon and M. J. Reiss, 3–25. Lincoln: University of Nebraska Press.

Sillitoe, Sir Percy. 1955. *Cloak without Dagger*. London: Cassell.

Silverstein, Michael. 1979. "Language, Structure, and Linguistic Ideology." In *The Elements: A Parasession on Linguistic Units and Levels*, edited by P. R. Clyne, W. F. Hanks, and C. C. Hofbauer, 193–247. Chicago: Chicago Linguistic Society.

———. 1995. "Shifters, Linguistic Categories, and Cultural Description." In *Language, Culture, and Society*, edited by Ben Bloun, 187–220. Prospect Heights, IL: Waveland.

Simmons, Russell. 2001. *Life and Def*. New York: Random House.

Simpson, J. A., and E. S. C. Weiner. 1989. "The Oxford English Dictionary." In *The Oxford English Dictionary*. New York: Oxford University Press.

Singer, Milton. 1984. *Man's Glassy Essence: Explorations in Semiotic Anthropology*. Bloomington: Indiana University Press.

Spencer, L. K., S. D. Dikinis, P. C. Keller, and R. E. Kane. 1998. "The Diamond Deposits of Kalimantan, Borneo." *Gems & Gemology* 24: 67–80.

Stewart, Kathleen. 2007. *Ordinary Affects*. Durham, NC: Duke University Press.

Susser, Ida, and Thomas C. Patterson, eds. 2001. *Cultural Diversity in the United States: A Critical Reader*. Malden, MA: Blackwell.

Szenburg, Michael. 1973. *Economics of the Israeli Diamond Industry*. New York: Basic Books.

Tavernier, Jean Baptiste. 2012 (1676). *Travels in India by Jean Baptiste-Tavernier, Baron of Aubonne*. Translated by Valentine Ball. Hong Kong: Forgotten Books.

Thomas, Nicholas. 1991. *Entangled Objects: Exchange, Material Culture, and Colonialism in the Pacific*. Cambridge, MA: Harvard University Press.

Tiffany and Co. N.d. "Lucida," http://www.tiffany.com/Engagement/Item.aspx?GroupSKU=GRP10003.

Trachtenberg, Carmel. 2004. "Antwerp Diamond Conference to Focus on Synthetics." *Rapaport Report,* June 2, http://www.diamonds.net/News/NewsItem.aspx?ArticleID =9678&ArticleTitle=Antwerp+Diamond+Conference+to+Focus+on+Synthetics.

Turner, Victor. 1986. *The Anthropology of Performance.* Baltimore, MD: Johns Hopkins University Press.

Turrell, Robert V. 1987. *Capital and Labor on the Kimberley Diamond Fields, 1871–1890.* Cambridge: Cambridge University Press.

United Nations. 2001 "Conflict Diamonds: Sanctions and War General Assembly Adopts Resolution on 'Conflict Diamonds.'" New York: United Nations: Security Council Affairs Division.

Veblen, Thorstein. 1973 (1899). *The Theory of the Leisure Class.* Boston: Houghton Mifflin.

Walker, Rob. 2004. "The Right-Hand Diamond Ring." *New York Times Magazine,* January 4, p. 16.

Walsh, Andrew. 2004. "In the Wake of Things: Speculating in and about Sapphires in Northern Madagascar." *American Anthropologist* 106, no. 2: 225–37.

Weiner, Annette B. 1992. *Inalienable Possessions: The Paradox of Keeping-While-Giving.* Berkeley: Univerisity of California Press.

Westwood, Sallie. 2000. "'A Real Romance': Gender, Ethnicity, Trust, and Risk in the Indian Diamonds Trade." *Ethnic & Racial Studies* 23, no. 5 (2000): 857–71.

———. 2002. "'Diamond Time': Constructing Time, Constructing Markets in the Diamond Trade." *Time and Society* 11, no. 1: 25–38.

Wharton-Tiger, Edward, and A. J. Wilson. 1987. *Burning Bright: An Autobiography of Edward Wharton-Tiger.* London: Metal Bulletin Books.

Wheatcroft, Geoffrey. 1987. *The Randlords.* New York: Simon & Schuster.

Williams, Raymond. 1980. "Advertising: The Magic System." In *Problems in Materialism and Culture,* edited by Raymond Williams, 170–95. New York: Verso.

Williamson, Judith. 1978. *Decoding Advertising: Ideology and Meaning in Advertising.* Salem, NH: Boyers.

Worger, William. 1987. *South Africa's City of Diamonds: Mine Workers and Monopoly Capitalism in Kimberley, 1867–1895.* New Haven, CT: Yale University Press.

Yee, Blythe. 2003. "Ads Remind Women That They Have Two Hands." *Wall Street Journal,* Eastern Edition, Aug. 14, p. B1.

Zapata, Janet. 1998. "Diamond Jewelry for Everyone." In *The History of Diamonds,* edited by George Harlow, Vladislav Shatsky, and Nikolai Sobolev, 186–98. Cambridge: Cambridge University Press.

Zoellner, Tom. 2006. *The Heartless Stone: A Journey through the World of Diamonds, Deceit, and Desire.* New York: St. Martin's.

Zwick, Edward, dir. 2006. *Blood Diamond.* 143 minutes. US: Warner Brothers Pictures.

INDEX

"A Diamond Is Forever," 11, 14, 83, 87, 135, 163
advertising, 3, 10, 22, 64, 71, 77, 81–82, 84, 95; "guy-humor," 93; images by Salvador Dali, 86; images by Pablo Picasso, 86; J. Walter Thompson, 90; N. W. Ayer & Son, 11, 37, 85–87; Raise Your Right Hand campaign, 96–97
Advertising Women of New York (AWNY), 96
Africa, 30, 31, 35, 46–47
agency, xiv, 4–5, 8, 17, 26, 79, 103
Amsterdam, 33
Anglo-American Corporation, 37
Angola, 48
Antwerp, 33, 49, 53, 55
archon, 46; volcanic process, 34n7, 45–46
art, 132, 141, 151n6, 181
Art as Technique, 131, 133
Austin, J. L., 25, 159
Australia, 38, 49; Argyle, 46, 49
authenticity, 153, 166–167, 170–171; fakes, 180

Baby Gangsta, 133
baguette, 91
Barnato, Barney, 35–36
Barnato, Harry, 36
Barthes, Roland, xiii
black market, 11, 32; De Beers International Diamond Security Organization, 30

blemish, 63
bling, 25, 129, 133; bling finger, 96
blood diamonds, 11, 32, 38, 85n3; Kimberley Process (KP), 11, 32
Boas, Franz, xiii
Bork, Robert, 137–138
Borneo, 31
bort, 10, 47
Botswana, 48, 50
Bourdieu, Pierre, 7, 164
bourse, 12
Boyd, Todd, 139
branding, 22–23, 33, 38, 68–69, 116; Forever Mark, 23; in cuts, 69
Brazil, 30–33, 90
brilliant, 1, 59, 67

Canada, 31, 38, 46, 49
capitalism, 7, 19–20, 70; kinship capitalism, 38
carat, 43, 55, 60–62, 74, 88
carbon, 38–41, 45–46
Catwoman, 97
celebrity, 86, 92, 95
certification, 13, 60, 61, 180; and price, 13
Chin, Elizabeth, 9
China, 11, 48
clarity, 43, 62, 64, 91; flaws, 62–64; features, 13
class, 9, 22, 31, 33, 67, 78, 86, 89–90, 106, 117; as style, 151

ABOUT THE AUTHOR

Susan Falls teaches anthropology at the Savannah College of Art and Design in Savannah, Georgia.